THE
THYROID
SOURCEBOOK
FOR WOMEN

THE
THYROID
SOURCEBOOK
FOR WOMEN

Second Edition

M. Sara Rosenthal, Ph.D.

McGraw·Hill

New York Chicago San Francisco Lisbon London Madrid Mexico City
Milan New Delhi San Juan Seoul Singapore Sydney Toronto

Library of Congress Cataloging-in-Publication Data

Rosenthal, M. Sara.
    The thyroid sourcebook for women / by M. Sara Rosenthal.—2nd ed.
       p.   cm.
    Includes bibliographical references and index.
    ISBN 0-07-144161-1
      1. Thyroid gland—Diseases—Popular works.   2. Women—Diseases—Popular works.
  I. Title.

    RC655.R673   2005
    616.4'4'0082—dc22   2004024945

1 2 3 4 5 6 7 8 9 0   FGR/FGR   3 2 1 0 9 8 7 6 5 4

ISBN 0-07-144161-1

McGraw-Hill books are available at special quantity discounts to use as premiums and sales promotions, or for use in corporate training programs. For more information, please write to the Director of Special Sales, Professional Publishing, McGraw-Hill, Two Penn Plaza, New York, NY 10121-2298. Or contact your local bookstore.

The purpose of this book is to educate. It is sold with the understanding that the author and publisher shall have neither liability nor responsibility for any injury caused or alleged to be caused directly or indirectly by the information contained in this book. While every effort has been made to ensure its accuracy, the book's contents should not be construed as medical advice. Each person's health needs are unique. To obtain recommendations appropriate to your particular situation, please consult a qualified health-care provider.

This book is printed on acid-free paper.

Contents

Foreword to the First Edition

SARA ROSENTHAL HAS done it again! Being a thyroid patient herself, she brings much-needed insight and a little humor to a very nonglamorous disease.

If you are a woman who is newly diagnosed with a thyroid disorder, this book will serve as your bible. Read it cover to cover. If you are a veteran thyroid patient, you may choose to use it as a reference when questions arise. Either way, it is an invaluable tool that no woman should be without. I say this because thyroid disease is estimated to affect some twenty-one million Americans (80 percent are women), and half of those twenty-one million are undiagnosed or misdiagnosed. The statistics only increase for women as we age; many of us will develop a thyroid condition at some point in our lifetime.

In fact, this book should be shared with family members and friends so that they can better understand your moods, energy levels (or lack thereof!), and gain the knowledge to provide understanding and moral support. In addition, it will increase awareness that thyroid disease has familial tendencies; if you should happen to be male, you are not immune to thyroid disease, either!

More than likely, most of us reading this book will deal with thyroid disease in some form or fashion for the remainder of our lives, as well as juggle a myriad of female hormone issues at any given stage of life.

Considering that thyroid disease is a lifelong condition, it is essential that we become better educated about our health condition while becoming more savvy medical consumers given the countless healthcare alternatives we face today.

It is my suggestion that you keep this book close at hand. It will be there for you, the hyperthyroid patient, wide awake at 4:00 A.M., when no one else will be; and for you, the hypothyroid patient, as you drag yourself out of bed wondering if you will ever have enough energy to keep up with your life as you knew it before, and who remembers reading about combination therapy. Take this book with you when you see your doctor and discuss the benefits of potential treatment mentioned herein.

This book provides the keys to unlock the mysteries and myths surrounding thyroid disease and women. Ms. Rosenthal provides easy-to-understand information, and I am particularly fond of the cross-reference annotations.

To thyroid patients everywhere—good reading and good health!

—Kelly R. Hale
Founder/President, American
Foundation of Thyroid Patients

Acknowledgments

I WISH TO thank my husband, Kenneth B. Ain, M.D., for his thorough review of the content in Chapters 1, 2, 5, 7, 9, 10, and 11 for this second edition. Dr. Ain is a unique thyroidologist I wish I'd known earlier in my life. He is currently Professor of Medicine and Director of the Thyroid Oncology Program, Division of Hematology and Oncology, Department of Internal Medicine, University of Kentucky Medical Center.

The following individuals served as medical advisers on previous works, which helped to lay much of the groundwork for the first edition of this book:

Robert Volpe, M.D., F.R.C.P., F.A.C.P.

Suzanne Pratt, M.D., F.A.C.O.G.

Masood Khathamee, M.D., F.A.C.O.G.

Gillian Arsenault, M.D., C.C.F.P., I.B.L.C., F.R.C.P.

Pamela Craig, M.D., F.A.C.S., Ph.D.

James McSherry, M.B., Ch.B., F.C.F.P., F.R.C.G.P., F.A.A.F.P., F.A.B.M.P.

Gary May, M.D., F.R.C.P.

Susan George, M.D., F.R.C.P., F.A.C.P.

Irving B. Rosen, M.D., F.R.C.S., F.A.C.S.

Matthew Lazar, M.D., F.R.C.P., F.A.C.P.

Debra Lander, M.D., F.R.C.P.

I'd also like to thank Kelly Hale, Founder and President, American Foundation for Thyroid Patients, for her unwavering support of this book. Judith McCarthy, my editor at McGraw-Hill, championed this new edition and recognized thyroid as a woman's book. For that, I thank her.

Introduction

A Woman's Disease

WELCOME TO THE second edition of *The Thyroid Sourcebook for Women*, a book that, to date, has surpassed *The Thyroid Sourcebook* in demand. This new edition is completely revised and expanded.

The inspiration to write about thyroid disease came from the women in my family. From my great-grandmother who developed a goiter in the 1930s. From my grandmother who developed Graves' disease in 1940 with her first pregnancy at twenty-four, had her thyroid removed, and was not given any subsequent medication because her doctor said she "didn't need it." From my mother, who developed Graves' disease in 1981, watched in dismay as her eyes bulged out like *her* mother's, and read through stacks of complicated medical texts to try to find out more about her illness. From my sister, who developed Graves' disease in 1991.

My family's thyroid heritage is statistically not remarkable. In 1983, when I turned twenty, my family's legacy was passed down to me as well: I was diagnosed with thyroid cancer.

The familiar feminist slogan "The personal is political" rings particularly true with thyroid disease. Within one woman's story about her feelings and struggles with her thyroid problem lies the story of all women's struggles with thyroid disease. It is both a social story and a medical story.

As a woman dealing with thyroid disease, you are also dealing with a myriad of other health concerns, and unfair social arrangements that create unique stresses for women.

This book is designed to help you make informed choices about your thyroid and general health care. "Informed consent" is a guiding principle for medical practitioners and researchers. It means that in order for someone to make an informed decision, there must be full disclosure of all risks and benefits; that person must completely understand what's being explained; that person must be fully competent; and that person must feel free to say yes or no according to his or her own wishes, values, and "gut feeling" without any coercion or coaxing.

Given the highly technical nature of some of this content, and the variety of tests and/or treatments you may undergo, is it even reasonable to expect that women can make informed decisions about thyroid health? Furthermore, are there gender differences in thyroid disease that we are only just discovering?

For example, much of what we know about general health is general health in a *white man's* body—because it was that body that participated in clinical trials looking at diseases, treatments, drug interactions, and so forth. Therefore, the "norms" for a healthy body are often based on a healthy white male body—one that does not menstruate, get pregnant, breast-feed, or go through menopause. The reason for this has to do with guidelines that were designed to protect women from participating in potentially risky research trials. In the past, women, the elderly, minorities, and other vulnerable populations had a long history of being abused in medical research—to such an extent that public outcry demanded stronger regulations to protect them. In response to the horrors of thalidomide (marketed in 1958), a sedating drug that was not properly tested prior to marketing (which caused severe limb deformities in the developing fetus), as well as DES (diethylstilbestrol—administered from the 1940s until the early 1970s), a miscarriage prevention drug that was later revealed to cause a rare form of vaginal cancer in DES daughters, legislation was passed to protect pregnant women and women of childbearing potential from the harmful effects of these drugs.

The ethics of excluding women from medical research were first questioned when basic diseases such as heart disease were shown to manifest in completely different ways in men than in women. For example, because men suffer from heart attacks much earlier than women, heart disease suddenly became a "man's disease," even though it kills just as many women. (In point of fact, women die from heart disease more than any other disease.) What we once knew about heart disease (symptoms, prevention, treatment, and so on), therefore, was based on a man's body, which later proved harmful to women, because treatments developed for men are often not appropriate for women. Unfortunately, the same can be said about thyroid disease. Not enough research has been done on thyroid diseases and their treatments in women. But slowly, we're getting there.

Women also report that their thyroid health complaints are often not taken seriously. Many women are given "fluffy" answers about their symptoms and told they are related to PMS or menopause or stress. Indeed, as you'll learn in this book, many physical and emotional ailments can mask thyroid disease in women, causing it to be missed. Or, more commonly, thyroid disease can aggravate other physical and emotional discomforts that are part of being female.

It's important to work with your doctor to be informed about your thyroid health or other health problems. Before consenting to treatments or tests surrounding your thyroid health, here are the questions you must ask yourself:

1. Do you understand the information relevant to your decision, and do you appreciate the reasonably foreseeable consequences of your decision, or *lack* of decision? This is what is known as your capacity to consent to procedures.
2. Do you understand what is being disclosed, and can you make your decision based on this information?
3. Are you being allowed to make your decision free of any undue influences? (For example, are you in pain? Is information being distorted or omitted? Are you being sedated?) This is what is known as *voluntariness*; involuntary "consent" means, of course, that you have *not* consented to a procedure.

If you answered no to any of these questions, you are probably not being given adequate information, or you are in no condition to make a decision about your health.

Doctors also have different medical personalities, which will affect how they disclose information to you. For example, a *paternalistic* doctor usually makes the decision for you or strongly suggests an approach. An *informative* doctor presents, in theory, enough information for you to make your own choice. Because your doctor knows more than you do, however, it may be unrealistic for you to actually make your own decision.

On that note, I leave it to you to use this book to help yourself better understand thyroid disease and how your thyroid condition will affect your health-care decisions throughout your life.

THE
THYROID
SOURCEBOOK
FOR WOMEN

1

All About Eve—and the Thyroid Gland

AT LEAST ONE in ten women can expect to suffer from some sort of thyroid disorder during her lifetime. Whether thyroid disorders strike at puberty, during peak reproductive years, during or after pregnancy, around menopause, or after the age of sixty, a woman's body is uniquely—and dramatically—affected. The most common thyroid disease (Hashimoto's thyroiditis, which causes an underactive thyroid gland) occurs three times more frequently in women than men, affecting roughly one in five women. The second most common thyroid disease (Graves' disease, which causes an overactive thyroid gland) occurs much more frequently in women. Thyroid nodules (lumps) and thyroid cancer are also much more common in women than men.

Thyroid disease can aggravate all kinds of health conditions that typically plague women, ranging from gynecological problems to eating disorders, depression (particularly postpartum depression), heart disease, and osteoporosis. Because thyroid disorders can affect one's appearance, women may suffer from body image problems or low self-esteem as a result of a change in appearance.

Women are more susceptible to autoimmune diseases in general, which means that the body attacks its own tissue. Lupus, multiple sclerosis, and rheumatoid arthritis are all examples of autoimmune diseases that strike women almost exclusively. Two of the most common thyroid disorders—Hashimoto's and Graves' disease—are also autoimmune. Stress, familial inheritance, and environmental factors such as smoking are believed to be the particular triggers of autoimmune diseases in women.

There is a separate issue with respect to thyroid disorders and women that affects a woman's emotional and physical health: validation. Since so many symptoms of thyroid disease are vague (see Chapter 2) and can be masked by other women's health problems (or ignored because of the existence of other health problems), many women suffer from these five horrible words: "It's all in your head!" Misdiagnosed thyroid disorders can worsen existing health problems and lead to unnecessary suffering. Many women continue to report that they find their health practitioners are dismissive of women's health interests, which can lead women down a frustrating path of "doctor bouncing" in order to obtain an accurate diagnosis of a thyroid disorder (discussed in Chapter 11).

This chapter is your starting point. It explains what your thyroid does, what your ovaries do, and how your unique physiology can be affected by a thyroid disorder. Symptoms of thyroid disease and the types of thyroid disorders that occur are discussed in Chapter 2. If you're suffering from a thyroid disorder, take heart: it's not all in your head—it's all in your *neck*. And it's treatable—which is something that cannot always be said about other women's health problems.

What Is a Thyroid?

The word *thyroid* was coined in the 1600s and is Greek for "shield" because of its shieldlike butterfly shape. Your thyroid gland is located in the lower part of your neck, in front of your windpipe (see Figure 1.1), and it makes two thyroid hormones (the word *hormone* is Greek for "stimulator")—thyroxine, known as T4 (because it has four iodine atoms) and triiodothyronine, known as T3 (which has three iodine atoms). Thyroid hormone (the two hormones are referred to in the singular) is then secreted into the circulatory system and becomes widely distributed throughout the body; it is one of the basic regulators of the function of every cell and tissue within the body, and a steady supply is crucial for good health. In essence, your thyroid affects you from head to toe—including skin and hair! (See Figure 1.2.)

Figure 1.1 *Where your thyroid lives.*

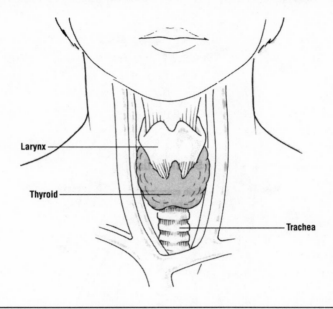

Reprinted from *Nichts Gutes im Schilde Krankheiten der Schiddruse.* Copyright 1994, Georg Thieme Publishing.

If you were to break down exactly how much T4 and T3 is secreted by your thyroid, you would find that 80 percent of the thyroid output is T4 and only 20 percent is T3. Although these hormones have the same effect in your body, T3 is four times as powerful as T4 and works eight times as fast. It is similar to comparing juice in a bottle and frozen concentrate. T4 works by turning into T3 by shedding an iodine atom if your body requires some thyroid hormone—fast!

Iodine

Your thyroid gland extracts iodine from various foods, including certain vegetables, shellfish, milk products, and anything with iodized salt or red dye number 3. Normally, we consume more than sufficient iodine in our daily diet. On the other hand, the diets of people in many parts of the developing world are iodine deficient, resulting in high rates of goiter (enlarged thyroid glands) and hypothyroidism.

Figure 1.2 The thyroid affects the body from head to toe.

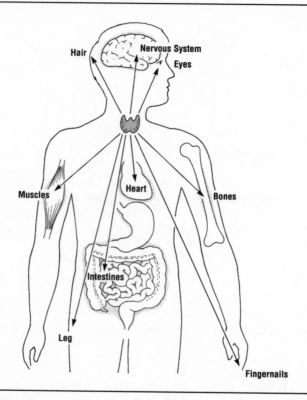

Reprinted from *Nichts Gutes im Schilde Krankheiten der Schiddruse.* Copyright 1994, Georg Thieme Publishing.

Our thyroids are very sensitive to iodine. When a person's thyroid gland is not able to obtain sufficient quantities of iodine, the thyroid can enlarge, and the person will develop a goiter. In this case, the thyroid gland gets too little iodine and produces too little thyroid hormone. On the flip side, too much iodine increases the chance of getting thyroid inflammation, and Hashimoto's thyroiditis can develop, which also causes hypothyroidism and goiter. Although it seems odd that both too much and too little iodine can produce the same results, the reason the goiter develops in each case is different.

Women with goiters are well-known throughout history, and as discussed in Chapter 5, the thyroid naturally enlarges during pregnancy. Goiters even appear in famous paintings and portraits of women, including Rubens's *Le Chapeau de Paille*, which hangs in the National Gallery in London.

Goiter Belts and Iodine Deficiency

A goiter belt is not a fashion accessory. You may be familiar with the term *goiter belt*, which refers to regions that typically suffer from insufficient iodine. The Great Lakes region, for example, used to be a goiter belt. The term originated because inhabitants of these regions would often develop goiters from a lack of iodine. Goiter belts are located far from seawater. In regions close to seawater, iodine gets into the soil and water supply from the wind and rain off the saltwater ocean. It also gets into plants eaten by people and livestock. It then travels into the milk and meat in people's diet.

The introduction of iodized salt in our diet has virtually eliminated goiters resulting from iodine deficiency in North America. But the problem of iodine deficiency is far from solved in other parts of the world. In fact, more than one billion people are at risk for iodine deficiency–related thyroid disease. Three hundred million people in Asia alone suffer from goiters, while twenty million people suffer from brain damage due to iodine deficiency in pregnancy and infancy. This is very disturbing because these problems can be completely prevented by the simple addition of iodized salt or iodized oil (proposed in some regions) to the diet. Goiters from iodine deficiency are regularly found in Asia, Africa, South America, and especially in mountainous regions such as the Himalayas and the Andes.

The first International Goiter Congress was held in 1929 in Bern after Switzerland and the United States introduced iodized salt. Many countries soon followed suit, and iodine deficiency has disappeared in many parts of the world. But not much happened to eliminate iodine deficiency in underdeveloped nations until 1985, when thyroid specialists established the International Council for Control of Iodine Deficiency Disorders (ICCIDD), a group of about four hundred members from seventy different countries.

While in North America only about one in four thousand newborns is born with hypothyroidism; in iodine-deficient areas 10 percent of all newborns are hypothyroid. Worse still, up to 70 percent of iodine-deficient populations become severely hypothyroid. Lack of thyroid hormone prevents proper brain development. As a result, iodine deficiency is now recognized as the most common cause of preventable mental defects. ICCIDD works with the World Health Organization and UNICEF to develop national programs in Africa, Asia, Latin America, and Europe with the goal of eliminating iodine deficiency in the near future. Most recently, the salt industry has joined the fight, too.

The Role of Calcitonin

Your thyroid gland "rents space" to nonthyroid cells called C cells, which make the hormone calcitonin. In many animals, this hormone helps to regulate calcium, but its importance in humans is debatable. Calcitonin is also used to treat Paget's disease, a bone disease that affects mostly men. Yet, to your bones, calcitonin can be likened to the tonsils. Calcitonin may in large amounts serve a useful purpose. But when the hormone is not manufactured due to the absence of a thyroid gland (if it's removed or ablated by radioactive iodine), you won't really notice any effects, just as you don't miss your tonsils if they are removed. Calcium levels are really controlled by the parathyroid glands, discussed later, and are much more dependent on the hormone estrogen and vitamin D, which helps with calcium absorption. Both diet and exercise build bone mass. There are also drug therapies on the market that can help to prevent osteoporosis, discussed in Chapter 6.

Calcitonin is only important in regard to the thyroid if you are discussing screening for a rare type of thyroid cancer called medullary thyroid cancer. When this kind of thyroid cancer develops, the tumor overproduces calcitonin, which is the telltale marker for this type of cancer. Once the thyroid and tumor deposits in it are removed, continued calcitonin secretions are a sign that this cancer is still in the body.

The Role of Thyroglobulin

Although this sounds like a Halloween candy, thyroglobulin is a specific protein made only by your thyroid cells and used by the thyroid gland itself to make thyroid hormone. Like calcitonin, this substance isn't all that important to your body once your thyroid is gone; you won't miss it. The only role thyroglobulin plays after your thyroid problem is treated is in screening for thyroid cancer recurrence. You see, when your thyroid gland is removed due to any type of thyroid cancer (see Chapters 10 and 11), this protein shouldn't be manufactured anymore. But when thyroglobulin shows up on a blood test after the thyroid gland has been removed surgically, it is a sign that some thyroid cancer cells are still in your body. For hyperthyroid or hypothyroid patients, however, screening for thyroglobulin is useless.

Hypothyroidism and Hyperthyroidism

The thyroid gland has one job to do: produce thyroid hormone on a supply-and-demand basis. But for many different reasons, the thyroid gland may either under- or overproduce thyroid hormone. *Hypothyroidism* means your thyroid is making too little or no thyroid hormone, which results in a slowing down of your bodily functions. In lay terms, hypothyroidism is known as an underactive thyroid. (The prefix *hypo-* means underactive.) *Hyperthyroidism* is the opposite: The thyroid gland is overactive, which results in *thyrotoxicosis*, or too much thyroid hormone. This leads to a speeding up of bodily functions. In lay terms, hyperthyroidism is known as an overactive thyroid. (The prefix *hyper-* means overactive.) Frequently patient literature will use the terms *hyperthyroidism* and *thyrotoxicosis* interchangeably, because thyrotoxicosis is one of the symptoms of hyperthyroidism. The causes, symptoms, and emotional effects of hypo- and hyperthyroidism are covered in depth in Chapter 2.

The Pituitary Gland

Your thyroid is under a lot of pressure to meet precise demand for a product it solely produces. That's where your pituitary gland comes in. Like a government, it controls and regulates all bodily functions and secretions (see Table 1.1). The pituitary gland (often referred to as the master gland) is situated under the brain, behind the eyes, and is, without question, the most influential gland in your body. Your thyroid gland reports directly to it. (So do your ovaries—which I will discuss later.)

Table 1.1 Your Hormones

The Gland	Hormones It Makes	What Hormones Do
Thyroid gland	thyroxine and triiodothyronine (T4 and T3)	control the heart and metabolic rate
	calcitonin	regulates blood calcium levels
Parathyroid gland	parathyroid hormone (PTH)	regulates calcium and phosphorus
Adrenal glands	stress hormones—adrenaline/ noradrenaline	regulate heart rate and blood pressure
	steroid hormones—e.g., cortisol and aldosterone	convert carbohydrate into energy
	sex hormones—androgens and estrogen*	control sexual development
Ovaries**	sex hormones—estrogen and progesterone	control menstrual cycle
Pancreas	insulin	maintains blood sugar levels
	glucagon	stimulates the liver to produce glucose
Pituitary gland	growth hormone	controls growth and aging
	prolactin	controls milk production
	antidiuretic hormone (ADH) (vasopressin)	regulates and controls urine production
	oxytocin	controls uterine contractions, breastfeeding, and childbirth
	thyroid-stimulating hormone (TSH)	controls thyroid hormone (T4, T3)

*In men, the sex hormone is testosterone.
**In men, the testicles produce the male hormone testosterone and sperm.
Source: Adapted by permission from Patsy Westcott, *Thyroid Problems: A Practical Guide to Symptoms and Treatment* (London: Thorsons/HarperCollins, 1995), 13.

The pituitary gland regularly monitors T4 and T3 stock in your body's blood levels. When stock is low, it sends a message to your thyroid gland—in the form of a stimulating hormone called TSH (thyroid-stimulating hormone)—and orders it to produce more.

Problems at the Helm

When hormone levels are adequate, TSH production is quite small; when hormone levels are too high, the pituitary gland stops all TSH secretion. This should alert the thyroid to stop production. But it doesn't always work, particularly when the thyroid gland is being turned on by the immune system (which occurs in Graves' disease) or learns to make T4 without the need for TSH. This latter situation occurs, for instance, with a multinodular goiter, meaning a bumpy or lumpy, enlarged thyroid gland. What happens here is that, for some unknown reason, a lump or nodule forms from your thyroid gland and is able to produce T4 and T3 on its own, no longer under the control of TSH from the pituitary gland. The pituitary gland sees this excess of T3 and T4 and appropriately stops the TSH secretion, which alerts the normal parts of the thyroid gland to slow down production. But T3 and T4 are still produced in uncontrolled quantities by the independent, or *autonomous*, nodule. So the system breaks down, and you wind up with too much thyroid hormone.

This same scenario can take place if you suffer from Graves' disease, which is an autoimmune or self-attacking disease, explained more thoroughly in Chapter 9. With Graves' disease, the body attacks its own thyroid gland. Something goes haywire in the immune system, and the thyroid gland is suddenly seen as an enemy. So an armed antibody is produced, called thyroid-stimulating antibody (TSA). TSA is then sent on a special search-and-destroy mission and launches a surprise attack on your poor thyroid gland, which is only doing its job. It latches on to the same "on" switch that TSH uses to turn on the thyroid. The result is that the pituitary gland sees all the extra T3 and T4 from the thyroid and again turns off its release of TSH. Confused and disoriented, the thyroid gland makes thyroid hormone like it's going out of style. Unfortunately, the white blood cells from the immune system, which make TSA, don't care how high the thyroid hormone levels get. You wind up hyperthyroid.

So, like any check-and-balance system, there is always a hole. When your thyroid is out of control, there is no way that your body can manage the situation without outside intervention. If there were, all it would have to do is get rid of all excess thyroid hormone. Unfortunately, it can't do that. As a result, overproduction or underproduction of thyroid hormone can cause trouble.

Functional Versus Structural Thyroid Disorders

Graves' disease is a good example of a functional thyroid disorder. In the early stages of Graves' disease, the thyroid might enlarge only slightly and would, perhaps, not be felt by your doctor. To the doctor, your thyroid appears normal in size and shape but is not properly controlled—it is overproducing thyroid hormone and causing your body to overwork itself. Function in this case is measured by blood tests. The opposite effect, underproduction of thyroid hormone, is measured by the same tests.

A goiter, which is an enlarged thyroid gland, is an example of a structural disorder. (Goiters can be caused by Graves' disease or other conditions that result in underproduction or overproduction of thyroid hormone.) In this case, your thyroid would grow noticeably larger in appearance, something your doctor could verify definitively by simply feeling your neck. If the goiter is a by-product of an overactive thyroid, for example, a blood test may determine that there is too much thyroid hormone in your bloodstream before the goiter grows too large. But many times an overactive thyroid gland isn't diagnosed by your doctor until the enlargement is so pronounced that the doctor can't miss it.

More often, a goiter is caused by a "broken" thyroid which has been attacked by antibodies from the immune system, causing it to be scarred and swollen. This is called *Hashimoto's thyroiditis*. (*Thyroiditis* means inflammation of the thyroid gland.) In other circumstances, particularly in mountainous parts of poorly developed countries, lack of iodine makes the thyroid unable to produce T3 and T4. The pituitary keeps trying to stimulate the thyroid by making more and more TSH. All the TSH can do is make the gland grow bigger and become a goiter, unless enough iodine is added to the diet.

Nodules

Your thyroid gland is also vulnerable to a hostile takeover. For reasons usually unknown (in some cases, exposure to radiation is a cause, discussed in Chapter 10), the tissue and cells in the thyroid gland change and start to overgrow, causing lumps. These lumps or nodules can sometimes make too much thyroid hormone, called "hot" nodules. On the other hand, sometimes these nodules forget how to make thyroid hormone and produce lumpy thyroids without changing thyroid hormone levels. When pictures (scans) are taken with special radiation cameras after the person swallows a small amount of radioactive iodine (see Chapter 11), these nodules don't glow as brightly as the rest of the gland and are called "cold" nodules.

Although a few "cold" nodules may be thyroid cancers, 90 percent of them are not and can usually be ignored. Before you panic or become too casual about it, your doctor has to take a very skinny needle to take out some pieces of these nodules and examine them under a microscope. This is the only way to tell if the nodule is or is not a cancer without doing surgery. It is known as *fine needle aspiration* (FNA).

The Parathyroid Glands

Everyone has at least four parathyroid glands that control the blood calcium level or calcium balance. (Some people have more than four.) Your parathyroid glands stimulate the release of calcium from bone to raise blood calcium levels; they also increase the absorption of calcium by producing vitamin D. Even more important, they tell your kidneys to keep the calcium in the blood from leaking out of your body into your urine.

These glands are located near the back of each lobe of your thyroid gland. The easiest way to grasp exactly where they are located is to imagine the capital letter H. At each tip of the H, imagine a circle. If the H is your thyroid gland, the circles at each tip are where your parathyroid glands are usually found.

Parathyroid glands usually come into play only when you undergo surgical treatment for a thyroid condition. Surgery is most commonly required when thyroid cancer is diagnosed or a goiter has grown out of control.

Because the parathyroid glands are so close to the thyroid gland, surgical complications could be serious. Essentially, if a surgeon is performing a thyroidectomy (removal of the thyroid gland) or simply removing benign or malignant growths on or around the thyroid gland, he or she must be careful not to touch or disrupt the parathyroid glands. As long as there is one good functioning parathyroid gland, there is no problem. However, these small glands are susceptible to either temporary or permanent damage during thyroid surgery.

If the parathyroid glands were accidentally removed or damaged during thyroid surgery, your blood calcium levels would drop. This could cause muscle spasms and contractions, seizures or convulsions called *tetany*, and cataracts. If the damage was temporary, you would need to take calcium intravenously and later, orally. If the damage was permanent, you would need to take calcium supplements as well as high doses of vitamin D for the rest of your life and have your calcium levels tested frequently. Vitamin D, in several forms, helps your body absorb large enough amounts of calcium to replace the losses. You may be low on calcium for other reasons, too. Diuretics can cause you to lose calcium in your urine, and kidney problems as well as certain medications can affect calcium levels. Diet, of course, is also key: when you are not eating enough calcium-rich foods, your calcium levels can drop.

Sometimes, however, tumors can develop in the parathyroid gland itself, causing calcium levels to become too high. These tumors are usually located outside of the thyroid gland and do not affect it. When this happens, surgical removal of the parathyroid gland tumor is required. Depending on whether the growths are benign (noncancerous) or malignant (cancerous—which is rare), removal of one or more of the parathyroid glands is sometimes necessary. Most of the time, parathyroid tumors are not cancerous and are easily treated with surgery.

Tracing Thyroid Disease in Your Family

Tracing thyroid disease in the family is important if you are either planning a family or already have children. That's because autoimmune thyroid disease runs in families. If you are pregnant, trying to get pregnant, or *unable* to get pregnant, it is important that your doctor be aware of your family's thyroid history. If you are prone to thyroid disorders, particularly autoimmune thyroid disease (such as Graves' disease or Hashimoto's thyroiditis), you are more vulnerable to them when you are pregnant. And as discussed in the next section, sometimes an infertility problem is linked to a thyroid disorder. (Pregnancy and thyroid are covered in detail in Chapter 5.)

If you already have children and you know your family has a history of thyroid disorders, you can alert them to that fact when they are older (particularly daughters, since thyroid disorders occur more frequently in women) and encourage regular testing of thyroid levels in their late teens and adulthood. You can also alert your children's doctors to your family's thyroid history. By doing this you can avoid unnecessary health problems that can arise through misdiagnosis of either specific thyroid disorders or related disorders.

Many different autoimmune diseases tend to cluster together in people and families. For example, *vitiligo* is an autoimmune disease in which antibodies attack the melanin pigment cells in your skin. It is a harmless condition characterized by patches of pigmentation loss (either white or pinkish patches) on the hands, arms, neck, and face. If this condition runs in your family, it's a sign that you are susceptible to autoimmune thyroid disease or other autoimmune diseases such as rheumatoid arthritis, myasthenia gravis, and lupus. These conditions are not always seen together in a person or family; however, they should make you more alert to the possibility of thyroid disease.

The Menstrual Cycle

The menstrual cycle can sometimes be an important element in detecting a thyroid problem. When you're moderately hypothyroid, periods may be heavier and longer, while cycles are often shorter. When hypothyroidism is in a more severe stage, you may experience amenorrhea—a lack of menstruation or the absence of periods.

Consequently, there also may be problems with ovulation and conception resulting from either the hypothyroidism itself or associated hormonal changes. For example, in some women with severe hypothyroidism, their pituitary gland produces increased amounts of the hormone prolactin. Increased prolactin secretions can block estrogen production and essentially turn off normal menstrual cycles.

When you have too much thyroid hormone, periods are irregular (usually the time between periods is longer), scanty, and shorter. Women with too much thyroid hormone can also experience amenorrhea and generally have a very difficult time getting pregnant. In fact, infertility is a common problem for hyperthyroid (or thyrotoxic) women.

Younger girls are also affected by hyper- or hypothyroidism. If girls develop a thyroid condition during puberty, for example, they may have delayed menstrual function. If you have a daughter who seems to be in this situation or are in your teens yourself and have not yet experienced your period, request a thyroid function test. A teenager who is hypothyroid, for example, may look like a ten-year-old at seventeen. Once the thyroid problem is resolved, however, she will begin her sexual development normally.

By the same token, if you are currently having problems getting pregnant or are experiencing problems with your menstrual flow, it is a good idea to get your thyroid checked first before you undergo more extreme tests. Once the thyroid condition has been treated, menstrual flows and fertility should return to normal.

If you are approaching menopause, you may be experiencing changes in your cycles as a result of your stage in life, rather than a thyroid disorder. What you may wish to do is ask your doctor to test your levels of follicle-stimulating hormone (FSH) to see if they are high—an indication that you are approaching menopause. Home FSH tests are also available through your pharmacy. This will help sort out whether your cycle changes are related to your thyroid or your age. In many cases they are, unfortunately, related to both.

Changes to your flow or cycle length can also be caused by stress, infections, and of course, early pregnancy (a clue that you are pregnant). Also, there are rare circumstances when there is a pituitary tumor (almost always benign) that interferes with both the thyroid and the ovaries, causing both hypothyroidism and loss of menstrual periods (amenorrhea). In this case, it is important that the pituitary tumor is fully evaluated and treated, rather than merely taking thyroid hormone.

There is much to say about the menstrual cycle and thyroid disease. For this reason, I've devoted Chapter 4 to the topic, which discusses all aspects of the menstrual cycle, normal versus abnormal cycles, PMS, and contraception.

The Breast Connection

There is a connection between thyroid hormone and breast development. Animal studies indicate that the thyroid hormone works with prolactin, the hormone that is key to breast development and milk production. In addition, research in many areas of breast health has linked thyroid and iodine to breast conditions.

Breast Cancer

At one time, there were confusing reports as to whether benign thyroid disease was associated with breast cancer. If you have a strong family history of endocrine cancers, which includes thyroid cancer (although a large percentage of thyroid cancer is caused by an external trigger, such as x-ray therapy in childhood or radioactive iodine fallout), then, statistically, you are at increased risk for developing an endocrine cancer of some kind. Thyroid hormone replacement pills do not cause breast cancer, nor does radioactive iodine therapy, based on fifty years of tracking patients who received it. While for the most part there are relatively few absolutes about the causes of breast cancer, at the present time thyroid sufferers do not appear to have a higher incidence of breast cancer than women in the general population. On the other hand, women with thyroid cancer have a higher risk of developing breast cancer. No one yet knows why. A study published in 2000 by Amy Chen, M.D., M.P.H., of the University of Texas M. D. Anderson Cancer Center in Houston found an association between RAI treatment for thyroid cancer and an increased incidence of breast cancer in women under forty. A theory is that breast tissue, like thyroid tissue, traps iodine, and thus radioactive iodine can predispose both normal thyroid and normal breast tissue to cancer. But no study has been able to make an absolute link, as indeed, 70 percent of all breast cancers are caused by unknown factors. There is no doubt that breast cancer is a risk for all women. Thus, women who are having RAI therapy for thyroid cancer should be doing breast self-exam at least once a month, and should consider earlier routine mammography beginning at age forty (or earlier, if you're concerned).

Breast Self-Examination (BSE)

Breast self-examination, or BSE, should be called "get to know your breasts." It involves specific steps of feeling your breasts at the same time each month and distinguishing suspicious lumps from normal lumpy/bumpy breasts. You can't know if a lump has remained unchanged unless you've been checking your breasts regularly. While ideally you should begin BSE by the age of twenty, starting now—however old you are—is just fine. That way, you will know what your breasts normally feel like, should something abnormal develop down the road.

While you're menstruating, you'll need to do a BSE after your period ends when your breasts are least tender and lumpy. When you're pregnant, BSE should be done monthly throughout all stages of your pregnancy. When you're breast-feeding, perform BSE on a monthly basis after a feeding, when your breasts aren't filled with milk. (And then, after your periods return, perform BSE after a feeding, after your period!) If you're past menopause, just pick the same time each month, like the first or fifteenth of the month, to do it.

Although the steps to BSE are outlined here, make sure your doctor shows you how to do it as well. In addition, there is a learning kit available through many breast health centers known as the Mammacare Learning System, which was developed at the University of Florida and partially funded by the National Cancer Institute. This kit was designed to teach you how to do a breast self-exam using a vertical grid pattern—currently the most effective pattern. Ask your doctor how to obtain this learning system.

At any rate, here are the steps to BSE:

1. Visually inspect your breasts. Stand in front of the mirror and look closely at your breasts. You're looking for dimpling, puckering (like an orange peel in appearance), or noticeable lumps (which are rare). Do you see any discharge that dribbles out on its own or bleeding from the nipple? Any funny dry patches on the nipple?

2. Now, raise your arms over your head in front of the mirror, and look for the same things. Raising your arms smoothes out the breast a little more so these changes are more obvious.

3. Palpation (feeling your breast). Lie down on your bed with a pillow under your left shoulder and place your left hand under your head. With the flat part of the fingertips of your right hand, examine your left breast for a lump, using a gentle circular motion. Imagine that the breast is a clock, and make sure you feel each "hour," as well as the nipple area and armpit area.

4. Repeat step 3, but reverse sides, examining your right breast with your left hand.

5. If you find a lump, note the size, shape, and how painful it is. A suspicious lump is usually painless, about a quarter to a half inch in size, and remains unchanged from month to month. If you find a lump, get it looked at as soon as you can.

6. If discharge oozes out of your nipple on its own, or if blood comes out, see your doctor immediately. Don't wait.

7. If your nipple is dry and patchy, see your doctor immediately. Don't wait.

How Effective Is a Manual Breast Exam?

Two-thirds of all breast cancers are discovered by women themselves— either accidentally or through BSE. And although you should also have a clinical breast exam (this is when your doctor manually feels your breasts for abnormalities) done with your annual Pap test, too, not all doctors are virtuosos in doing clinical breast exams. That's why doing a BSE yourself is an extremely important screening method. BSE is also important in areas where doctors or routine mammography are not widely available.

Breast-Feeding

The first connection thyroid has to breast-feeding is a postpartum connection: if you have just delivered a child, you may be suffering from postpartum thyroid disease, which may, in turn, be interfering with your ability to care for your infant or breast-feed properly. Breast-feeding also delays the return of your periods, which means that you cannot rely on irregular cycles to be a clue that your thyroid is out of whack. For pregnancy and postpartum issues, see Chapter 5.

Another point about thyroid disease and breast-feeding is that you should not undergo either a radioactive iodine scan (thyroid scan) or be treated with radioactive iodine (see Chapter 11) while breast-feeding. Radioactive isotopes are secreted into breast milk and can be passed on to your child.

Antithyroid drugs (see Chapter 11) can be used if absolutely necessary when you are breast-feeding, although a small amount may pass into the breast milk. Taking thyroid hormone is also safe and will not harm your child in any way.

Fibrocystic Breast Condition (FBC)

You may have been diagnosed with fibrocystic breast condition, which is a broad term that refers to six separate benign breast conditions, including noncyclical breast pain. Some women with this particular breast problem may be put on an iodine treatment that has proven helpful. Outside of the United States, iodine therapy is widely used and has proven helpful for some women with this particular breast problem (although many U.S. breast specialists are not aware of iodine therapy for any breast condition whatsoever).

Again, the breasts—like the thyroid gland—trap iodine from the blood, and iodine treatment has been shown to improve fibrocystic breast condition as well as various other breast conditions. The catch is this: if you have iodine treatment for breast pain caused by cysts, you may risk a thyroid problem if you are predisposed to thyroid disease. Therefore, if you have a thyroid problem, please notify whoever is treating your breast condition prior to consenting to any treatment.

2

Signs of Trouble

It Is Not All in Your Head

WHAT ARE THE signs of thyroid trouble? They are symptoms of either an underactive thyroid gland, known as *hypothyroidism* (when the thyroid gland makes too little or no thyroid hormone), overactive thyroid gland, known as *hyperthyroidism* (when the thyroid gland makes too much thyroid hormone), or *thyrotoxicosis* (when too much thyroid hormone is in your body from too much medication or other reasons).

In most cases, overactive and underactive thyroid glands are symptoms of specific thyroid diseases; they are not the cause of a disorder, however. The best way to explain it is to imagine yourself with a cold; your throat is sore, your nose is stuffed, and your chest might feel congested. Here, the sore throat and congestion are cold symptoms; the cold itself is caused by a virus. Similarly, hyperthyroidism, thyrotoxicosis, or hypothyroidism are manifestations of thyroid disease; the thyroid disorders themselves are caused by particular malfunctions outlined later on. Sometimes, to simplify explanations, doctors may choose only to tell patients that they are hyperthyroid (most doctors do not use the term *thyrotoxic*) or hypothyroid, sparing them details of the actual malfunction that caused their over- or underactive symptoms. However, it is not possible to spontaneously produce too much or too little thyroid hormone without the existence of a particular disorder.

19

Often, treatment for a specific thyroid disorder results in hypo- or hyperthyroidism. When this is the case, the under- or overactivity of the thyroid gland is a temporary side effect of the treatment, just the same as drowsiness can be a side effect of a particular cold medicine. This chapter explains what happens to your body when you are either hyper- or hypothyroid, and outlines possible causes of either condition. Chapter 3 covers the role of stress in thyroid disease, while Chapter 9 examines two of the main causes of hypo- or hyperthyroidism in greater detail: Hashimoto's disease and Graves' disease. Both are autoimmune and believed to be triggered by stress. Chapter 11 outlines tests and treatments for hypothyroidism and hyperthyroidism.

Cold Women: The Hypoalphabet Soup

When you are hypothyroid, everything slows down—including your body temperature. Feeling cold all the time is one of the more classic hypothyroid symptoms. When your body slows down, there are equal but opposite symptoms to the hyperthyroid/thyrotoxic scenario. So again, I will discuss these symptoms alphabetically so that you can find the information you need faster (see also Table 2.1). And also again, these symptoms disappear once the thyroid hormone level is restored to normal.

Cardiovascular Changes

Hypothyroid people will have an unusually slow pulse rate (between 45 and 75 beats per minute) and blood pressure that may be too high.

More severe or prolonged hypothyroidism could raise your cholesterol levels as well, and this can aggravate blockage of coronary arteries. In severe hypothyroidism, the heart muscle fibers may weaken, which can lead to heart failure. This scenario is rare, however, and one would have to suffer from severe and obvious hypothyroid symptoms long before the heart would be at risk.

If you're past menopause, this may aggravate your risk for heart disease since women's risk of heart disease increases with age, particularly postmenopause. For example, it's not unusual if you are hypothy-

Table 2.1 Hypothyroidism at a Glance

Women are five times more likely to experience hypothyroidism than men. Here's a quick checklist of symptoms.

What You May Notice
- Changes in skin pigmentation
- Chest pain after physical activity
- Constipation
- Depression
- Difficulty managing hair, brittle nails
- Difficulty concentrating
- Extreme tiredness and slowness
- Eyelids that feel sticky
- Feeling cold
- Headaches, problems focusing
- Irregular periods or infertility
- Loss of interest in sex
- Muscle spasms
- Shortness of breath
- Slow healing, frequent infections
- Tingling in hands and feet
- Weakness and muscular aches and pains
- Weight gain

What Others May Say
- You look pale.
- Your face is puffy.
- Your eyes are swollen.
- Your hair looks/feels coarse. Are you losing hair?
- Your voice is husky.

continued

Table 2.1 Hypothyroidism at a Glance (continued)

- You snore!

- You used to love doing X or Y—why aren't you interested anymore?

- Did you hear what I said? (meaning that you can't hear well)

What Your Doctor Should Watch For

- Delayed reflexes

- Goiter (enlarged thyroid)

- Milk leaking from breasts (when you are not breast-feeding)

- Muscle weakness

- Slowed pulse

- Soft abdomen

- Tingling or numbness in the hands (sign of carpal tunnel syndrome)

Source: Adapted from Patsy Westcott, *Thyroid Problems: A Practical Guide to Symptoms and Treatment* (London: Thorsons/HarperCollins, 1995), 35.

roid to notice chest pain (which may be confused with angina), or shortness of breath when you exert yourself, or notice some calf pain as well, which is caused by hardening of the arteries in the leg. Fluid may also collect, causing swollen legs and feet.

Cold Intolerance

You may not be able to find a comfortable temperature and may often wonder "why it's always so freezing in here." Hypothyroid people carry sweaters with them all the time to compensate for continuous sensitivity to cold. You'll feel much more comfortable in hot, muggy weather, and may not even perspire in the heat. This is because your entire metabolic rate has slowed down.

Depression and Psychiatric Misdiagnosis

Hypothyroidism is linked to psychiatric depression more frequently than hyperthyroidism. The physical symptoms associated with major depression (discussed in Chapter 3) lead to the psychiatric misdiagnosis. Sometimes, psychiatrists find that hypothyroid patients can even exhibit certain behaviors linked to psychosis, such as paranoia or aural and visual hallucinations (hearing voices, seeing things that are not there). This used to be called *myxedema madness*. Interestingly, roughly 15 percent of all patients suffering from depression are found to be hypothyroid.

Digestive Changes and Weight Gain

Because your system has slowed down, you'll suffer from constipation, hardening of stools, bloating (which may cause bad breath), poor appetite, and heartburn. The heartburn results because your food is not moving through the stomach as quickly, so acid reflux (where semi-digested food comes back up the esophagus) may occur.

Because the lack of thyroid hormone slows down your metabolism, you might gain weight as well. But often—because your appetite may decrease radically—your weight will stay the same. Hypothyroid patients can experience some or all of these symptoms, and sometimes, if the hypothyroidism is caught early enough, patients may not be conscious of any of these symptoms until their doctor specifically asks if they have noticed a particular change in their metabolism or energy. You'll need to adjust your eating habits to compensate, which is discussed in more detail in Chapter 8. The typical scenario is to gain roughly ten pounds during a period of about a year, even though you may not be eating as much. Some of the weight gain, however, is due to bloating from constipation.

Enlarged Thyroid Gland

Your thyroid gland often enlarges, either because it is scarred from Hashimoto's thyroiditis (discussed in Chapter 9) or from constant stimulation from high TSH levels. But sometimes, the destruction of the thyroid tissue can actually cause the thyroid gland to shrink.

Fatigue and Sleepiness

The most classic symptom of hypothyroidism is a distinct, lethargic tiredness or sluggishness, causing you to feel unnaturally sleepy. I refer to my own hypothyroid symptoms as "draggy." Your doctor may also notice that you exhibit very slow reflexes. Researchers now know that when you are hypothyroid, you are unable to reach the deepest "Stage 4" level of sleep. This is the most restful kind of sleep. Lack of it will explain why you will remain tired, sleepy, and unrefreshed.

Fingernails

Fingernails become brittle and develop lines and grooves to the point where applying nail polish may become impossible.

Hair Changes

When you are hypothyroid, hair may become thinner, dry, and brittle, causing you to need additional hair conditioner. Hair loss may also occur to the point where balding sets in. (See "Hair Changes" under "Fast Women: The Hyperalphabet Soup" for more details.) You will also lose body hair such as eyebrow, leg, and arm hair, as well as pubic hair. Much of this grows back after some time on thyroid hormone replacement.

High Cholesterol

Hypothyroid people often have high cholesterol that can lead to a host of other problems, including heart disease. This should be controlled through diet until your thyroid problem is brought under control. It's generally recommended that anyone with high cholesterol be tested for hypothyroidism. Cholesterol lowering medications should not be started unless the high cholesterol levels persist a few months after sufficient thyroid hormone replacement therapy.

Menstrual Cycle Changes

Menstrual periods become much heavier and more frequent than usual, and sometimes ovaries can stop producing an egg each month. This can make conception difficult if you are trying to have a child. Anemia, resulting from heavy periods, may also develop. See Chapters 4 and 5 for more details on menstrual cycle changes and infertility.

Milky Discharge from Breasts

Hypothyroidism may cause you to overproduce prolactin, the hormone responsible for milk production. Too much prolactin can also block estrogen production, which will interfere with regular periods and ovulation. As a general rule, when you notice discharge coming out of your breast by itself and you are not lactating or deliberately expressing your breasts, please have it checked by a breast specialist or gynecologist (who should also perform a thorough breast exam to rule out other breast conditions).

Muscles

Common complaints from hypothyroid people are muscular aches and cramps (which may contribute to crampier periods). Joints may also start to hurt. In fact, many people believe they are experiencing arthritic symptoms, when, in fact, this condition completely clears up once hypothyroidism is treated. But the aching can be severe enough to wake you up at night. Muscle coordination is also a problem, causing you to feel "klutzy" all the time while finding it increasingly difficult to perform simple motor tasks. This can result from the effects of hypothyroidism on the coordination center in the brain, the cerebellum.

Numbness

This is combined with a sensation of "pins and needles" as well as a tendency to develop carpal tunnel syndrome, characterized by tingling and numbness in the hands. It is caused, in this case, by compression on nerves in the wrist due to thickening and swelling of the body tissues under the skin. This condition also plagues pregnant women who suffer from water retention. Carpal tunnel syndrome can also be a repetitive strain injury and can be aggravated by working at a computer keyboard, for example. This condition should resolve itself once your hypothyroidism is treated.

Poor Memory and Concentration

Hypothyroidism causes a "spacey" feeling, where you may find it difficult to remember things or to concentrate at work. This is especially scary for seniors, who may feel as though dementia is settling in. In fact, one of the most common causes of so-called senility is undiagnosed hypothyroidism. (So before you shout "Alzheimer's," get a thyroid function test for the loved one you suspect is "losing it.") See Chapter 6 for more details about thyroid disease and aging.

Skin Changes

Skin may feel dry and coarse to the point where it flakes like powder when you scratch it. Cracked skin will also become common on your elbows and kneecaps. Your skin will also sport a yellowish hue as the hypothyroidism worsens. The yellow color results from a buildup of carotene, a substance in our diet that is normally converted into vitamin A, but slows because of hypothyroidism. Because your blood vessels are more tightly constricted, diverting blood away from your skin, you will appear pale and washed out.

Other symptoms more obvious to a physician will be the presence of a condition known as *myxedema*, a thickening of skin and underlying tissues. Myxedema is characterized by a puffiness around the eyes and face, and can even involve the tongue, which will also swell. See the section "Easy Bruising" as well, under "Fast Women: The Hyperalphabet Soup."

Stunted Growth in Children

The classic scenario is wondering why your twelve-year-old son still looks like he's only nine years old. So you take him to the doctor—and find out that his thyroid petered out and he has stopped growing! This will completely reverse itself once treatment with thyroid hormone begins.

Voice Changes

If your thyroid is enlarged, it may affect your vocal cords and cause your voice to sound hoarse or husky.

What Causes Hypothyroidism?

Hypothyroidism is often caused by an autoimmune disorder known as Hashimoto's thyroiditis, which causes inflammation of the thyroid gland (see Chapter 9). There are other causes of thyroiditis as well.

Ironically, the treatment for a hyperthyroid condition often causes hypothyroidism because the thyroid is often ablated to treat the hyperthyroid condition. (See Chapter 11 for more information on the treatment of thyroid disorders.) Also, anyone who has a thyroidectomy (surgical removal of the thyroid gland) will be hypothyroid. Thyroidectomy is standard as part of the treatment for thyroid cancer.

Sometimes a baby is born with no thyroid gland. This is one cause of congenital hypothyroidism, discussed in Chapter 5. In many parts of the world, iodine deficiency causes hypothyroidism in both newborns and adults. Postpartum hypothyroidism can also develop, which occurs when the thyroid gland becomes inflamed after delivery, known as postpartum thyroiditis. (See Chapter 5.)

Finally, a significant portion of people who have received external radiation therapy to the head and neck area for cancers such as Hodgkin's disease, for example, tend to develop hypothyroidism within ten years after treatment. It is recommended that this group have an annual TSH test.

Other Forms of Thyroiditis

Although the most common form of thyroiditis is Hashimoto's disease, there are other kinds of thyroiditis that can occur that can cause either hypothyroidism or thyrotoxicosis. Depending on what kind of thyroiditis you have, a goiter and symptoms of either hyperthyroidism or hypothyroidism can develop. Other forms of thyroiditis include the following:

• *Subacute viral thyroiditis* (also known as de Quervain's thyroiditis). It is suspected that subacute (or "not-so-severe") viral thyroiditis is probably caused by one or more viruses. Although there is no final proof that this condition is viral in origin, several possible viruses have been implicated that are similar to the measles or mumps viruses, and certain common cold viruses. The condition ranges from extremely mild to severe and usually runs its course as will a normal flu virus. When the thyroid gland gets inflamed, thyroid hormones leak out—the way fluid oozes out of a blister. Then, of course, your system has too much thyroid hormone in it, and you experience all the classic hyperthyroid/thyrotoxic symptoms outlined above. But sometimes damage to the thyroid gland can result in permanent hypothyroidism, which means that you will need to be on thyroid hormone replacement for the rest of your life.

• *Silent thyroiditis.* The silent form of thyroiditis is so named because it is tricky to diagnose. Silent thyroiditis runs a painless course but is otherwise similar to subacute viral thyroiditis. With this version, there are no symptoms or outward signs of inflammation but mild thyrotoxicosis still occurs—for the same leakage reasons. Usually silent thyroiditis sufferers are women, and it is common in the postpartum period (discussed further in Chapter 5). This is sometimes referred to as *spontaneously resolving thyrotoxicosis.*

Secondary Hypothyroidism

Sometimes hypothyroidism occurs because of a pituitary gland disorder that may interfere with the production of thyroid-stimulating hormone (TSH). This is pretty rare, however. Tumors or cysts on the pituitary gland can also interfere with production of hormones from the gonads and the adrenal glands. This can also occur from damage to the hypothalamus region of the brain.

Subclinical Hypothyroidism

Subclinical hypothyroidism refers to hypothyroidism that has not progressed very far, meaning that you currently have few or no symptoms. On a blood test, your free T4 (thyroid hormone) readings would be very close to normal but your thyroid-stimulating hormone (TSH) readings would be higher than normal. Right now, there is much discussion in clinical circles about doing routine TSH testing in certain groups of people for subclinical hypothyroidism. This would include anyone with a family history of thyroid disease, women over forty, women after childbirth, and anyone over age sixty. Because the TSH test is simple and can be added to any blood laboratory package, it presents an opportunity to catch hypothyroidism before serious symptoms develop, and hence prevent it and all the symptoms discussed under "Cold Women: The Hypoalphabet Soup."

Fast Women: The Hyperalphabet Soup

When you are hyperthyroid due to an overactive thyroid gland, or are making too much thyroid hormone for other reasons (called thyrotoxicosis), everything speeds up. As a result, there are numerous physical symptoms that you can experience when you are hyperthyroid—so many, in fact, that I am going to discuss them alphabetically (see also Table 2.2). This will hopefully give you faster access to the information you may need now! The good news is that the vast majority of these symptoms disappear once your thyroid problem is treated. Again, all of the following symptoms are signs of either thyrotoxicosis (too much thyroid hormone) or an overactive thyroid gland which results in thyrotoxicosis.

Behavioral and Emotional Changes

You may experience a host of emotional symptoms such as irritability, restlessness, sleeplessness, anxiety, depression, and sadness. See the sections "The Emotional Effects of Hyperthyroidism" and "Hyperthyroidism and Psychiatric Misdiagnosis" later in this chapter for details.

Bowel Movements

Increased frequency of bowel movements, known as hyperdefecation, is another sign of too much thyroid hormone. This is different than diarrhea because the bowel movements will not be loose but appear to be normal. They'll just appear more often—even if your diet is normal and hasn't changed. Because your digestion speeds up, so does your bowel habit. Sometimes the buildup of thyroid hormone will prevent your

Table 2.2 Hyperthyroidism at a Glance

Nine out of ten hyperthyroid people are women. Here's a quick checklist of hyperthyroid symptoms.

What You May Notice

- Anxiety and irritability
- Changes in menstrual cycle, such as no periods, longer or shorter cycle
- Dry, thin skin that turns red more easily
- Enlarged thyroid
- Eye problems or irritations
- Feeling hot all the time
- Hair loss
- Increased appetite
- Increased sex drive
- Increased sweating
- Insomnia
- Muscle weakness
- Palpitations
- Staring eyes
- Warm, moist palms
- Weight loss

What Others May Say

- You're moody.
- You're so talkative lately!
- You seem agitated.
- Your neck looks swollen.
- Why are you staring like that? (your eyes have a "staring" look)
- You've lost weight.
- You're shaking.

What Your Doctor Should Look For

- Fast pulse

- Irregular heartbeat (atrial fibrillation)

- Low blood pressure

- Quick reflexes

- Tremor

Source: Adapted from Patsy Westcott, *Thyroid Problems: A Practical Guide to Symptoms and Treatment* (London: Thorsons/HarperCollins, 1995), 45.

small intestine from absorbing certain nutrients from food as well. If you suffered from chronic constipation prior to your thyroid problem, you may notice simple regularity without laxatives or fiber. You may even notice that you have magically lost seven to ten pounds, although you have been eating more than usual. You may also crave sweets.

Easy Bruising

Platelet disorders tend to be more common in people with either hyper- or hypothyroidism because the number of platelets—which help your blood to clot—is reduced. Aspirin or nonsteroidal anti-inflammatory drugs (NSAIDs), such as ibuprofen, can make the bruising worse. Your platelet function can be checked via a bleeding time test. This disorder can exist without a thyroid problem. However, this does not pose any danger to your health unless very large numbers of platelets are destroyed (which is a pretty rare occurrence). A watchful eye (yours and your doctor's) remains the best approach for now.

Enlarged Thyroid Gland

As discussed in Chapter 1, an enlarged thyroid gland is called a *goiter*, where your thyroid will enlarge and may swell in the front of your neck. Here, a goiter (an overgrown thyroid gland) develops because too much stimulation of the thyroid causes the gland to enlarge. In extreme cases, a goiter can swell to the diameter of a midsize balloon. Goiters are also caused by iodine deficiency, as well as by hypothyroidism.

Exhaustion

When your body is overworked, this can lead to exhaustion, which will affect your sleep patterns, energy levels, and your general emotional well-being. See the separate section on emotions, "The Emotional Effects of Hyperthyroidism," later in this chapter for details.

Eye Problems

If you are hyperthyroid due to Graves' disease, an autoimmune or self-attacking disorder, you may also notice changes in your eyes; they can become irritated, itchy, watery, and bulging. Sometimes double vision occurs. This is known as *exophthalmos* and is explained in detail in Chapter 7.

Fingertip and Fingernail Changes

Many people with too much thyroid hormone notice that they have swollen fingertips to the point where they look "clubbed." This is known as *achropachy* or clubbing. Nail growth also increases, while the nails become soft and easy to tear off. In addition, an alarming condition known as *onycholysis* can occur where the fingernails become partially separated from the fingertips.

Hair Changes

Hair often becomes softer and finer and may not be as easy to style as it once was. In some cases you may notice hair loss and find clumps of it on your pillow, clothing, tub, or hairbrush. It may also become grayer and may not take to perms or color. In appearance, there will be a general thinning of your hair, but once your thyroid is treated, your hair should grow as it once did. To create less stress on the hair, you should avoid coloring or perms until your hair follicles are stronger. If you are self-conscious, get a wig and take it to your hairdresser to be styled to match your normal hair. You can also contact the American Hair Loss Council at 800-274-8717.

Heart Palpitations

One of the first signs of too much thyroid hormone is a rapid, forceful heartbeat. Increased levels of thyroxine released from the thyroid gland stimulate the heart to beat faster and stronger. Initially, you will not notice an increase in your heart rate until it becomes severe.

When a heartbeat is noticeably fast and you are conscious of it beating in your chest, you will experience what is called a *palpitation*. Generally, palpitations can occur from excessive exercise, sexual activity, alcohol, caffeine, or smoking. It is abnormal for a palpitation to occur when your body is inactive, not anxious, or not exposed to substances known to increase your heart rate. Yet people with too much thyroid hormone often experience palpitations when they are reading, sleeping, or involved in other relaxing activities. Palpitations caused by an overactive thyroid gland do not mean you have a serious heart condition. Once your thyroid problem is treated, your heart will resume its normal rate.

If untreated, however, palpitations caused by hyperthyroidism can lead to serious heart problems and eventually cause heart failure. Normally, hyperthyroidism is caught in its early stages—long before any serious heart problem develops from palpitations. In fact, permanent changes in the heart are unusual in patients with normal, healthy hearts, unless hyperthyroidism is particularly severe and left untreated.

If you have normal thyroid function and take synthetic thyroid hormone when it is not prescribed (helping yourself to a friend's or relative's supply, for example), you will most likely overwork your heart and put yourself at risk unnecessarily. This is why it is dangerous to misuse synthetic thyroid hormone and why it should never be used as a weight control pill. In addition, women who use synthetic thyroid hormone as a weight control pill can worsen their health out of proportion to any weight loss results.

As many as 15 percent of all hyperthyroid people experience atrial fibrillation, a common heart rhythm abnormality. This means that your heart may pause slightly, followed by bursts of pounding, rapid heartbeats. While this may be only an occasional symptom, it is not unusual for it to be continuous until the thyroid problem is treated.

Another problem with a fast pulse (which may be as high as 150 beats per minute) is that the speed of the heartbeat may create congestive heart failure, which can cause swollen ankles and even a collection of fluid in the chest. Shortness of breath may also develop, particularly if you are over age sixty-five. For this reason, it is not unusual for hyperthyroidism to be misdiagnosed as asthma, bronchitis, or heart disease. Thyroid-related heart problems are treated with beta-blockers that slow the heart down.

Heat Intolerance

A classic physical sign of hyperthyroidism or too much thyroid hormone is an intolerance to heat. Your body temperature rises, and normal temperatures feel too warm. As a result, you sweat far more than usual. The feeling is unpleasant because you feel isolated in your discomfort. Typically, someone who is hyperthyroid is constantly wondering, "Is it me or is it really hot in here?"

This single symptom is responsible for misdiagnosis of hyperthyroidism or thyrotoxicosis in women approaching menopause whose complaints of feeling hot are mistaken for hot flashes, a classic menopausal symptom.

Infertility

Hyperthyroidism can interfere with a woman's ovulation cycle, resulting in temporary infertility. Once the thyroid problem is treated, however, fertility is restored.

An undiagnosed thyroid problem in early pregnancy can lead to miscarriage; repeated miscarriage is often considered a form of infertility. If this is a problem for you, please have your thyroid checked to rule out an underlying thyroid problem.

Menstrual Cycle Changes

Hyperthyroid women will find that their periods are lighter and scantier, and they may even skip periods. This is why thyroid problems can affect fertility—because it interferes with ovulation and regular cycles.

Once the thyroid problem is treated, cycles should return to normal. (See Chapter 4 for more details.)

Muscle Weakness

Muscle weakness is especially noticeable in the shoulders, hips, and thighs, which can make it difficult to climb stairs. Thigh muscles may burn or feel soft. Shoulder weakness is noticed when you brush your hair or do upper arm movements for long periods of time. This may greatly exacerbate osteoporosis, discussed in Chapter 6, as well as fibromyalgia, discussed in Chapter 3. Muscle weakness is due partly to an overworked, exhausted body, and will resolve once the thyroid problem is treated.

Paralysis

This is a rare symptom of Graves' disease, where you may experience episodes of paralysis following exercise or after eating a lot of starches and sugars. This particularly affects people of Asian descent, but once the thyroid problem is brought under control, the paralysis will resolve. This usually involves changes in the blood potassium levels.

Skin Changes

Your skin may develop a fine, silky texture, and you may also notice patches of either pigmentation loss or darkening. People with Graves' disease may notice thick or swollen skin over their shin bones.

You may be sweating more than usual, causing your skin to become soft, warm, and damp. The palms of your hands may also look flushed, and little spidery veins may pop up on your cheeks.

Some women notice unsightly patches of thick red skin over the shins and feet, and a thickening of the skin on the fingers and feet.

Tremors

Trembling hands is one of the classic signs of hyperthyroidism. You may notice that you have an "internal tremor"—meaning that you feel a little nervous and uneasy all the time.

Weight Loss

Sometimes the hyperdefecation, combined with heavy sweating, contributes to weight loss—in spite of a healthy appetite. Women, in particular, find weight loss an unexpected, welcome bonus, but it is this single hyperthyroid trait that is responsible for a misunderstanding of thyroid and weight loss. Usually, weight loss is limited to ten to twenty pounds, and not all patients necessarily lose weight. Hyperthyroidism often causes excessive exhaustion, and some patients wind up gaining weight because they become less active. Unfortunately, some women with normal thyroid function take synthetic thyroid hormone to induce weight loss. This is a big mistake and can cause (among a host of other unpleasant side effects) heart trouble. (Weight is discussed in more detail in Chapter 8.)

The Emotional Effects of Hyperthyroidism

Normally, cells in the body use thyroid hormone to regulate the "rate of life" known as metabolism. When the body speeds up from abnormally high thyroid hormone levels, there is a rapid consumption of energy. As a result, exhaustion can set in because the body simply cannot supply the excess energy. This is the paradox of hyperthyroidism: on the one hand, bodily functions speed up; on the other, mental and physical energy levels are literally exhausted. Consequently, hyperthyroid patients experience a range of emotional symptoms. Nervousness, restlessness (unable to keep still, to sit quietly and calmly), anxiety, irritability, sleeplessness (not able to sustain sleep for long periods of time—waking up every hour), or insomnia (not able to fall asleep at all) are common problems. Basically, these are linked to a general fatigue caused by very real physical exhaustion. A hyperthyroid person may exhibit some, all, or none of these characteristics; it depends solely on the individual.

Most hyperthyroid patients do experience loss of sleep, however. When you are hyperthyroid, the body continues its rapid speed during sleep, and patients often feel more tired when they wake up. This is another reason why irritability, anxiety, and general restlessness persist.

Hyperthyroidism and Psychiatric Misdiagnosis

When women experience the exhaustion of hyperthyroidism and the natural anxiety that accompanies it, but do not notice or report other physical manifestations such as a fast pulse or hyperdefecation (which can also be attributed to anxiety), they are often misdiagnosed. One reason for this is that hyperthyroid disorders occur much more frequently in women (see Chapter 1). Another reason is that hyperthyroid symptoms often imitate the symptoms of major, or unipolar, depression and bipolar disorder (discussed in Chapter 3).

The symptoms of major depression are a flat or depressed mood, which can include irritability and sadness. Physical symptoms that accompany depression also mimic symptoms of hyperthyroidism, such as poor appetite, weight loss, sleeplessness, and having no energy. Cognitive and perceptual changes can also occur with both depression and thyroid disease. Anxiety (or persistent worry) as well as disordered thinking or paranoia may complicate matters, as well as euphoric mood swings more typical in bipolar disorder. Until the mid-1970s, hyperthyroid women were indeed misdiagnosed as hysterical, depressed, or emotionally unbalanced. They were often referred to psychiatrists instead of thyroid specialists. As stress-related ailments have become

Will I Become Hyperthyroid?

You are more likely to develop hyperthyroidism or thyrotoxicosis if you:

- Are between the ages of twenty and forty
- Had a baby less than six months ago
- Had a thyroid condition in the past or are being treated for hypothyroidism
- Have another autoimmune disease (Addison's disease, type 1 diabetes, rheumatoid arthritis, lupus)
- Have vitiligo
- Have other family members with thyroid disease

more prevalent in recent years, hyperthyroid women are now often told they are under too much stress. I discuss the overlapping of fatigue, types of depression, and stress in Chapter 3, including information on the effects of lithium on thyroid function.

What Causes Hyperthyroidism?

Although there can be several reasons why a thyroid gland would become overactive, in 80 percent of cases the cause is an autoimmune disorder known as Graves' disease (discussed in Chapter 9).

A toxic multinodular goiter or a benign nodule on the thyroid gland can also cause thyrotoxicosis or too much thyroid hormone. See Chapter 10 for more information on thyroid nodules.

Thyrotoxicosis also results from taking too much thyroid hormone. Thyroid hormone is prescribed as a replacement hormone when treating hypothyroidism or when the thyroid is either surgically removed or deadened by radioactive iodine. (See Chapter 11 for more details on the treatment of thyroid disorders.)

Inflammation of the thyroid gland, called *thyroiditis*, can also cause thyrotoxicosis, usually lasting for a limited time. (See the section "Other Forms of Thyroiditis" earlier in this chapter.)

The Three Faces of Eve

There are three faces of a woman with thyroid disease. The first face is your normal face: the euthyroid face. The second face is the hypothyroid face and the third face is the hyperthyroid face.

The Hypothyroid Face

If you look in the mirror, you may notice the following changes in your appearance when you are severely hypothyroid, compared to a photo taken when your thyroid was functioning normally:

- *Face:* Full and puffy, with pads of skin around the eyelids, as well as little yellow lumps around the eyes (called *xanthelasma*), which is caused by cholesterol buildup.
- *Complexion:* Pale and porcelain-like, with a pink flush in the cheeks. It may also have a yellowish tint to it, due to a buildup of carotene.
- *Lips:* They may appear to be swollen and a little purple due to poor circulation. Your tongue may also be slightly enlarged.
- *Eyebrows:* You may notice that you have fewer brow hairs.
- *Expression:* Sad, lackluster.
- *Hair:* It may lose its sheen, becoming dull. Hairspray will not hold, and you may not be able to have a successful permanent.
- *Skin:* Thick, dry, and peeling with possible patches of pigmentation loss.

The Hyperthyroid Face

If you look in the mirror, you may notice the following changes in your appearance when you are thyrotoxic or hyperthyroid, compared to a photo taken when your thyroid was functioning normally:

- *Face:* A little gaunt due to weight loss (in most cases).
- *Eyes:* They may appear to be bulging with the lids slightly retracted. This is a sign of Graves' disease or thyroid eye disease (see Chapter 7).

continued

- *Complexion:* You may notice soft, sweaty skin that is almost silky because you are sweating more. You may also notice that it is either increasingly "tanned" or that you have patches of pigmentation loss.
- *Expression:* Staring and almost "mad" looking because of your eyes.
- *Hair:* It may become softer and finer, and you may even notice it is falling out. It may become grayer as well and not take to being colored or permed.

3

Stress, Fatigue, and Depression

Do They Collide with Your Thyroid?

IF YOU LOOK at the list of symptoms in Chapter 2 that comprise hypothyroidism and hyperthyroidism (or thyrotoxicosis) many of them overlap, and collide, with symptoms of stress, fatigue, and depression. There are syndromes with nonspecific symptoms that are often confused with hypothyroid symptoms in particular. For example, chronic fatigue syndrome, allergies, and environmental sensitivities can often be labeled as hypothyroid symptoms when they are not. And just because you have thyroid disease does not mean that you cannot also be suffering from another organic illness or even a situational depression, the symptoms of which are covered later in this chapter. Indeed, being ill is often the situation that triggers your depression. But when you are referred to a psychiatrist when all you need is thyroid hormone, or a well-earned vacation for that matter, it can be enough to . . . drive you crazy!

This chapter is designed for two groups: women who have been told they're stressed, depressed, or have "unexplained fatigue" when, in fact, they are suffering from a thyroid disorder, and women who are coping with stress, fatigue, or depression as well as a thyroid problem. In either case, a thyroid function test (see Chapter 11) can verify whether your symptoms are thyroid related, or aggravated by a thyroid problem.

Women, Stress, and Thyroid Disease

The extensive literature on women and stress, and the fact that autoimmune thyroid diseases such as Hashimoto's thyroiditis and Graves' disease occur so much more frequently in women, begs the question: Can stress-linked autoimmune thyroid diseases be considered socially produced? Are the unfair social arrangements that typically place "double duty" burdens on women partly responsible for the burden of autoimmune thyroid disease in women? Furthermore, do these "double duty" roles predispose women to more depression or fatigue-related disorders such as chronic fatigue or fibromyalgia as well as other syndromes with nonspecific symptoms?

As a woman, a medical sociologist, and bioethicist, I have researched the subject of women and stress in great depth. I argue that stress is so much a part of "being a woman" that most women are not even aware of how much it affects them until their bodies tell them so.

What Is a Woman's Stress?

Stress affects women's bodies in unique ways, which are not adequately covered in the reams of stress management books available. For example, one early 2000 study reported by Time Health Media found that women were more likely than men to react to stress with a nurturing impulse, looking after others before themselves. This has been dubbed the "tend and befriend" response.

Generally, stress is defined as a negative emotional experience associated with biological changes that allow you to adapt to challenging life circumstances. In response to these circumstances, your adrenal glands pump out "stress hormones" that speed up your body: your heart rate increases and your blood sugar levels increase so that glucose can be diverted to your muscles in case you have to act quickly or run. This is known as the "fight or flight" response. These hormones are called the *catecholamines*, which are broken down into epinephrine (adrenaline) and norepinephrine. (I discuss these hormones, too, in Chapter 4 in the section "PMS and Thyroid Disorders.") It's crucial to note that adrenaline is also pumped out when you have too much thyroid hormone in your body. Therefore, always rule this out first, before assuming you are suffering from just plain "stress."

Stress hormones actually put a physical strain on our bodies, and can lower our resistance to disease. Initially, stress hormones stimulate our immune systems. But after the stressful event has passed, the overworked immune system can become suppressed, leaving us open to a wide variety of illnesses and physical symptoms. Hans Selye, considered the father of stress management, defined stress as the "wear and tear" on the body. Once we are in a state of stress, the body adapts to the stress by depleting its resources until it becomes exhausted, which can leave us vulnerable to a host of physical symptoms, which indeed can be manifested as autoimmune disorders, fatigue, and depression.

Current statistics from the Duke Center of Integrative Medicine reveal that 90 percent of women ignore clear physical signs of stress.

Types of Stress

There are different types of stress: acute stress and chronic stress. Acute stress results from an acute situation, such as a sudden, unexpected negative event, organizing a wedding, or planning for a conference. When the event passes, the stress will pass. Acute stress occurs when you're feeling the pressure of a particular deadline or event. But there is an end to the stress. Symptoms of acute stress include anger or irritability, anxiety, and depression; tension headaches or migraines; back pain, jaw pain, muscular tension; digestive problems; cardiovascular problems; and dizziness.

But acute stress can be what's known as *episodic*, meaning that there is one stressful event after another creating a continuous flow of acute stress. Someone who is always taking on too many projects at once is likely to suffer from episodic acute stress. Workaholics and those with the so-called type A personality are classic sufferers of episodic acute stress.

Chronic stress results from boredom and stagnation, as well as from prolonged negative circumstances. Chronic stress tends to have no end in sight; no growth occurs from the stressful event. When negative events don't seem to yield anything positive in the long term, but more of the same, the stress can lead to chronic and debilitating health problems. When nothing positive is associated with the stress, it has a much more negative effect on our health. Some examples of chronic stress include stagnant jobs or relationships, disability from accidents or diseases, or long-term unemployment.

In addition to acute and chronic stress, stress can be defined in even more precise ways:

- Physical stress (physical exertion)
- Chemical stress (when we're exposed to a toxin in our environment, including substance abuse)
- Mental stress (when we take on too much responsibility and begin worrying about all that has to be done)
- Emotional stress (when our feelings stress us out, such as anger, fear, frustration, sadness, betrayal, bereavement)
- Nutritional stress (when we're deficient in certain vitamins or nutrients or experience food allergies)
- Traumatic stress (caused by trauma to the body such as infection, injury, burns, surgery, or extreme temperatures)
- Psycho-spiritual stress (caused by unrest in our personal relationships or belief system, personal life goals, and so on—in general, this is what defines whether we are happy)

Emotional Signs of Stress

When we're under stress, we feel more things. We may be more irritable, sleep-deprived, and fatigued—which can make us feel things more intensely. But—and this is a big *but*—it's also accurate to say that when we're feeling a lot of emotions, we can become stressed. Emotional upset takes a real, calculable, physical toll on our bodies. The lines between stress and powerful emotions blur; they are interconnected. Not only are they hard to separate, but I wonder if they're even worth separating. The emotional signs of stress are anxiety, panic, and depression. All three problems come with their own set of physical and emotional sensations.

Anxiety

It's normal to worry about a lot of things. Worry crosses over into anxiety when the worry persists after the problem you worried about has resolved or ended. *Generalized anxiety disorder* (*GAD*) is characterized by extreme worry about things that are unlikely to happen. The worries begin to be persistent and to interfere with your normal functioning. Always there is a sense of dread, a constant fretting, restlessness, and uneasiness about your personal security or safety. As discussed in the previous chapter, signs of too much thyroid hormone in your body due to hyperthyroidism or thyrotoxicosis can cause you to feel very anxious. So thyroid disease can mimic anxiety or aggravate anxiety.

Panic Attacks

When you suffer from anxiety, you may also suffer from panic attacks. If you do suffer from panic attacks, it's crucial to rule out hyperthyroidism or thyrotoxicosis as the cause, since panic attacks can be caused by the adrenaline rush that occurs with thyrotoxicosis. In this case, taking a beta-blocker will alleviate the problem and probably put an end to your panic attacks. Panic attacks are essentially an adrenaline response. When the adrenaline pumps out and the "fight or flight" response is triggered, you will first feel an accelerated heart rate, which often feels not like a palpitation but a "fluttery" heartbeat; it can also feel racing, pounding, or skipping. This is accompanied by a cold sweat or excessive sweating, chills or flushes (also called cold or hot flashes), and possibly tingling or numbness in parts of your body. Vertigo or a choking feeling can accompany these symptoms, and some people faint, vomit, and even convulse while unconscious. Although chronic panic attacks often occur before age twenty-four, many people suffer their first attacks in their thirties or forties, while under extreme stress, in the absence of hyperthyroidism or thyrotoxicosis.

Causes of "Normal" Stress for Women

If you're a healthy, socially well-adjusted woman, the normal pressures that go with the territory can be overwhelming as it is. But women who are in negative relationships, going through a divorce or breakup, moving, or who have suffered loss will have all the normal stress other women have on top of their unique circumstances. I outline the "normal" causes of stress here to punctuate how numerous they are and how they can indeed predispose women to stress-related illnesses and symptoms, which include thyroid disease and nonspecific symptoms that can mimic hypothyroidism, as well as fatigue and depression.

The majority of women who are asked in surveys about what causes them stress report family life and relationships as the chief cause. Married women who are working report that their stress stems from the torn-apart feeling they have over working and being mothers. No woman feels she can perform both roles to her satisfaction, which creates a great deal of inner turmoil. Child care in North America is in crisis, leaving most women with few choices. Mothering duties are also distinct from household chores; in all studies and surveys of heterosexual relationships, women do the majority of the housework, even when they are with supportive partners. The mothering, combined with the housework, is why the terms "second shift," "double duty," and "Supermom" have entered into our vernacular in the last ten years. Most women do not believe they will become trapped in this classic dilemma until they bring home the baby—and find themselves living the life they thought was extinct: the 1950s suburban housewife, with twenty-first century pressures. Many women who make the decision to stay home with children are stressed by underchallenge and boredom in their new role as mother, yet feel tremendous guilt over wanting more. At the same time, there are many women who find full-time parenting very rewarding, but in recent years, the "happy homemaker" role has been splashed over so many magazines that women who are not happy being at home feel they are bad people.

Many women don't realize the bigger social picture behind their limited choices. Women who experience their options "collapsing" are also experiencing a world that was not built for, and is not even remotely accommodating to, mothers, children, or vulnerable people such as the elderly and disabled.

The Mother Load

When women make the transition into motherhood, the stress can be incapacitating as they cope with postpartum life (fatigue, not getting out, and the demands of a new baby), all the while struggling with the dilemma of returning to work. If they don't return to work, they feel judged by working colleagues, and must face that terrible question, "What do you do all day?" If they return to work they must cope with the schizophrenic existences they lead at work and at home, and cope with the guilt they feel over leaving their child each morning. Housework issues, competing work demands, and a host of problems can ensue when Junior arrives. The "mother load" is the source of much stress for women.

The Workload

Since the 1970s, women have been brainwashed into thinking that they would be happier and more fulfilled people if they joined the workforce. Many women are fulfilled by their work, but made sick with stress by the *places* they are forced to work in and the people they are forced to work with. Two-thirds of mothers with children under six are working at full-time jobs. Many women report that they feel they are going mad weighing the choices and options of working or staying home.

Women are plagued by incorrect definitions of feminism that assert that women are exactly the same as men and require no special treatment. This is the "dino-definition" of feminism from the 1970s—what working women cling to in order to have equal pay in the workplace. Most feminist scholars worth their salt will tell you that feminism means exactly the opposite of "women are equal to men in every way." The real definition is more like this: because women are biologically different, socialized differently, and emotionally wired differently (which, most believe, has to do with how we're socialized), feminism means that the interests of women should be equal to the interests of men. Therefore, since women are mothers and men are not, the interests of mothers and their children ought to be equally considered in our society. But, they're not.

Living Single

Single working mothers are the most stressed: they do everything. They have to find suitable child care, work, and go home to the second shift with no help or support. Many women are single mothers by choice: they may have become mothers with the aid of a friend's sperm or a sperm bank. Women who are single mothers by chance may have been abandoned by their partner or left with no choice but to leave a troubled or violent relationship. More common these days than ten years ago, many women in their thirties and forties are also widowed due to increasing rates of cancer in young adults, random accidents, and, of course, war, violence, and terrorism.

Then there are single women who are not mothers, who also report that the main source of their stress stems from their relationships (or lack thereof). Single women by chance—meaning that they are single because they have not found a suitable life partner—find relationships, the dating scene, and the continuous waiting or watching for Mr. Right extremely stressful. There are also many single women in unsatisfying and unfulfilling relationships, or who find themselves wandering in relationship "purgatory," going from one relationship to the next in an endless stream of serial romances and repeated patterns.

The Supermom Disease

What I call the "Supermom disease" mental health professionals call the "pleasing disease." Women who feel they are failures because they haven't completed every item on a to-do list, or feel they can't give themselves permission to relax, are doing so because they are conditioned to nurture and to please. When they can't manage all of the tasks at work and at home, instead of slowing down, many women tend to speed up, becoming better at multitasking and taking on even more. Women who say yes to everything are also trying to avoid the terrible guilt they feel when they can't do everything.

Housework Issues

Housework contributes to a great deal of stress. It's not the individual chores themselves, but the distribution of housework and the arguments over it that leads to stress. In studies and surveys about housework among heterosexual couples, roughly 66 percent of women report that they're responsible for cooking and grocery shopping, including meal organization, and household budgeting. The only job that falls consistently to the man is household repairs. Men are frequently responsible for car maintenance and repairs as well. The "housework" argument is about power relations between the couple, not about the actual chores.

Fatigue

If you can relate to these causes of stress, it's only natural to feel a little tired or fatigued. Fatigue is a by-product of stress. There is a difference between feeling normal fatigue and chronic fatigue, which is characterized by continuous low energy and lethargy—also signs of hypothyroidism and depression. This section outlines some of the factors responsible for normal fatigue that can be remedied by making lifestyle changes.

Sleep Deprivation

Many women with multiple demands suffer from sleep deprivation, which refers to being deprived of the recommended hours of sleep for healthy adults. *Sleep deprivation can dramatically worsen fatigue in women who are hypothyroid.* In women who are thyrotoxic, sleep deprivation can contribute to exhaustion, but sleep is difficult anyway because the body is "racing" at night, which interferes with a good night's sleep.

In the absence of hypothyroidism or thyrotoxicosis, sleep deprivation can have serious health repercussions. In fact, some research suggests that chronic fatigue as well as fibromyalgia may be directly linked to chronic sleep deprivation. One Canadian study deliberately deprived a group of medical students of non-REM sleep over a period of several nights. Within the next few days, each of the study participants developed symptoms of Chronic Fatigue Syndrome (CFS) and/or fibromyalgia.

There is a misconception that as we get older, we need less sleep. This is not so; we need just as much sleep as always, but we often get less sleep. What happens is that our ability to achieve quality sleep for long periods of time diminishes as we age. The older we get, the more fragile our sleep becomes, which means it can be more easily disturbed by light, noise, and pain (for example, arthritis). It's common for various medical conditions to interfere with sleep, and in the case of thyroid disease, this is usually the restlessness, anxiety, and "racing heart" from thyrotoxicosis. Whether you have normal thyroid function, are hypothyroid, or are thyrotoxic, for a better sleep, try:

- *Regular bedtime hours:* Go to bed at the same time every night.
- *Regular wake-up hour:* Try to wake up around the same time every morning.
- *Daily sun exposure:* Exposure to natural outdoor light during the day helps with sleep.
- *A cool, dark, and quiet room at bedtime:* Lower the temperature at night or open a window. Use earplugs if necessary and pull down shades or draw curtains.

If you're getting regular sleep and have normal thyroid levels, but find you're dosing off during the day or still feel tired, you may have a sleep disorder, which is present in roughly 40 million North Americans. Sleep disorders such as apnea, restless leg syndrome, insomnia, or coping with partners who snore, can all affect quality sleep.

Burnout

When women have no autonomy or control in their jobs, are overworked or poorly paid, they can suffer from burnout. The term *burnout* is now a common term in all health-care literature, and is characterized by physical and emotional exhaustion, feeling personally disconnected from one's friends and family, and feeling nonproductive.

Signs of burnout include low morale, exhaustion, poor concentration, feelings of helplessness and depression, and physical problems such as bowel problems, poor appetite, cramps, headaches, and so on.

Another chief cause of burnout is caregiving. Burnout tends to be highest in caring professions, where people are around nonstop suffering. In this case, burnout has been described as a feeling of being spiritually drained, meaning that all energies are being poured into meeting the needs of others, leaving no room to fulfill one's own needs. The feeling of being "used up" emotionally as well as feeling as though there is no control over the work is also an important distinction between burnout and depression. Some articles refer to burnout as *carers' fatigue* (defined as a hemorrhaging of oneself for others), suggesting this is a long-known problem among women who are in the role of either nonprofessional caregiver or professional caregiver. In North America, nonprofessional caregivers are responsible for 80 to 90 percent of the assistance provided to elderly persons in their homes;

the majority of caregiving is provided by women. In almost all cases, it is the woman who takes on the role of unpaid caregiver. Frequently she is a working mother, trying to balance a job and child care on top of caregiving. Caregiving, understandably, burns women out, and largely goes unrecognized and unacknowledged.

Abnormal Fatigue: Chronic Fatigue Syndrome (CFS)

Seventy percent of people who suffer from chronic fatigue are women under age forty-five. Many of them may be misdiagnosed as having a thyroid condition or depression.

CFS has been around longer than you might think. In 1843, for example, a curious condition called *fibrositis* was described by doctors. It was characterized by symptoms similar to those now seen in *fibromyalgia* (chronic muscle and joint aches and pains) and *chronic fatigue syndrome* (symptoms of fibromyalgia, accompanied by flulike symptoms and extreme fatigue). The term *rheumatism*, now outdated, was frequently used as well to describe various aches and pains with no specific or identifiable origin.

In the late 1970s and early 1980s, a mysterious virus, known as Epstein-Barr virus, was being diagnosed in thousands of young, upwardly mobile professionals—at the time known as *yuppies*—the so-called baby boom generation. People were calling this condition the "yuppie flu," "yuppie virus," "yuppie syndrome," and "burnout syndrome." Many medical professionals were stumped by it, and many disregarded it as a phantom or psychosomatic illness. Because so many women were dismissed by their doctors as hypochondriacs, or not believed to be ill or fatigued, the physical symptoms triggered self-doubts, feelings of low self-esteem, self-loathing, and so on, which often triggered depression. But even given the most sensitive medical attention, depression seems to go hand in hand with CFS simply because the disorder leaves so many sufferers at home in bed, isolated from the active lifestyle so many CFS sufferers once had. In other words, some believe that in the case of CFS, depression is a normal response to "feeling rotten" every day of your life. It's an example of the adage "If you weren't depressed, you'd be crazy."

A lot of people with CFS were also misdiagnosed with various other diseases that shared some of the symptoms we now define as CFS. These diseases included mononucleosis, multiple sclerosis, HIV-related illnesses (once called AIDS-related complex, or ARC), Lyme disease, post-polio syndrome, and lupus. If you have been diagnosed with any of these diseases, please take a look at the established symptom criteria for CFS as outlined in the sidebar. You may have been misdiagnosed—an extremely common scenario.

Chronic Fatigue Syndrome or Thyroid?

The following symptoms can indicate CFS as well as hypo- or hyperthyroidism or thyrotoxicosis.

- An unexplained fatigue that is new
- Poor memory or concentration*
- Sore throat (possible if you have inflammation of the thyroid gland)*
- Mild or low-grade fever
- Tenderness in the neck and underarm area (tenderness in the neck may occur with an enlarged thyroid gland)*
- Muscle pain*†
- Pain along the nerve of a joint*
- A strange and new kind of headache you have never suffered from before
- You sleep but wake up unrefreshed (a sign of insufficient amounts of non-REM sleep).*
- You feel tired, weak, and generally unwell for a good twenty-four hours after you have had even moderate exercise.*

*Signs of hypothyroidism
†Signs of hyperthyroidism or thyrotoxicosis
*†Signs of either hypo- or hyperthyroidism or thyrotoxicosis

In the early 1980s, two physicians in Nevada, who had treated a number of patients who shared this curious condition (after a nasty winter flu had hit the region), identified it as chronic fatigue syndrome. This label is perhaps the most accurate, and the one which has stuck.

But there are other names for CFS, such as the United Kingdom label, *M.E.*, which stands for *myalgic encephalomyelitis*, as well as *post-viral fatigue syndrome*. CFS is also known as *chronic fatigue immune deficiency syndrome (CFIDS)*, because it's now believed that CFS sufferers are immune suppressed, although this fact is still being debated. For the purposes of this chapter I'll refer to the simpler label that seems to tell it like it is: chronic fatigue syndrome.

Fibromyalgia Versus CFS

Fibromyalgia is a soft tissue disorder that causes you to hurt all over—all the time. It appears to be a condition that is triggered and/or aggravated by stress. If you notice fatigue and more general aches and pains, this suggests CFS. If you notice primarily joint and muscle pains, *accompanied* by fatigue, this suggests fibromyalgia.

Fibromyalgia is sometimes considered to be an offshoot of arthritis, and it is not unusual to be misdiagnosed with rheumatoid arthritis. Headaches, morning stiffness, and an intolerance to cold, damp weather are common complaints associated with fibromyalgia. It is also common to suffer from irritable bowel syndrome or bladder problems with this disorder.

Causes of CFS

Newer thinking about chronic fatigue suggests that it is directly linked to chronic sleep deprivation. Some experts who treat chronic fatigue syndrome (CFS) and fibromyalgia believe that a lack of non-REM sleep may be a trigger for these disorders. In other words, some believe that CFS is really a sleep-related disorder. One Canadian study deliberately deprived a group of medical students of non-REM sleep over a period of several nights. Within the next few days, each of the study participants developed symptoms of CFS and/or fibromyalgia.

There are CFS sufferers who have an impaired immune system, similar to what occurs with HIV infection. This suggests there may be some viral agent(s) at work. But there are other CFS sufferers who have an overactive immune system. This would seem to suggest that CFS may be an autoimmune condition.

Depression and Thyroid Disease

It's important to understand that depression is a vast topic, and there are many different types of depression. For the purposes of this section, I'll be limiting the discussion to two types of depression that can be confused with, mask, or aggravate hypothyroidism and hyperthyroidism or thyrotoxicosis. *Unipolar depression*, sometimes called *major depression*, is characterized by one low or "flat" mood. This is distinct from *bipolar depression*, which is characterized by two moods: a high mood and a low mood. Unipolar depression has many of the same symptoms as hypothyroidism, while hypothyroidism can also trigger depression. Bipolar depression has many similarities with symptoms of hyperthyroidism (or thyrotoxicosis), but cannot be triggered by hyperthyroidism.

Unipolar Depression and Hypothyroidism

Most cases of unipolar or major depression are caused by life circumstances and/or situations. For this reason, the term *situational depression* is used by mental health experts to describe most cases of mild, moderate, or even severe unipolar depression. Situational depression can first mean that your depression has been triggered by a life event. Examples of a "life event" include the following:

- Illness (including thyroid disease)
- Loss of a loved one (the relationship may have ended, or a loved one may have died)
- Major life change
- Job loss or change
- Moving

Situational depression can also be triggered by the *absence* of change in your life, meaning that you are living in a state of continuous struggle, unhappiness, or stress in which no light appears at the end of the tunnel. Examples of continuous struggle include the following:

- Chronic illness (including untreated thyroid disease)
- Unhealthy relationships
- Poverty and/or economic worries
- Job stress
- Body image problems, such as feeling fat or unattractive

A third trigger for situational depression is an absence of resolution regarding past traumas and abuses suffered as a child or younger adult.

In the absence of thyroid disease, one out of five people in North America suffer from at least one episode of depression in their lifetime. At least twice as many women suffer from depression as men, which may be due to the social roles women play in our society, as explained earlier. For example, from 1994 through 1997, 72 percent of reported depressive episodes were in women.

Sadness Versus Depression

The million-dollar question is, are you depressed or "just sad"? Everyone experiences sadness, bad days, and bad moods. Feeling sad is not the same thing as being depressed. Sadness is characterized by sad *feelings*, which is opposite from numbness—the main feature of depression. The main thing to remember about sadness versus depression is this: sadness lifts, depression persists. That's how you can tell if you're just feeling sad or are actually depressed. Feelings of sadness and grief are definitely common and normal in an infinite variety of circumstances.

Signs of Unipolar Depression

It's impossible to define what a "normal mood" is since we all have such complex personalities and exhibit different moods throughout a given week, or even a given day. But it's not impossible for *you* to define what a normal mood is for *you*. You know how you feel when you're functional: you're eating, sleeping, interacting with friends and family, being productive, active, and generally interested in the daily goings-on in life. Well, depression is when you feel you've lost the ability to function for a prolonged period of time, or you're functioning at a level reasonable to the outside world, but you've lost *interest* in participating in life.

The symptoms of unipolar depression can vary from person to person, but can include some or all of the following:

- Feelings of sadness and/or "empty" mood
- Difficulty sleeping (usually waking up frequently in the middle of the night)
- Loss of energy and feelings of fatigue and lethargy
- Change in appetite (usually a loss of appetite)
- Difficulty thinking, concentrating, or making decisions
- Loss of interest in formerly pleasurable activities, including sex
- Anxiety or panic attacks (see earlier in the chapter; this may also be a symptom of hyperthyroidism)
- Obsessing over negative experiences or thoughts
- Feeling guilty, worthless, hopeless, or helpless
- Feeling restless and irritable
- Thinking about death or suicide

When You Can't Sleep

The typical sleep pattern of a depressed person is to go to bed at the normal time, only to wake up around two o'clock in the morning and find that she can't get back to sleep. Endless hours are spent watching infomercials to pass the time, or simply tossing and turning, usually obsessing over negative experiences or thoughts. Lack of sleep affects our ability to function and leads to increased irritability, lack of energy, and fatigue. Insomnia by itself is not a sign of depression, but when you look at depression as a package of symptoms, the inability to fall or stay asleep can aggravate all your other symptoms. In some cases, people who are depressed will oversleep, requiring ten to twelve hours of sleep every night.

When You Can't Think Clearly

Another debilitating feature of depression is finding that you simply can't concentrate or think clearly. You feel scattered, disorganized, and unable to prioritize. This usually hits hardest in the workplace or a center of learning, and can severely impair your performance on the job. You may miss important deadlines, important meetings, or find you can't focus when you do go to meetings. When you can't think clearly, you can be overwhelmed with feelings of helplessness or hopelessness. "I can't even perform a simple task such as X anymore" may dominate your thoughts, while you become more disillusioned with your dwindling productivity.

Anhedonia: When Nothing Gives You Pleasure

One of the most telling signs of depression is a loss of interest in activities that used to excite you, enthuse you, or give you pleasure. This is known as *anhedonia*, derived from the word *hedonism* (meaning the "philosophy of pleasure"); a *hedonist* is a person who indulges her every pleasure without considering (or caring about) the consequences. Anhedonia simply means "no pleasure."

Different people have different ways of expressing anhedonia. You might tell your friends, for example, that you don't "have any desire" to do X or Y; you can't "get motivated"; or X or Y just doesn't "hold your interest or attention." You may also notice that the sense of satisfaction from a job well done is simply gone, which is particularly debilitating in the workplace or in a place of learning. For example, artists (photographers, painters, writers, and so on) may find the passion has gone out of their work.

Managing Unipolar Depression

When your depression is related to life events, talk therapy is the first logical step. (See the section "Finding Someone to Talk To" later in this chapter.) Talk therapy can be combined with antidepressant medications, but consider the adage "Start low, go slow" when you're seeking treatment for depression. Remember that life events and hypothyroidism can collide. It's imperative that all women who have been diagnosed with depression have a thyroid function test (see Chapter 11) to check for mild, moderate, or severe hypothyroidism. Many women diagnosed with depression who have mild hypothyroidism report improvement when they are treated with thyroid hormone. It's also important to note that you can have a thyroid condition and

Depression or Thyroid?

The following symptoms can indicate major depression as well as hypo- or hyperthyroidism (or thyrotoxicosis):

- Feelings of sadness and/or "empty" mood*
- Difficulty sleeping (waking up frequently in the middle of the night)†
- Loss of energy and feelings of fatigue and lethargy*
- Change in appetite (usually a loss of appetite)*†
- Difficulty thinking, concentrating, or making decisions*
- Loss of interest in formerly pleasurable activities, including sex*
- Anxiety or panic attacks (characterized by a racing heart)†
- Obsessing over negative experiences or thoughts
- Feeling guilty, worthless, hopeless, or helpless
- Feeling restless and irritable†
- Thinking about death or suicide

*Indicates signs of hypothyroidism
†Indicates signs of hyperthyroidism or thyrotoxicosis

depression independently of one another. The fact that your depression persists after your thyroid problem is treated does not necessarily mean your thyroid is acting up again.

Antidepressants

Many women with hypothyroidism are prescribed antidepressants, which work on brain chemistry, before they are prescribed thyroid hormone. Clearly, this is a troubling phenomenon. In the absence of thyroid disease, frequently antidepressants are prescribed for people who could manage their depression by making lifestyle changes with the right support through proper counseling.

Antidepressants are typically overprescribed to women who have real social causes for their depression (which could be alleviated through real social changes), PMS, anxiety, or other normal mood responses to difficult circumstances. That said, there is a role for antidepressants, but they should be reserved for severe cases of depression, where possible.

There are several types of prescription antidepressants, known as heterocyclics, monamine oxidase inhibitors (MAOIs), and selective serotonin reuptake inhibitors (SSRIs). A subtype of SSRIs, called MSRIs, which stands for mixed serotonin reuptake inhibitors, is also popular, and includes serotonin-norephinephrine reuptake inhibitors (SNRIs).

Support Groups

When your depression is not caused by an untreated thyroid problem, social support can do wonders. The "sharing" approach has been shown to be highly beneficial—particularly in cases where women share difficult circumstances or have difficulties in common. One example is the support many women coping with thyroid disease find online or through thyroid organizations. Professionals who provide counseling for women report that the support and confidence gained from other women, including woman-centered counseling, is very helpful.

Family Support

Depression changes spousal/partner relationships, as well as other family relationships. When you're going through a depression, knowing that things won't fall apart can be the source of greatest comfort. Unfortunately, too many women are subjected to "family harassment" in the sense that they are not given the space to go through their depression. Being continuously told to "snap out of it," "get out of the house," "go for a walk," or "What you need is a nice big cup of . . ." isn't what family support is about. There are things family members can do that *are* supportive, which will give you the space to feel you are allowed to go through what you are going through.

Small gestures such as the following can work wonders to support a depressed family member:

1. Becoming the homemaker without asking. When family or friends look after as many of the meals or chores as they can, it takes pressure off the depressed or hypothyroid person. People who are depressed have trouble asking for help and may worry about how to get everything done, which only adds to the burden; it may also increase anxiety, which frequently accompanies depression.

2. Offer to go to support groups or counseling with your depressed family member; this says: "I want to understand what's going on with you."

3. Check in instead of checking up. Asking how someone is feeling is supportive. Badgering someone with unwanted opinions or advice, or asking "what did you do today" in a tone that is judgmental is not fine or supportive.

4. Let the depressed person feel "allowed" to set the pace of his or her day. When family members try to force someone to go on an outing, eat, etc., it just puts more pressure on the depressed person and emphasizes their inability to function or cope.

5. If your depressed family member wants to tell others about her depression or feelings, she should feel supported to do so. People have different ways of coping, and some choose to be more open about mood disorders. So if she wishes to talk about her depression, she doesn't need to feel as though it's a dirty secret and hide the fact that depression is at her house.

Finding Someone to Talk To

When you're looking for a therapist, you should focus on finding someone you can relate to and who is a "good fit." The pitfall you want to avoid is winding up with a therapist who is not helpful. Unhelpful therapy does not mean that your therapist is a poor therapist or unethical; it means that the style of therapy is not well-suited to you, and/or your therapist is not someone with whom you feel entirely comfortable. There can be many reasons for this, and they are often difficult to nail down. In other words, what one woman finds helpful therapy another woman may not. Therapists and styles of therapies are highly individual and so is their impact. For information on where to find good talk therapy, please consult Appendix B.

Bipolar Disorder and Thyroid Disease

Bipolar disorder involves two moods, one high and the other low, with symptoms mirroring those described for unipolar depression earlier. Think of it is as the North Pole and South Pole; the North meaning high moods (mania), the South meaning low moods (depression). Bipolar disorder is the new label that has replaced an older, probably more accurate one: *manic depression,* which means that the moods fluctuate between mania (incredible highs) and depression (incredible lows). How "incredible" the high or low is can dramatically vary, which has given rise to different classifications of bipolar disorders—bipolar I and bipolar II. For the purposes of this book, however, it's important to note the signs of mania, which can often be confused with the emotional symptoms of hyperthyroidism or thyrotoxicosis (see Chapter 2).

Studies also reveal that 25 to 50 percent of all people with bipolar disorder also suffer from a thyroid problem; *lithium can trigger Hashimoto's-induced hypothyroidism* (as outlined in Chapter 11). In other words, if you have underlying Hashimoto's disease with no symptoms, the lithium you take to manage your bipolar disorder may unveil hypothyroidism. In this case, you would exhibit the signs of hypothyroidism discussed in Chapter 2, but they could be mistaken for a low mood. It's critical to be tested for hypothyroidism on at least an annual basis if you're taking lithium.

What Is Bipolar Disorder?

Over two million people in North America suffer from bipolar disorder. Right now, psychiatrists believe that bipolar disorder is an inherited disease because it is seen in families. In other words, it's not unusual to see this condition across the generations, as in a grandmother, mother, and daughter. Researchers believe that like multiple personality disorder, which is almost exclusively a response to child abuse, bipolar disorder may also be a response to other unusual conditions. Bipolar disorder occurs with greater frequency among high achieving individuals, and may be seen across the generations because of the special talents and gifts that are inherited across the generations. There may also be pressure to achieve in such families.

Episodes of mania are characterized by a speeding up, while the depression is the biological "payback" for the bursts of energy, creativity, and euphoria seen during the manic period. For now, the "genetic versus situational" aspect of bipolar disorder remains in question; to date, no genetic defect associated with bipolar disorder has been found, despite intensive research efforts to find genes associated with this disease.

Women with bipolar disorder suffer from dramatic mood swings ranging from euphoria (known as mania), accompanied by irritability, to the depths of depression. For most, there are also periods in between where the mood is completely normal—neither depressed nor euphoric.

Signs of Mania in Bipolar Disorder

Some of the following signs of mania can also be seen in women who have hyperthyroidism or who are thyrotoxic:

- Erratic behavior, characterized by wild spending sprees, sexual flings, and impulsive acts
- Incredible bursts of energy and activity (in hyperthyroidism, there is exhaustion rather than energy)
- Restlessness (constantly looking for something to do; not able to focus for a long time on one activity)
- Fast talking to keep up with a "racing mind"
- Acting and feeling "high" or euphoric (again, in hyperthyroidism or thyrotoxicosis, exhaustion would likely prevent this)
- Extreme irritability and distractibility
- Not requiring sleep (in hyperthyroidism or thyrotoxicosis, sleep is interrupted by a "racing body"; in genuine mania, you feel there is too much to do in life, and that sleep is a waste of time, even though lack of it may lead to irritability and agitation)
- Deluded thoughts or distorted and disordered thinking (in hyperthyroidism or thyrotoxicosis, delusions can lead to para-

noia; in genuine mania, delusions lead to feelings of
grandeur)
- Making decisions and judgments that seem out of character
  or "not like you"
- Increased need or desire for sex (many women with hyperthyroidism or thyrotoxicosis have an increased desire for sex,
  which is the opposite of what occurs in hypothyroidism)
- Behavior that pushes other people's buttons (aggressive or
  intrusive acts)
- Increased sensitivity to sound, and easily irritated by various
  sounds (in hyperthyroidism or thyrotoxicosis, there is also an
  intolerance or sensitivity to heat)

Ruling out hyperthyroidism or thyrotoxicosis when these symptoms
present is the best approach, since it's much easier to treat hyperthyroidism or thyrotoxicosis than bipolar disorder. For more information
on bipolar disorder, consult the National Depressive and Manic-
Depressive Association, listed in Appendix B.

4

Thyroid Disease and the Menstrual Cycle

TO UNDERSTAND HOW the thyroid gland uniquely affects a woman's body, it is important to first review how the female hormones work (see Table 1.1 in Chapter 1). Low levels of sex hormones are produced continuously during a woman's reproductive years. But it is the continuous fluctuation of these hormones that establishes the menstrual cycle, which can become affected when the thyroid gland is either over- or underactive. Most important, women frequently have other gynecological problems which may or may not be related to a thyroid disorder.

The Moon Cycle

A normal menstrual cycle is similar to a moon cycle. Interestingly, the only event in human life that corresponds to the lunar calendar is menstruation. Time itself was probably first measured by the moon's phases. One of the problems with the current English calendar is that the months don't coincide exactly with the solar year. In our current system, the months have been made to fit the year by Gregory XIII, who gave them an arbitrary number of days unrelated to the moon calendar. So our calendar actually puts us out of sync with the moon.

The word *menstrual* comes from the Latin word *mens*, meaning "month"; the word *month* comes from the root word *moon*. The Greek word for moon is *mene*, while *menstruation* actually means "moon-change." (In some dictionaries, the root word for *month* and *menstruation* is *measure*.) The point of all this is to simply establish that an accurate and positive interpretation of menstruation was recorded in our history through language.

Countless other languages and cultures link menstruation to the moon as well. German peasants refer to menstruation literally as "the moon," while the French term for menstruation is *le moment de la lune* ("the moment of the moon"). The Mandingo, Susus, and Congo tribes also call menstruation "the moon," while in parts of East Africa, menstruation is thought to be *caused* by the new moon. The Papuans believe that the moon has intercourse with girls, triggering their periods; the Maori call menstruation "moon sickness;" the Fueginas call the moon "The Lord of the Women." Clearly the belief that the lunar cycle is identical to the menstrual cycle is universal. There is even some remarkable physical evidence that connects the moon to menstruation even more. For example, the cervix, *metra* in Greek, referring again to the word *measurement*, and also called the "meter of a woman," changes color, size, and position during menstruation. In fact, when it's viewed with a speculum (an instrument doctors use to open up the vagina) the cervix has been said to resemble a globe. Even in pregnancy, the embryo is shaped like the moon; the embryo starts out round and full, and as it becomes a fetus, curves like the half-moon.

All this evidence suggests that women are perhaps far more in tune to the natural rhythms of the universe than they think. Meanwhile, comprehending the similarities between the menstrual and lunar cycles is crucial in order to understand what a healthy, normal menstrual cycle really is. Women are also in tune with other women's cycles; two women living together will often synchronize cycles. The rhythmic timing of menstruation also provided women with a sense of their own timing, other than just day and night.

What Is "Normal"?

It's more accurate to call a menstrual cycle a "hormonal cycle" because that is in fact what the menstrual cycle is. The menstrual cycle is driven by a symphony of hormones, which trigger each other, stopping and starting, flooding and tapering in a regular rhythm each month.

The main organs involved in the menstrual cycle are the hypothalamus (a part of the brain), the pituitary gland, and the ovaries. The hypothalamus is like an omniscient figure, watching over the cycle and controlling the symphony of hormones from above. It tells the pituitary gland to start the hormonal process, which signals the ovaries to "do their thing." The hypothalamus is sensitive to the fluctuating levels of hormones produced by the ovaries. When the level of estrogen drops below a certain level, the hypothalamus turns on gonadotropin-releasing hormone (GnRH). This stimulates the pituitary gland to release FSH, follicle-stimulating hormone. FSH triggers the growth of ten to twenty ovarian follicles, but only one of them will mature fully; the others will start to degenerate some time before ovulation. As the follicles grow they secrete estrogen in increasing amounts. The estrogen affects the lining of the uterus, signaling it to grow or proliferate (called the *proliferatory phase*). When the egg approaches maturity inside the mature follicle, the follicle secretes a burst of progesterone in addition to the estrogen. This progesterone-estrogen combo triggers the hypothalamus to secrete more GnRH, which signals the pituitary gland to secrete FSH and LH (luteinizing hormone) simultaneously. The FSH-LH levels peak and signal the follicle to release the egg. (This is *ovulation*.)

To simplify this process, think of it as a thunderstorm. The lightning that precedes the storm is the hypothalamus sending out GnRH. The thunder that follows is the pituitary gland, answering with FSH, which is the rain starting, lightly at first. This rain grows follicles and trickles estrogen and progesterone into the bloodstream. This light rain goes on for a few minutes until, suddenly, two bright bursts of lightning ignite the sky: the hypothalamus again with GnRH. Then, *bang, bang*—the pituitary gland answers the lightning by sending out FSH and LH simultaneously. Then the intensity of this rain increases and it starts pouring—the follicles burst and estrogen and progesterone pour out into the bloodstream, which is when you ovulate. Slowly the rain dies down as hormonal levels taper off until the storm stops. It is at this point that you menstruate.

Under the influence of LH, the follicle changes its function and is now called a corpus luteum, secreting decreasing amounts of estrogen and increasing amounts of progesterone. The progesterone influences the estrogen-primed uterine lining to secrete fluids that nourish the egg (the *secretory phase*). Immediately after ovulation, FSH returns to normal, or base levels, and LH decreases gradually, as the progesterone increases. If the egg is fertilized, the corpus luteum continues to secrete estrogen and progesterone to maintain the pregnancy. In this case, the corpus luteum is stimulated by human chorionic gonadotropin (HCG), a hormone secreted by the developing placenta. If the egg is not fertilized, the corpus luteum degenerates until it becomes nonfunctioning, at this point called a *corpus albicans*. As degeneration progresses, the progesterone levels decrease. The decreased progesterone fails to maintain the uterine lining, which causes it to shed. Then the whole process starts again. Menstrual cycles range anywhere from twenty to forty days, and the bleeding lasts anywhere from two to eight days (four to six days being the average). It is important to count the first day of bleeding as day 1 of your cycle.

Every woman's hormones dance to a different tune—but rarely does it correspond to the English calendar. Women with completely different cycles may even synchronize cycles after living together as roommates. In this case, women's cycles become in tune with each other on levels not understood.

Although many women count the first day of clear discharge *after* their periods as day 1, this is not as accurate. Since ovulation always takes place roughly fourteen days before your period, five days off in your counting could radically interfere with your family planning. Secondly, if you're on the pill, the first day of bleeding is *always* counted as day 1. If you're planning to go on or off the pill, your cycle is more accurately tracked by using the same counting method. Thirdly, doctors always count the first day of bleeding as day 1 of the cycle.

Many of us assume that our menstrual flow is strictly blood, but this is not so. The menstrual fluid is made from a variety of ingredients: cervical and vaginal mucus, degenerated endometrial particles, and blood. The fluid does not smell until it makes contact with the bacteria in the air and starts to decompose.

Irregular Cycles: Metorrhagia

When you have a thyroid disorder, you cycles can become irregular, as discussed in Chapter 2. That said, an irregular cycle does not mean you have a thyroid problem, and the following section outlines the more common culprits behind irregular cycles.

It's important to remember that being regular doesn't mean your cycle is the same number of days each time. One month your cycle may be twenty-nine days, and the next month it may be thirty-one days. This is still considered the norm. It's also normal to be lighter one month and heavier the next. So long as you're menstruating every twenty to forty days, it's a sign that you're ovulating. Another common misperception about irregular cycles is the belief that unless you have a period every four weeks (again, the statistical average) you're irregular. This is not true. Some women menstruate every three weeks, which is normal for them; some menstruate every five weeks, which is also normal for them. The only times you should be concerned is if your period consistently yo-yos: three weeks, then four weeks, then five weeks, then three weeks, and so on. When this happens, it's usually a sign that you're not ovulating regularly. This is common in young girls when they first begin menstruating. If your period only jumps around once or twice a year, there isn't anything to worry about. Occasional stress is usually the culprit when this happens.

Once in a while, women may skip a period and then experience a heavier flow with their next period. Skipping one period in most cases is caused by stress. The flow is heavier after a skipped period because the estrogen has been building up in the endometrium longer, and there is more lining than usual that needs to be shed. In essence, you would have built up two cycles' worth of lining, so the flow is naturally heavier than normal.

It's also common to skip a period altogether and not experience a heavier flow the next time around. This means you actually skipped an ovulation cycle, and had not produced a lining in your endometrium that would support a pregnancy. In this case, there wasn't a lining to shed. It's not unusual to skip one or two periods a year; it is unusual to skip them more often than that, however.

Common Causes of Irregular or Missed Cycles

In the absence of a thyroid problem, the number one cause of irregular or skipped periods is emotional stress, discussed more in Chapter 3. The typical scenario is worrying that you might be pregnant, and then actually missing your period because you're worried. Other stress-related situations revolve around career changes, job loss, death in the family, moving, exams, and stressful workloads. It's not really understood why stress can cause you to miss a cycle, but it is considered a protective mechanism, a sort of prehistoric parachute in the female body. The body senses the stress levels and decides somehow to stop ovulation for that month, preventing a stressed pregnancy.

Overdieting and overexercising can also affect your cycle. For example, sudden weight loss could cause you to miss your period, or cause a long bout of irregular cycles. Overexercising can also cause you to miss your period, and it's actually not unusual for female athletes to stop menstruating when they're in training.

Finally, irregular cycles may be normal for your age. For example, it often takes young women several years before they establish a regular menstrual cycle, and many times young women will be put on oral contraceptives to regulate their periods. Then, women beyond forty could begin menopause at any time, and irregular cycles may be a sign of perimenopause, discussed more in Chapter 6.

Amenorrhea: No Menstrual Cycle

There is such a thing as having no menstrual cycle. However, today, if you don't begin menstruating by the age of eighteen, there's usually a hormonal imbalance. As discussed in Chapter 1, young girls should have a thyroid function test to rule out an underlying thyroid disorder that could be delaying puberty or menstruation. In the absence of a thyroid disorder, there could be other problems interfering with menstruation which hormonal supplements or oral contraceptives can remedy. If you're menstruating regularly and are between twenty and forty, it's unusual to simply stop menstruating. If this does occur, in the absence of a thyroid problem, an eating disorder such as anorexia nervosa (food refusal) is the most common cause, triggering a protective mechanism in the body. When the female body is malnourished, it stops ovulating because it can't sustain a pregnancy. One doctor told me about an aboriginal tribe in Australia that demonstrates this unique protective mechanism. Women of that particular tribe only menstruate at certain times of the year, when the food cycle is abundant.

Athletes may also experience amenorrhea. Generally, in the absence of a thyroid disorder, all cases of a stopped or stunted menstrual cycle can be remedied with progesterone supplements. You can take synthetically produced progestin or natural progesterone from botanical sources.

The Need to Bleed

Today, women have to deal with more periods in their lifetime than women did in the past due to fewer pregnancies and a longer life cycle. Also, in the past century, women have experienced a radical change in their diet, environment, stress levels, and career and family expectations. Understandably, the accumulated effect of all these factors has affected the hormonal cycle of women, which of course affects the menstrual cycle.

Again, it's fine to skip a period once in a while, or experience some occasional fluctuation. But if you've missed more than two periods, and know for certain that you're not pregnant and have normal thyroid function, then you should investigate having your period induced with a progesterone supplement, which will kick-start your cycle again. It's dangerous to go longer than three months without a "bleed"; if the uterus isn't regularly cleaned out, your risk of uterine cancer can increase.

Heavy Flow: Menorrhagia

If you have an extremely heavy flow, it may be normal for you. This is known as *primary menorrhagia*, which means that your flow has been heavy since you first began menstruating. If this is the case, there isn't anything to worry about. You should regularly (every six months) have your blood levels checked, however, because consistent heavy flows could cause anemia. In fact, the number one cause of anemia is a heavy menstrual flow.

If a lighter flow slowly *develops* into a continuous heavy flow, this is known as *secondary menorrhagia*. When this happens, as long as you're having annual pelvic exams and biannual blood tests, you shouldn't be concerned. If, however, your flow *suddenly* becomes unexplainably heavy, see your doctor. This kind of menorrhagia may signify other problems, which may include a thyroid problem or other gynecological problems, such as fibroids. Flows are considered dangerously heavy if you need to change your pad or tampon every hour.

Some women are concerned about clots. A clot looks like a tiny sample of raw liver or raw oyster, and often comes out with a heavy menstrual flow. Clots are normal, and do not mean you're hemorrhaging. Blood naturally clots, and often when you're sleeping during a heavy period, the blood will collect in clots and expel in the morning. The only time you need to worry about clots is if you're passing them after your period is over, passing them with a prolonged period, passing them midcycle, or while you're pregnant. (Similarly, if you're bleeding at all during these times you should see a doctor.)

When You Experience Abnormal Heavy Bleeding

Abnormal heavy bleeding is when your bleeding is suddenly heavy or significantly heavier than what your normal menstrual flow pattern is. In fact, it is your own perception of what's heavy that's more important than your doctor's perception. Good doctors will try to get you to describe your impression of "heavy" and have you compare it to your normal pattern. If your doctor tries to determine exactly how much blood you've lost, this is a waste of time for both of you.

Clinically, abnormally heavy menstrual bleeding is defined by more than eighty cubic centimeters of blood lost per cycle. But studies show that many women who complain of an abnormally heavy flow have lost much less than that. In fact, a more helpful measurement is to simply take inventory of the number of pads and tampons you're going through and compare that with your normal pattern.

In the absence of a thyroid problem, your age has a lot to do with your menstrual flow. In fact, teenaged women and women approaching menopause will have similar cycles, often characterized by changes in flow. Women between twenty and forty will have (or should have!) regular patterns that do not fluctuate that much from period to period.

If you're under twenty and are noticing heavy bleeding, ask your doctor to check you out for a blood coagulation disorder known as von Willebrand's disease, or other platelet disorders. Most of the time, however, abnormal heavy bleeding is caused by some sort of hormonal disorder, which can be investigated by a reproductive endocrinologist.

If you're over forty, abnormal heavy bleeding is usually caused by what's known as the *anovulatory period*. Here, you make estrogen in the first part of your cycle but for some reason (often unknown) you just don't ovulate. Therefore, you do not produce progesterone and develop an unusually thick uterine lining, which is expelled during your period. This translates into abnormally heavy bleeding.

No matter how old you are, one of the chief culprits of abnormally heavy bleeding in women is often high doses of aspirin. So if you're fighting off headaches or other ailments before your period, you may want to use an alternative pain reliever.

Sometimes your contraception method can affect your menstrual cycle. For instance, an IUD (intrauterine device) or hormonal contraception can sometimes trigger heavy bleeding. Changes in exercise patterns (usually less exercise) can also affect your menstrual flow.

If you notice abnormal bleeding either during or between periods, make sure your doctor rules out the following: hyperthyroidism (and thyrotoxicosis) or hypothyroidism; ovarian cysts; abnormal tissue within your uterus, such as endometriosis (discussed further on). Your doctor should also perform a pelvic exam, as well as a transvaginal ultrasound, a procedure in which a transducer is inserted into your vagina. Transvaginal ultrasound produces much sharper images than abdominal ultrasound.

And, of course, your doctor should be ruling out symptoms of possible sexually transmitted diseases (STDs).

Dysmenorrhea: Painful Periods

Primary dysmenorrhea means that you've always had painful periods—ever since you started menstruating. *Secondary dysmenorrhea* means that your periods have become more painful with time. In either case, painful periods are common, and cramps are simply caused by uterine contractions, which is how the lining is pushed out; some uteri contract more than others. It is also believed that cramps may be caused by low levels of calcium.

By regulating the cycle and reducing the flow, cramping can be reduced as well. Taking an analgesic such as ibuprofen before your period starts can really help; this will also reduce flow. Oral contraceptives also reduce cramping and flow, which is known as one of their noncontraceptive benefits.

It's also important to differentiate normal cramping from unusual, debilitating pain during your periods. Endometriosis, a serious disease, is often the culprit behind severe pain during your period. If you suspect your dysmenorrhea is a sign of something more serious, let your doctor know your suspicions and have it checked out.

PMS and Thyroid Disorders

When you are suffering from either hypo- or hyperthyroidism, PMS can be aggravated, thus worsening your symptoms. On the flip side, your PMS can mask your thyroid disorder, and symptoms of thyroid disease can be deemed to be PMS-related when in fact they are not. So the first order of business is to review all of the symptoms that fall into the category of PMS. Then, you can cross-reference PMS symptoms with thyroid symptoms.

What Is PMS?

The most important piece of information you can get from this section is this: menstruation, and all of the bodily changes that occur before, during, and after, are normal. The term *PMS* is more commonly known as *premenstrual syndrome* (in the United Kingdom it is also known as *premenstrual tension*, or *PMT*). In my work, I prefer to call PMS "premenstrual signs," since they occur in virtually all women. Premenstrual signs refer to the many physical discomforts, shifts in moods, and emotional responses women experience during this time due to the normal fluctuations of hormones. That happens to us during pregnancy, breast-feeding, menopause, and throughout our life cycle as we age. We are human women on the planet Earth who experience our hormones. This is normal and natural and not a syndrome or a disease.

It's important to recognize there are other things going on before and during our periods than simply our periods; there are social causes for mood swings, and social causes that exacerbate the normal physical discomforts that we go through during the various stages of our lives. In other words, your premenstrual signs may be aggravated by the conditions of your life. For example, we are also living in a world that was not built for us: our economy and the buildings we work in, for example, were designed for males, and not for bodies that menstruate, get pregnant, breast-feed, and go through menopause. There are also unfair power arrangements in both our working and intimate relationships that predispose women to more stress depression (see Chapter 3). Our current health-care system also medicalizes normal premenstrual discomforts. For example, the term *premenstrual dysphoric disorder* (PDD) simply means "unhappy before your period." Makers of antidepressants have suggested in commercials and other marketing materials that normal premenstrual discomforts may be improved by antidepressants, which creates ethical problems surrounding labeling normal female physiology as a "disease" requiring these drugs.

Virtually all women in their childbearing years have premenstrual signs. As we age, our premenstrual signs can become more severe, especially as we approach our *perimenopause*, a term that means "around menopause," which is usually somewhere in our mid- to late forties. Premenstrual signs occur roughly fourteen days before your period and disappear when you get your period, or just after. Traditionally, women's complaints about premenstrual signs have been either viewed as psychological or written off as part of the biological lot of women. Many women have difficulty admitting they suffer from them for fear of compromising their position in the workplace. But virtually all women experience some premenstrual signs. It's how *you* experience these signs, and how severely they affect you, that determines whether these premenstrual signs warrant remedying with other therapies.

Ninety percent of women who menstruate experience premenstrual signs of some sort. Of this group, half will experience the more traditional premenstrual signs, such as breast tenderness, bloating, food cravings, irritability, and mood swings. These signs, for many women, are often perceived as a sign that their bodies are "in tune" or "on schedule" and that all is well. In other words, these signs are natural markers of a healthy menstrual cycle. If you fall into this group, you may find that moderately adjusting your diet can dramatically improve your premenstrual discomforts.

Thirty-five to forty percent of menstruating women experience the same signs as the first group, but in a more severe form. In other words, they have *really* tender breasts, so sensitive that they hurt if someone just lightly touches them; severe bloating, to the extent that they gain about five pounds before their periods; instead of just food cravings, they may suddenly find that they have voracious appetites; instead of just being irritable, they may find that they become impossible to be around; and so on. Even these more severe signs are considered to be very normal experiences. If you fall into this group, you may find that more rigorous dietary adjustments and supplements, in combination with herbal remedies and physical activity, can dramatically improve your level of discomfort. You may also benefit from ruling out other causes for your discomforts, and may even want to explore natural progesterone supplements.

Roughly 3 to 10 percent of menstruating women (the latest statistics hover around 3 to 4 percent) suffer from incapacitating discomforts that affect their ability to function. In this case, these women would experience discomforts that interfere with their quality of life, such as profound mood swings; sudden, unexplainable sadness; irritability; sudden or unexplainable anger; feelings of anxiety or being on edge; depression; hopelessness; self-deprecating thoughts, and more extreme physical discomforts. In the psychiatric literature, even women with hysterectomies and oophorectomies (removal of their ovaries) were found to experience these symptoms. It is considered sound, and good medicine to offer this group of women antidepressants as a treatment for their PMS, even though incapacitating discomforts can still be managed through natural remedies. If you fall into this group, it's important to first rule out other causes for your physical and emotional discomforts, such as stress or an underlying depression that has social causes and has more to do with your life's conditions; or you may have reactions to synthetic hormones or medications you are taking that get aggravated by fluctuating hormones around the time of your period. Next, take a long hard look at your diet and activity patterns. Adjusting your diet, adding supplements and herbs, and becoming more active can really make a difference. Finally, rule out other causes for your symptoms, such as thyroid disease.

The Syndrome Label

PMS was first labeled *premenstrual syndrome* in 1953 by British physician Dr. Katharina Dalton. Dalton began treating premenstrual discomforts as early as 1948; she was working during a time when virtually no women were doctors, and when most women were dismissed by male doctors as "crazy" when they reported premenstrual complaints. It was Dalton who validated women's premenstrual discomforts and mood changes by recognizing a group of symptoms that were universal to premenstrual women. She was the first to carefully itemize a set of symptoms and labeled them a syndrome. Dalton's definition, which is still used today, is that PMS means "the recurrence of symptoms before menstruation with complete absence of symptoms after menstruation." The symptoms comprise all the premenstrual mood changes and physical discomforts I discuss here. Dalton established that PMS is a problem with inadequate levels of progesterone, due to inadequate functioning of progesterone receptors (what carries the hormone to the various parts of the body).

Her first book, *The Premenstrual Syndrome*, was published in 1964. She added *The Menstrual Cycle* in 1969. Dalton is most famous for her pioneering work in treating PMS with progesterone therapy, and her book *Once a Month: Understanding and Treating PMS*, first published in 1978, is in its sixth edition and still going strong.

The Adrenaline-Thyroid Connection

Dalton's research revealed two core findings: (1) progesterone receptors can't work when the blood sugar is low; (2) progesterone receptors can't work in the presence of adrenaline, which we pump out while under stress, when we are hyperthyroid or thyrotoxic, or when our blood sugar is low (in women with diabetes or insulin resistance). John Lee, M.D., known for his work on establishing how estrogen overload can wreak havoc on women's bodies, noted that adequate levels of progesterone are apparently necessary in order to regulate thyroid function. What does all this mean? Both Dalton and Lee made a similar observation: thyroid and progesterone seem to be linked in significant ways. Thyroid researchers I've interviewed have indeed confirmed that too much thyroid hormone can trigger an adrenaline surplus in the body, creating the classic adrenaline "attacks" we typically associate with low blood sugar (that shaky, headachy, irritable feeling). If Dalton's theories are correct, then indeed, too much thyroid hormone can dramatically affect PMS. Clearly, more research needs to be done in this area.

When we are fearful, or under physical stress from low blood sugar, or have too much thyroid hormone, and for many other causes, adrenaline is pumped out. As discussed in Chapter 3, this "stress hormone" speeds up your body: your heart rate increases and your blood sugar levels increase so that glucose can be diverted to your muscles in case you have to "fight" or run. Indeed, women who are hyperthyroid or thyrotoxic frequently experience panic attacks, which is purely an adrenaline reaction (discussed more in Chapter 3). Many women are falsely diagnosed with low blood sugar (or hypoglycemia) because adrenaline can mimic hypoglycemic reactions. Women often report to their doctors episodes of getting shaky, dizzy, nauseated, and irrational when hungry, yet are frustrated when blood sugar tests reveal normal levels of blood sugar. The symptoms they are reporting, however, are caused by excess adrenaline, not hypoglycemia. Today's health-care practitioners all acknowledge the role of diet (maintaining stable levels of blood sugar) and stress (trying to reduce situational stress before your period) in controlling the severity of PMS, but the connection between thyroid hormone and progesterone is not well researched. Of note, the thyroid and ovaries are considered "linked organs systems" in traditional Chinese medicine.

If you suffer from severe PMS that you think is adrenaline-linked, here are some causes to rule out:

1. *Hyperthyroidism or thyrotoxicosis.* If you are hyperthyroid or are taking thyroid hormone replacement pills, you may be on too high a dose that is resulting in too much circulating thyroid hormone in your body, which could be triggering adrenaline release. In most cases, going on a beta-blocker, which simply blocks adrenaline, can take care of the problem. In some cases you may be able to lower your dose as well.

2. *Low blood sugar.* Request a fasting blood glucose test, and rule out signs of impaired glucose tolerance or full-blown type 2 diabetes, which could mean that you are prone to episodes of low blood sugar or *hypoglycemia.* This can be remedied by eating balanced meals or snacks at regular intervals, avoiding simple carbohydrates in favor of more complex. For more information, consult my book *The Type 2 Diabetes Sourcebook for Women.*

3. *Situational stress.* In the absence of any organic disease, you may be going through a period of unusual stress due to a move or job change that may be creating unusually severe PMS. Stress can also trigger an adrenaline response, and there is also evidence that it may trigger autoimmune thyroid disease, discussed more in Chapter 9.

PMS Subclassifications

PMS has been classified into subcategories, according to the cluster of discomforts women experience.

- *PMS-A.* The *A* is for *anxiety*, and women with PMS-A are said to suffer from premenstrual anxiety, irritability, and emotional instability related to too much estrogen and not enough progesterone.
- *PMS-C.* The *C* is for *cravings*, and women with PMS-C are said to experience increased appetite, cravings for sweets, headaches, fatigue, fainting spells, and heart palpitations. These, by the way, are all signs of an adrenaline rush, which could be triggered by hyperthyroidism or low blood sugar.
- *PMS-D.* The *D* is for *depression*. Women with PMS-D are said to be suffering from decreased levels of estrogen premenstrually that cause changes in serotonin levels. The depression will disappear when the period starts.
- *PMS-H.* The *H* is for *hyperhydration*, which means bloating. (It would make more sense to label it *PMS-B*, which would neatly fit between *PMS-A* and *PMS-C*!) Women with PMS-H are said to suffer from water retention symptoms, such as bloating, breast tenderness, congestion, and swollen hands and feet due to an excess in androgen levels which could be stress-related.

The Discomforts of PMS

PMS is associated with a range of physical and emotional changes seven to ten days before the menstrual period starts. Of course, these can aggravate existing thyroid disease symptoms, mask them, or mimic them.

The Physical Signs

This list is not exhaustive, but women report the following physical premenstrual signs (listed alphabetically):

- Abdominal bloating (which may also cause weight gain)
- Acne or other skin eruptions
- Asthma
- Backache
- Breast swelling and tenderness
- Changes in sex drive (either more or less)
- Chills, shakiness, and dizziness
- Clumsiness and poor coordination
- Constipation or diarrhea
- Eye problems
- Fatigue (also see Chapters 2 and 3)
- Headaches
- Heart pounding (see Chapter 2)
- Hoarseness
- Increased appetite and weight gain
- Insomnia
- Joint and muscle pain (see Chapter 3)
- Menopausal-like hot flashes
- Nausea
- Seizures
- Sensitivity to noise
- Sugar and salt cravings

The Emotional Signs

Of course, it is the emotional premenstrual signs that cause the most problems. They include (in alphabetical order):

- Aggression (physical or verbal) toward others
- Anger, rage
- Anxiety
- Confusion (extremely rare)
- Decreased concentration
- Depression, melancholy, unexplained crying (see Chapter 3)
- Emotional overresponsiveness
- Forgetfulness
- Irritability
- Loss of control
- Nightmares
- Restlessness
- Sudden mood swings
- Suicidal thoughts (extremely rare)
- Withdrawal

The best way to determine whether your symptoms are directly related to your periods is to chart them. Women suffering from PMS would see their symptoms vanish with the onset of their periods. If the symptoms seem to be chronic and are not related to your periods, then you can probably rule out PMS and investigate other causes for your symptoms, such as a thyroid condition.

Charting Premenstrual Signs

Use the charts titled "My Emotional Cycle Chart" and "My Physical Cycle Chart" to help you determine when in your cycle your mood changes begin, end, peak, and valley. Remember that day 1 of your cycle is the first day of bleeding, or day 1 of your period.

Use one chart for each week of your cycle. Indicate the day of your cycle above the day of the week. Then write in a rating under each date for the feelings, perceptions, or experiences you have that day. A rating of 10 means "really severe" and 1 means "really mild." Leave the space blank for feelings that do not seem to differ from your everyday experience.

My Emotional Cycle Chart

Month: _____

Week: _____

	Sun.	Mon.	Tues.	Wed.	Thurs.	Fri.	Sat.
Aggression							
Anger, rage							
Anxiety							
Confusion							
Decreased concentration							
Depression, melancholy							
Forgetfulness							
Irritability							
Loss of control							
Overreacting							
Restlessness							
Sudden mood swings							
Suicidal thoughts							
Unexplained crying							
Withdrawal							

For each day of your cycle, answer the following questions:

Describe your dreams. If you can remember your dreams, describe them here. Dreams change according to the cycle and can be valuable clues to what you are working on in your inner life. Pick up a dream dictionary to help you with symbols.

_____

_____

_____

What did you eat today? Moods can be linked to blood sugar swings, too. List your meals and snacks and times you ate them.

_____

_____

_____

Are there any special circumstances? Did anything out of the ordinary occur today? If so, explain.

_____

_____

Where is the moon in its cycle? Take note of the moon's position (new moon, half-moon, etc.) so you can chart your emotional changes in accordance with moon changes. Remember, the Greek word for "moon" is *mene*, while *menstruation* actually means "moon change."

_____

_____

continued

My Physical Cycle Chart

Month: _____

Week: _____

	Sun.	Mon.	Tues.	Wed.	Thurs.	Fri.	Sat.
Acne, other skin eruptions							
Asthma							
Backache							
Bloating							
Breast swelling, tenderness							
Changes in sex drive							
Chills							
Clumsiness, poor coordination							
Constipation							
Diarrhea							
Dizziness							
Eye problems							
Fatigue							
Headaches							
Heart pounding							
Hoarseness							
Increased appetite							

	Sun.	Mon.	Tues.	Wed.	Thurs.	Fri.	Sat.
Insomnia							
Joint and muscle pain							
Menopausal-like hot flashes							
Nausea							
Salt cravings							
Seizures							
Sensitivity to noise							
Shakiness							
Sugar cravings							
Weight gain							

For each day of your cycle, consider the following questions:

What medications did you take today? Aspirin and Tylenol count! List all prescription and over-the-counter medications you're taking.

_____

_____

Are you taking supplements? List any herbal or vitamin supplements you're taking.

_____

_____

_____

continued

What did you eat or drink today? List your meals and snacks and times you ate them.

_____

_____

Are there any special circumstances? Did anything out of the ordinary occur today? If so, explain.

_____

_____

Where is the moon in its cycle? Take note of the moon's position so you can chart your physical changes in accordance with moon changes. Remember, *menstrual cycle* means "moon cycle."

_____

_____

5

Fertility, Pregnancy, and the Thyroid

THERE ARE TWO groups of women reading this chapter. The first group is concerned about first developing a thyroid problem during or after pregnancy, while the second group is concerned about how a diagnosis of thyroid disease prior to conception will interfere with conception or pregnancy. This chapter will address all of these concerns.

If you are in the first group, you have reason to worry about a thyroid problem because autoimmune thyroid disorders such as Hashimoto's or Graves' disease are most likely to strike during the first trimester of a pregnancy and within the first six months after delivery. If you are in the second group, you have less reason to worry because once your thyroid condition is brought under control, it shouldn't interfere with conception or pregnancy if you're under the care of a good doctor. That said, you should note that autoimmune disorders tend to improve anyway during a pregnancy but can worsen after delivery. So don't be surprised if you suddenly notice a flare-up of thyroid symptoms after delivery. Hashimoto's thyroiditis, postpartum thyroiditis, and Graves' disease are the most common thyroid problems that will develop during or after pregnancy.

Getting Pregnant

As discussed in Chapter 1, when your thyroid gland is over- or under-active, it can interfere with your menstrual cycle and subsequently interfere with ovulation. This could make conception difficult. So the first rule when planning a pregnancy is to have your thyroid checked, especially if thyroid disease runs in your family. Your partner should also have his thyroid checked, as thyroid disease in men may interfere with sperm count and libido.

Infertility

If a thyroid problem is interfering with your menstrual cycle, it's important to remember that infertility is always temporary when it's caused by either hypo- or hyperthyroidism. Once the thyroid problem is treated, your cycles should return to normal. That said, there could be other causes for your ovulation problems. Currently, the most common reason for difficulty ovulating is age. Fertility actually begins to decline after age twenty-five and continues to decline considerably after age thirty. Ninety-seven percent of all twenty-year-old women are fertile; by age forty-five that number dwindles to 5 percent. As women age, there is also an increase in conditions such as endometriosis, where pieces of uterine lining (the endometrium) grow outside of the uterus and can block the fallopian tubes or scar the ovaries. In short, delaying childbearing is probably the most common reason why women suffer from infertility (see Table 5.1).

Casual, unprotected sexual encounters earlier in life have also led to an explosion in sexually transmitted diseases (STDs), which can damage women's reproductive organs, causing infertility in the thirties and forties. It's estimated that at least half of all infertility is preventable through safe sex.

It's important to note that hypothyroidism is more common in women with polycystic ovary syndrome, as well as women with Turner's syndrome, a genetic disorder where the ovaries do not make eggs without female hormone supplements.

Table 5.1 Thyroid or Age?

Fertility declines naturally as you age. Before you blame your thyroid gland, read this:

Age	Likelihood of Fertility*	Likelihood of Infertility
20–24	100%	3%
25–29	94%	5%
30–34	86%	8%
35–39	70%	15%
40–44	36%	32%
45–49	5%	69%
50	0%	100%

*Presumes optimal health
Source: Adapted from Masood Khatamee, M.D., "Infertility: A Preventable Epidemic?" *International Journal of Fertility* 33, no. 4 (1988): 246–51.

Having Sex

Conceiving may be difficult when you are hypothyroid because your desire for sex can be diminished. Because of the fatigue that sets in, you might find that you simply don't have the energy or desire for sex. This is a temporary problem that clears up when your thyroid problem is treated. Women who are hyperthyroid or thyrotoxic, however, frequently have an increased desire for sex.

Other Causes of Infertility

It's important to rule out male infertility first, before you undergo an invasive workup. This is done through a simple semen analysis. Male infertility is often structural, too, caused by blockages within the male reproductive tract. There is also a problem with declining sperm counts, which have been linked to environmental pollution.

In general, when infertility is caused by a male or female hormonal disorder, only a small fraction of these disorders are due to a thyroid problem.

Bad Habits

Eating well and cutting down on the "bad stuff" can also improve your chances for conception. For example, smoking, alcohol, and caffeine can impair fertility.

A Word About Contraception

Preventing unintended pregnancy is still a high priority for most women. But which contraceptive methods are best for women with thyroid problems?

If you've been treated for a thyroid condition and are currently on thyroid replacement hormone, so long as you don't smoke and do not have other risk factors preventing you from taking hormonal contraception, you can take oral contraceptives or other forms of hormonal contraception. If you are hyperthyroid or hypothyroid, using a barrier method of contraception is best since either state can reduce the effectiveness of hormonal contraception. If you are currently undergoing scans or treatment with radioactive iodine, a double barrier method is recommended, such as a diaphragm and condom. Alternatively, use a barrier method in addition to hormonal contraception.

If You Have Already Been Treated for Thyroid Disease

If you are hypothyroid or are taking thyroid replacement hormone for a thyroid condition prior to pregnancy, thyroid hormone replacement (levothyroxine sodium)—the usual treatment—is fine. Although very little thyroid hormone will cross over from you to the fetus, this small amount is critical for proper fetal development until the fetus develops its own thyroid gland. Sometimes a change in dosage is needed because requirements for thyroid hormone can increase during pregnancy. It's normal to require as much as a 40 to 50 percent increase in your dosage. In this case, doctors generally monitor the TSH level anyway and should increase your dosage as necessary. Since prenatal vitamins often contain iron, it's important to take them at night so that the iron doesn't interfere with the absorption of the morning thyroid pill.

If you've been treated for hypothyroidism and are planning to get pregnant, you should have your thyroid levels checked again while you are trying to conceive. To make sure you're taking enough thyroid hormone replacement, request a TSH test. That way, you will minimize any possible risk to yourself or your baby from hypothyroidism during pregnancy. Since you naturally feel increasingly tired when you're pregnant, fatigue caused by hypothyroidism could severely lower your energy levels.

If you're being treated for hyperthyroidism via radioactive iodine, you shouldn't plan to get pregnant for about six months. As a precaution, all doctors screen for pregnancy first before radioactive iodine is administered.

If you're taking antithyroid medications and are planning to get pregnant, you can safely become pregnant while continuing to take this medication as long as you're under the supervision of a physician. In fact, this medication may protect the baby in your womb from the effects of thyroid-stimulating antibody, which crosses from you into the baby's circulation.

Being Pregnant

It was customary in ancient Egypt to tie a fine thread around the neck of a young bride; when it broke, it meant she was pregnant. It's normal for the thyroid gland to enlarge slightly during pregnancy because the placenta makes a hormone, human chorionic gonadotropin (HCG), which stimulates the mother's thyroid gland. Researchers have found that HCG has a very similar molecular structure to thyroid-stimulating hormone (TSH). The more iodine-deficient a woman is (especially if she lives in an iodine-deficient area), the more enlarged her thyroid becomes because of increased TSH levels. The thyroid usually increases in volume by 30 percent between eighteen and thirty-six weeks into pregnancy. (As a precaution, however, even a modestly enlarged thyroid gland or goiter should be checked. And, of course, iodine deficiency should be treated with iodine immediately.)

Normal, healthy pregnant women often develop symptoms and signs that suggest hyperthyroidism, such as a rapid pulse or palpitations, sweating, and heat intolerance. This is because the metabolic rate increases during pregnancy. Despite this, hyperthyroidism occurs only in about one in a thousand pregnancies. Thyroid hormone levels also increase during pregnancy because of the high levels of estrogen a pregnant body secretes. This is due to an increase in a binding protein in the blood that holds thyroxine there. The amount of free thyroxine available to the tissues, however, is not increased, and the increased total thyroid levels would not interfere with the health of normal pregnant women.

Gestational Thyroid Disease
(Thyroid Disease During Pregnancy)

If hypothyroidism is suspected while you're pregnant, your doctor will give you a TSH test. Just as in nonpregnant women, your TSH levels will be increased if you're hypothyroid, and you'll be treated with thyroid hormone replacement. Sometimes, pregnancy itself can mask hypothyroid symptoms. For example, constipation, puffiness, and fatigue are all traits of pregnancy as well. If this is what's happening, your hypothyroidism is probably not that severe, but the symptoms will persist after delivery.

Hyperthyroidism during pregnancy is more complex, and when it does happen, it's usually due to Graves' disease. Diagnosis and treatment of hyperthyroidism during pregnancy presents some unique fetal and maternal considerations, however.

First, the risk of miscarriage and stillbirth is increased if hyperthyroidism goes untreated. Second, the overall risks to you and the baby increase if the disease persists or is first recognized late in pregnancy. As in nonpregnant women, specific hyperthyroid symptoms usually indicate a problem, but here again, some of the classic symptoms such as heat intolerance or palpitations can mirror classic pregnancy traits. Usually, symptoms such as bulgy eyes or a pronounced goiter give Graves' disease away. But because radioactive iodine scans or treatment are never performed during pregnancy, hyperthyroidism in this case can only be confirmed through a blood test. (If, by some fluke, you are exposed to radioactive iodine during pregnancy because the pregnancy was not suspected, you may want to discuss the possibility of a therapeutic abortion with your practitioner.)

The treatment for Graves' disease in pregnancy is antithyroid medication. Propylthiouracil (PTU) or methimazole are most commonly used, but PTU is the one usually used during pregnancy. The antithyroid medication in pregnancy is used first to control the hyperthyroidism. Then, the aim is to administer the lowest dose possible to maintain the thyroid hormone levels in the "high normal" or maximum-without-risk range. Because thyroid-stimulating antibodies cross the placenta, they can cause fetal hyperthyroidism, which is very dangerous and may even cause fetal death. Therefore, the PTU, by suppressing the fetal thyroid, actually benefits the fetus. Since the fetal thyroid is slightly more sensitive to PTU than the mother's thyroid, the dose is slightly less than would completely normalize the mother's thyroid hormone levels.

Sometimes women discover they are allergic to PTU. If this happens, methimazole is used instead. When there is a problem with both drugs, sometimes a thyroidectomy is performed during the second trimester. This is rare, though. In general, surgery is avoided during pregnancy because it can trigger a miscarriage.

Many times, hyperthyroidism becomes milder as the pregnancy progresses. When this happens, antithyroid medication can be tapered off slowly as the pregnancy reaches full term, and often normal thyroid function resumes after delivery.

On the other hand, when Graves' disease is the cause of hyperthyroidism in pregnancy, the hyperthyroidism will need to be controlled throughout pregnancy to avoid either severe hyperthyroidism or complications during labor and delivery. Sometimes, beta-blockers (heart medication) such as propanalol are added to PTU, which can be continued safely during the nursing period.

A Word About Morning Sickness

If you are suffering from severe morning sickness in early pregnancy, this may be a sign of thyrotoxicosis. It's believed that morning sickness can become increasingly severe because of the overproduction of thyroid hormone. See your doctor if your morning sickness is severe. Even if you do not have hyperthyroidism, severe morning sickness can lead to dehydration and should be treated.

The Risk of Miscarriage

Studies indicate a 32 percent risk of miscarriage in women with antithyroid antibodies compared to a 16 percent risk in women without them. The risk of miscarriage rises with age. In the general population, one in six pregnancies ends in miscarriage with risk highest during the first trimester.

Bleeding in the First Trimester

Bleeding during pregnancy is not normal, but it's not unusual either. Nor does it mean that a miscarriage is imminent. It's also important to note whether any pain accompanies your staining or bleeding. Staining or bleeding with no pain is better news than staining or bleeding and cramps. Bleeding or spotting of *any* kind during this stage should be reported immediately to avoid any risk.

The most dangerous kind of bleeding at this point is heavy bleeding. The definition of heavy bleeding means that you need to change your pads about every hour. Other danger signs to watch out for are other symptoms accompanying the bleeding such as cramps, pain in the abdomen, fever, weakness, and possible vomiting. If the blood has clumps of tissue in it, this is also a bad sign. If this is the case, save your pad. Just stick your whole pad—clumps and all—in a plastic bag and save it for the doctor to inspect. The clumps may provide important clues as to what is going on. You may also notice an unusual odor. If light bleeding or spotting continues for more than three days, this is another, less obvious danger sign.

Symptoms of Miscarriage

Heavy bleeding and cramping anywhere between the end of the second month to the end of the third month are classic signs that you're in the process of miscarrying. Cramps without bleeding are also a danger sign that you're miscarrying. The bleeding can be heavy enough to saturate several pads within an hour or may be manageable and more like a heavy period. You may also be experiencing unbearable cramping that renders you incapacitated. Sometimes, you can pass clots, dark red clumps that look like small pieces of raw beef liver. You may even pass gray or pink tissue. A miscarriage can also be occurring if you have persistent, light bleeding and more mild cramping at this stage. The medical term for a miscarriage prior to twenty weeks is *spontaneous abortion.*

Finding a Solitary Thyroid Nodule During Pregnancy

If you discover a lump on your thyroid gland during pregnancy, investigation and treatment will vary depending on what stage you are in.

If you are in the first trimester, a needle biopsy will be done to determine whether the lump is benign or malignant. If it is malignant, surgery will probably be performed during the second trimester, which is considered the safest time for surgery. If a cancerous nodule is confirmed in the second trimester, surgery may still be performed if there is time. Otherwise, you might simply have to wait until you deliver. As will be discussed in Chapter 10, thyroid cancer grows very slowly and the extra few months won't usually make a difference in the overall treatment scenario.

After the Baby Is Born

During pregnancy, your immune system is naturally suppressed to prevent your body from rejecting the fetus. After pregnancy, your immune system "turns on" again. But this has a rebound effect in that it is so alert, it is almost too powerful and can develop antibodies that attack normal tissue. This is what's known as an autoimmune disorder and may be one reason why women are more prone to autoimmune disorders after pregnancy. I liken the scenario to having a guard dog tied up for nine months (during the pregnancy) and then let out. The dog will be more feisty and may even attack his owner.

If you first developed an autoimmune thyroid disease such as Hashimoto's or Graves' disease after you delivered, you would undergo normal treatment for either disease. If you developed Graves' disease after delivery, however, you may not have to discontinue breast-feeding; the antithyroid medication, propylthiouracil, doesn't cross into your milk and is safe for lactating women. However, radioactive iodine therapy must wait until after breast-feeding has ended because breasts trap iodine.

If you had developed Graves' disease during pregnancy, the condition can get worse after delivery unless antithyroid drugs are continued.

If you were diagnosed and successfully treated for Graves' disease prior to pregnancy, you can sometimes suffer a relapse after delivery. But depending on the severity of Graves' disease after delivery, some women can choose to postpone treatment until they are finished breast-feeding.

Postpartum Thyroiditis

Postpartum thyroiditis means "inflammation of the thyroid gland after delivery." It is a general label referring to silent thyroiditis (see Chapter 2) occurring after delivery, causing mild hyperthyroidism, or a short-lived Hashimoto's type of thyroiditis, causing mild hypothyroidism. Postpartum thyroiditis occurs in 5 to 18 percent of all postpartum women and usually lasts two to eight months before it resolves on its own. (This statistic does not include the many women who develop Graves' disease either during or after pregnancy.) Until quite recently, the mild hypo- and hyperthyroid symptoms were attributed simply to symptoms of postpartum depression, those notorious "postpartum blues" thought to be caused by the dramatic hormonal changes women experience after pregnancy.

Usually, the silent thyroiditis or short-lived Hashimoto's thyroiditis lasts for only a few weeks. Often, women don't even realize what's wrong with them, because the symptoms are mild and usually associated with the natural fatigue that accompanies taking care of a newborn.

These conditions clear up by themselves. Short-lived Hashimoto's thyroiditis is usually more common than silent thyroiditis after delivery, and, in more severe cases, thyroid hormone is administered temporarily to alleviate the hypothyroid symptoms. Women who experience this sudden thyroid flare-up tend to reexperience it with each pregnancy, however. Women who do experience postpartum thyroiditis are predisposed to thyroid disorders and seem to be vulnerable in that particular area. Since it's not feasible to screen for this condition in advance, there's really no way to prevent it.

Diagnosing Postpartum Thyroiditis

Today, it should be standard practice for all pregnant women in North America to have their thyroid glands tested after delivery. Regardless of how you feel, request that your doctor perform a thyroid function test within a few days. This is a simple, easy-as-pie blood test. The test will determine whether you're either over- or underproducing thyroid hormone. If your thyroid test is normal, yet you still have symptoms of PPD or maternal blues, then you can rule out a thyroid condition as a physical cause for your symptoms.

Treating Postpartum Thyroiditis

Most women will experience hypothyroid symptoms (see Chapter 2). In this case, you may be monitored and given no medication unless the symptoms are severe enough to warrant it. Medication is one tiny pill that is thyroid replacement hormone: it simply replaces or supplements the thyroid hormone your body makes naturally. Often postpartum thyroiditis resolves on its own.

If your hyperthyroid symptoms are severe, you may be placed on beta-blockers until the excess thyroid hormone is depleted. Regardless of whether you are given thyroid hormone or beta-blockers, you can still breast-feed safely.

Postpartum Thyroiditis, Maternal Blues, or Postpartum Depression?

If you look at the symptoms of hypothyroidism in Chapter 2, it's easy to see how they can be confused with symptoms of postpartum depression—especially since fatigue and depression are symptoms of hypothyroidism! True postpartum psychological and emotional disturbances range from what's known as "maternal blues" to true postpartum depression, where one experiences symptoms ranging from unipolar depression (see Chapter 3) to something known as postpartum psychosis, the diagnosis made in a situation where a woman loses touch with reality and becomes psychotic, believing, for example, that her newborn is evil or abnormal in some way. Postpartum psychosis occurs in two of every thousand deliveries, not as uncommon as one is led to believe.

Maternal Blues

As many as 70 percent of all women will suffer from *maternal blues* after delivery. The maternal blues are common, nothing to worry about, mild, and transitory, meaning short-term. This condition usually occurs within the first ten days (averaging three or four days) after delivery.

Symptoms of maternal blues are frequent crying episodes, mood swings, feelings of sadness, low energy, anxiety, insomnia, restlessness, and irritability. Women who experience these feelings should feel comforted that these feelings are normal and will pass. It will last for a couple of weeks.

Maternal blues are most likely caused by enormous hormonal shifts in your body. There is not any real documented proof that what you're feeling is hormonal, however. Since we do know that hormonal shifts definitely cause premenstrual mood swings as well as menopausal mood swings, and we know that estrogen levels are depleted after childbirth, it's likely that hormones are the culprit.

Nevertheless, there are other causes that have to do with an enormous lifestyle shift. This includes an increase in stress and responsibility, worry about your newborn, physical discomfort associated with your postpartum physique, and possible exhaustion following labor and delivery.

Postpartum Depression (PPD)

Postpartum depression is more serious and persistent, and affects 10 to 15 percent of the postpartum population. Depression can begin at any time after delivery—from the first few hours afterward to a few weeks after. These symptoms include sadness, mood changes, lack of energy, loss of interest, change in appetite, fatigue, guilt, self-loathing, suicidal thoughts, and poor concentration and memory. When these feelings last for more than a couple of weeks, the consequences can be truly negative, leading to problems in bonding with the baby and relationship trouble. However, women don't go from the maternal blues to depression. In fact, you can feel well after delivery and then *suddenly* develop postpartum depression.

The causes of postpartum depression are possibly similar to those cited as causes for the milder maternal blues. But women at risk for this more serious depression are those with a family history of depression and women who have a poor support system at home (spouseless, bad relationship with partner, teenage mothers, and so on).

Study after study makes this fact official: most women are unprepared for the life they begin to lead after the baby is brought home from the hospital. One alarming study of fourteen hundred U.S. couples revealed that following the birth of a baby, 70 percent of couples reported that their marriages had worsened to the point where both people were unhappy. Eighty percent of women experience the blues after delivery; one in four first-time mothers will go on to develop full-blown depression.

Treating PPD

If you do begin to notice these feelings, treatment is available with a qualified mental health practitioner. You may just need some counseling or to be put on antidepressant medication. Counseling can vary from short-term "sorting out your life" chats (interpersonal therapy) to cognitive behavioral therapy. It really varies depending on the severity of your symptoms. In addition, there are now a number of postpartum support groups where you can talk to other women in the same boat. (For more information about depression, see Chapter 3 and consult Appendix B.)

Unfortunately, many women who have postpartum thyroiditis are misdiagnosed as having postpartum depression. For these women, a diagnosis of postpartum depression can be enough to . . . drive them crazy!

Postpartum Psychosis

Postpartum psychosis is very serious and requires hospitalization. This affects a very small portion of women and usually begins in the first month after delivery. Basically, this is when you're usually totally out of touch with the world around you. This condition usually indicates other psychiatric disorders, but women can suddenly develop the following psychotic symptoms: delusions that the child is dead or defective, denial that the birth ever took place, or hearing voices inside their head that tell them to harm the infant. Accompanying symptoms include sleep disorders, intense confusion, loss of energy, and hence, difficulty caring for the child.

This is a serious psychiatric illness that needs to be treated with medications and therapies. In some cases, the infant may need to be cared for temporarily by another family member.

Your Baby's Thyroid

The baby's thyroid begins to function somewhere between the tenth and twelfth week of pregnancy. Thyroid hormones are important for the development of the fetal nervous system. The hormones at this stage come primarily from the baby's thyroid gland secretions; only very small amounts of the mother's thyroid hormone cross the placenta.

Iodine in the mother's diet will also cross the placenta and is used by the fetal thyroid gland to make thyroid hormone. Iodine deficiency, on the other hand, can cause newborn hypothyroidism or mental retardation and is a major health problem in underdeveloped countries. But since there is an overabundance of iodine in the North American diet, disorders caused by a lack of dietary iodine don't happen here. (See Table 5.2 for what can cause thyroid disease in your baby.)

Table 5.2 Mother and Child and Thyroid Disease

When Baby Has . . .	You May Have . . .
Fetal hyperthyroidism	Graves' disease (your antibodies crossed the placenta)
Fetal hypothyroidism	Hashimoto's disease (your antibodies crossed the placenta)
	Taken too high a dosage of antithyroid pills
	Taken drugs containing too much iodine
Fetal goiter	A goiter
	Hashimoto's disease
	Taken drugs containing too much iodine
	Taken too high a dosage of antithyroid pills
Neonatal hyperthyroidism	Graves' disease or Hashimoto's disease (your antibodies crossed the placenta)
Neonatal hypothyroidism	A goiter caused by a shortage in iodine
	Hashimoto's disease

Source: Adapted from Patty Westcott, *Thyroid Problems: A Practical Guide to Symptoms and Treatment* (London: Thorsons/HarperCollins, 1995), 91.

Fetal Hypothyroidism

Antithyroid medications, ordinary or nonradioactive iodine, and sometimes maternal thyroid antibodies can cross the placenta and cause hypothyroidism in the baby.

Plain iodine, which is present in medications including some cough syrups, for example, can cause a goiter in the fetus, making delivery difficult or causing respiratory obstruction. For this reason, drugs that contain iodine should never be used in pregnancy except in the case of extreme hyperthyroidism—sometimes called thyroid storm.

Unfortunately, there is no simple blood test to assess the baby's thyroid function in the womb, although measurements of thyroid hormone or TSH levels in the amniotic fluid sac have been used in research studies. Plain x-ray will sometimes show delayed bone development in fetal hypothyroidism, but this test is usually not recommended because the x-ray itself can cause more damage to the fetus than the underlying condition. Screening for hypothyroidism at birth—now done routinely in North America on all newborns—is still the best method for determining whether your baby is hypothyroid and whether the infant needs short-term or long-term treatment in the form of thyroid replacement hormone.

Fetal Hyperthyroidism

When the fetus is hyperthyroid the condition is known as *fetal thyrotoxicosis*. This happens when maternal thyroid-stimulating antibodies cross the placenta, as in the case of Graves' disease. Fetal hyperthyroidism is unusual, though. In most cases when the mother herself is hyperthyroid and is being treated with antithyroid drugs, the drugs wind up treating the baby as well by crossing the placenta. However, if the mother's hyperthyroidism occurred in the past and was already treated via radioactive iodine or surgery, she could potentially have thyroid-stimulating antibodies in her blood even though she's no longer hyperthyroid. Since the mother is well and isn't exhibiting any hyperthyroid symptoms, fetal hyperthyroidism is simply not suspected. When the fetus is hyperthyroid, the fetal heart rate is consistently above the normal limit of 160 beats per minute, and elevated levels of thyroid-stimulating antibodies will be present in the mother's blood.

All women with Graves' disease or a history of Graves' disease should be tested for thyroid-stimulating antibodies late in pregnancy. The consequences of untreated fetal hyperthyroidism can lead to low birth weight and small head size, fetal distress in labor, neonatal heart failure, and respiratory distress. Putting the mother on antithyroid drugs during pregnancy will treat the baby in this situation, but after delivery it will be necessary to continue treatment for the baby as well as perform follow-up tests.

Neonatal or Congenital Hypothyroidism

Roughly one in four thousand babies is born with either neonatal or congenital hypothyroidism. In neonatal hypothyroidism, the baby is born without a thyroid gland. In congenital hypothyroidism, the baby is born with what appears to be a normal thyroid gland but then develops symptoms of hypothyroidism after its first twenty-eight days of life. In this case, while the condition was present at birth, the symptoms didn't manifest until later. The treatment is the same for the two conditions.

Neonatal hypothyroidism or congenital hypothyroidism are very serious conditions that can lead to severe brain damage and developmental impairment, and may not be obvious until brain damage has already occurred. They can occur from an iodine deficiency in the mother's diet. This is common in more remote or mountainous areas of the world where iodine is not readily available. In fact, iodine deficiency is the most common cause of mental retardation in underdeveloped countries. Fortunately, this is not a problem in North America because most of our salt is iodized. (And low-salt diets still contain enough iodine for our needs.)

Neonatal Screening for Hypothyroidism

The wonderful news is that neonatal screening for hypothyroidism in newborns was introduced in the mid-1970s, and usually catches neonatal hypothyroidism while preventing congenital hypothyroidism from developing. In North America, all babies are given a "heelpad" test approximately two days after birth to check for hypothyroidism.

The heelpad test involves a blood sample taken via a small heel prick and sent to a laboratory for analysis. Usually the test confirms that your baby's thyroid gland is functioning normally. In rare instances, the initial tests may be unclear or inconclusive. If this happens, the laboratory usually notifies the hospital where your child was born, as well your family physician. Then, someone contacts you to request another blood sample from your baby. If your child is in fact hypothyroid at birth, an endocrinologist and pediatrician will be consulted, and your baby will be given thyroid replacement hormone daily.

As a precaution, before you leave the hospital with your newborn, ask your doctor whether the heelpad test or thyroid test was administered. If for some reason the test was not done, request it, and make certain that you find out the results of the test. If hypothyroidism is diagnosed at birth, any serious consequences are preventable by administering thyroid replacement hormone to the baby. In this case, intellectual and physical growth will be normal.

A Word About Down Syndrome

At one time, it was believed that fetal or neonatal hypothyroidism caused Down syndrome. In the nineteenth century, animal thyroid hormone was administered to children with Down syndrome in the belief that it would normalize their development. We now know that hypothyroidism has absolutely nothing to do with Down syndrome. Down syndrome is caused by a chromosomal abnormality in which there is an extra chromosome.

Neonatal Hyperthyroidism

Hyperthyroidism only occurs in infants born to mothers who are hyperthyroid. Most cases are not reported, and it occurs in one of seventy babies born to hyperthyroid mothers. As discussed, neonatal hyperthyroidism occurs when fetal hyperthyroidism is not caught. Fortunately, this type of hyperthyroidism in a newborn lasts only as long as the mother's antibodies remain in the baby's bloodstream—usually from three to twelve weeks. As well, this condition is usually mild, since most women who are hyperthyroid produce only low levels of thyroid-stimulating antibodies.

Occasionally, if the hyperthyroidism is severe at birth, babies can be born with prominent eyes, irritability (they cry a lot), flushed skin, and a fast pulse—all classic hyperthyroid symptoms. These babies tend to be long and scrawny and, although they have large appetites, may not gain any weight. The cranial bones may also be malformed. Some fetuses die before birth because of this illness, though. Infants who are hyperthyroid are always treated with antithyroid medication; radioactive iodine is never given to infants, and performing a thyroidectomy on an infant is unnecessary since the disease runs its course in eight to twelve weeks. Sometimes plain iodine is used, too.

6

Thyroid Disease and Menopause

WHEN IT COMES to menopause, women with thyroid disease have a little more to be concerned about than women without thyroid disease. First, all women postmenopause are at an increased risk of heart disease, which is the major cause of death for postmenopausal women. But in postmenopausal women with untreated hypothyroidism or hyperthyroidism (or thyrotoxicosis), cardiovascular changes with possible damage to the heart can result, magnifying the normal risk of heart disease that exists in the general female population. Hyperthyroidism or thyrotoxicosis can also speed the process of osteoporosis, also a risk for women after menopause.

In women with normal thyroid function prior to menopause, the signs of thyroid disease can be masked by perimenopausal symptoms. Thus, thyroid disease can be missed, which can aggravate menopause and postmenopause risks of other diseases, such as osteoporosis or heart disease. Or, you may be mistakenly told you are perimenopausal when you are not. It's important to note that mild hypothyroidism, or subclinical hypothyroidism (meaning that symptoms may not be obvious but still contribute to general malaise), steadily rises with age, increasing from 10 percent in the premenopausal age group to 20 percent in the postmenopausal age group.

Finally, in light of the 2002 studies on hormone replacement therapy (HRT) and heart disease, managing menopause for all women presents a challenge. But we also know that the roughly 5 percent of post-menopausal women on thyroid hormone also taking HRT typically need to increase their thyroid hormone dosages, similar to the scenario during pregnancy.

Natural Menopause

When menopause occurs naturally, it tends to take place anywhere between the ages of forty-eight and fifty-two, but it can occur as early as your late thirties or as late as your midfifties. When menopause occurs before age forty-five, it is technically considered early menopause, but just as menarche is genetically predetermined, so is menopause. For an average woman with an unremarkable medical history, what she eats or the activities she engages in will not influence the timing of her menopause. However, women who have had chemotherapy or who have been exposed to high levels of radiation (such as radiation therapy in their pelvic area for cancer treatment) may go into earlier menopause. In any event, the average age of menopause is between fifty and fifty-one.

Other causes that have been cited to trigger an early menopause include mumps (in a small number of women, the infection causing the mumps has been known to spread to the ovaries, prematurely shutting them down) and specific autoimmune diseases, such as lupus or rheumatoid arthritis (some women with these diseases find that their bodies develop antibodies to their own ovaries and attack the ovaries).

The term *perimenopause* refers to women who are in the thick of menopause—their cycles are wildly erratic and they are experiencing hot flashes and vaginal dryness. This label is applicable for about four years, covering the two years prior to and the two years following the official "last" menstrual period. Women who are perimenopausal will be in the age groups discussed above, averaging to about fifty-one. The term *menopause* refers to your final menstrual period. You will not be able to pinpoint your final period until you've been completely free from periods for one year. Then you count back to the last period you charted, and that date is the date of your menopause. The term *post-menopause* refers to the last third of most women's lives and includes women who have been free of menstrual periods for at least four years to women celebrating their hundredth birthday.

Signs of Natural Menopause

There are really just three classic short-term symptoms of menopause: erratic periods, hot flashes, and vaginal dryness. All three of these symptoms are caused by a decrease in estrogen. As for the emotional symptoms of menopause, such as irritability, mood swings, melancholy, and so on, they are actually caused by a rise in FSH. As the cycle changes and the ovaries' egg supply dwindles, FSH is secreted in very high amounts and reaches a lifetime peak—as much as fifteen times higher; it's the body's way of trying to "jump-start" the ovarian engine.

Decreased levels of estrogen can make you more vulnerable to stress, depression, and anxiety because estrogen loss affects REM sleep. When we're less rested, we're less able to cope with stresses that normally may not affect us. Stress can also increase blood sugar.

Every woman entering menopause will experience a change in her menstrual cycle. However, not all women will experience hot flashes or even notice vaginal changes. This is particularly true if a woman is overweight. Estrogen is stored in fat cells, which is why overweight women also tend to be more at risk for estrogen-dependent cancers. What happens is that the fat cells make estrogen, creating a type of estrogen reserve that the body will use during menopause and that can reduce the severity of estrogen loss symptoms.

Cycles may become longer or shorter with long bouts of amenorrhea. There will also be flow changes, where periods may suddenly become light and scanty, or very heavy and crampy. Of course, all of this could be masking thyroid disease; or, thyroid disease may be the cause of your symptoms and you may be misdiagnosed as being menopausal when you are not.

Roughly 85 percent of all pre- and perimenopausal women experience hot flashes. They can begin when periods are either still regular or have just started to become irregular. The hot flashes usually stop between one and two years after your final menstrual period. A hot flash can feel different for each woman. Some women experience a feeling of warmth in their face and upper body; some women experience hot flashes as a simultaneous sweating with chills. Some women feel anxious, tense, dizzy, or nauseous just before the hot flash; some feel tingling in their fingers or heart palpitations just before. Some women will experience their hot flashes during the day; others will experience them at night and may wake up so wet from perspiration that they need to change their bedsheets and/or nightclothes.

A hot flash is not the same as being overheated. Although the skin temperature often rises between 4° and 8°F (1° and 3°C), the internal body temperature drops, creating this odd sensation. Certain groups of women will experience more severe hot flashes than others:

- Women who are in surgical menopause.
- Women who are thin. When there's less fat in the body to store estrogen reserves, estrogen loss symptoms are more severe.
- Women who don't sweat easily. An ability to sweat makes extreme temperatures easier to tolerate. Women who have trouble sweating may experience more severe flashes.

You can lessen your discomfort by adjusting your lifestyle to cope with the flashes. The more comfortable you are, the less intense your flashes will feel. Once you establish a pattern by charting the flashes, you can do a few things around the time of day your flashes occur. Some suggestions:

- Avoid synthetic clothing, such as polyester, because it traps perspiration.
- Use only 100 percent cotton bedding if you have night sweats.
- Avoid clothing with high necks and long sleeves.
- Dress in layers.
- Keep cold drinks handy.
- If you smoke, quit. Smoking constricts blood vessels and can intensify and prolong a flash.
- Avoid "trigger" foods such as caffeine, alcohol, spicy foods, sugars, and large meals.
- Substitute herbal teas for coffee or regular tea.

- Discuss with your doctor the benefits of taking vitamin E supplements. Evidence suggests that vitamin E is essential for proper circulation and the production of sex hormones.
- Exercise to improve your circulation.
- Reduce your exposure to the sun; sunburn will aggravate your hot flashes because burnt skin cannot regulate heat as effectively.

Other Changes

Estrogen loss will also cause vaginal changes. Since it is the production of estrogen that causes the vagina to continuously stay moist and elastic through its natural secretions, the loss of estrogen will cause the vagina to become drier, thinner, and less elastic. This may also cause the vagina to shrink slightly in terms of width and length. In addition, the reduction in vaginal secretions causes the vagina to be less acidic. This can put you at risk for more vaginal infections. As a result of these vaginal changes, you'll notice a change in your sexual activity. Your vagina may take longer to become lubricated, or you may have to depend on lubricants to have comfortable intercourse.

Estrogen loss can affect other parts of your sex life as well. Your libido may actually increase because testosterone levels can rise when estrogen levels drop. (The general rule is that your levels of testosterone will either stay the same or increase.) However, women who *do* experience an increase in sexual desire will also be frustrated that their vaginas are not accommodating their needs. First, there is the lubrication problem: more stimulation is required to lubricate the vagina naturally. Secondly, a decrease in estrogen means less blood flows to the vagina and clitoris, which means that orgasm may be more difficult to achieve or may not last as long as it normally has in the past. Other changes involve the breasts. Normally, estrogen causes blood to flow into the breasts during arousal, which makes the nipples more erect, sensitive, and responsive. Estrogen loss causes less blood to flow to the breasts, which makes them less sensitive. And finally, since the vagina shrinks as estrogen decreases, it doesn't expand as much during intercourse, which may make intercourse less comfortable, particularly since it is less lubricated.

Mood Swings

Mood swings can be an especially tricky symptom of both menopause and thyroid disease. While irritability and depression can be symptoms of menopause, they may also be signs of thyroid disease.

Surgical Menopause or Premature Menopause

Surgical menopause occurs when you've had your ovaries surgically removed, or chemically shut down as a result of certain medications, such as chemotherapy for cancer. In this case, you will likely experience all of the symptoms of natural menopause but in the extreme. Most women in surgical menopause report far more severe menopausal symptoms because the process of estrogen loss has been sudden rather than gradual. Surgical menopause or premature menopause before the age of forty-five are best managed using traditional hormone replacement therapy until the natural age of menopause (fifty to fifty-five). In this case, HRT simply replaces what your body should have been making naturally, were it not for illness or premature ovarian failure. Once

Menopause or Thyroid?

The following menopausal symptoms can also be confused with symptoms of hypo- or hyperthyroidism:

- Erratic periods
- Hot flashes (women who are hyperthyroid will feel hot all the time)
- Vaginal dryness and/or changes in libido
- Muscle aches and pains (could be signs of bone loss)
- Skin changes
- Irritability
- Mood swings

you reach the natural age of menopause, you can decide whether it is risky for you to continue HRT in light of the heart disease risks and the status of your thyroid condition. The 2002 Women's Health Initiative (WHI) study looked at the long-term use of HRT in women over fifty-five, and the results do not affect women on HRT to correct premature menopause due to surgery, chemotherapy, or premature ovarian failure caused by other factors.

HRT, Menopause, and Thyroid Disease

The average woman will live until age seventy-eight, meaning that she will live one-third of her life after her menopause. Since thyroid disorders affect women so much more frequently, balancing thyroid hormone replacement with the confusion surrounding traditional estrogen and progesterone hormone replacement is challenging. Since heart disease can be a major complication of hypothyroidism, thyrotoxicosis, or hyperthyroidism, in the 1980s and 1990s, women with thyroid disease were encouraged to seriously consider hormone replacement therapy after menopause, because it was believed that long-term HRT protected women from heart disease. *That's all changed.*

In July 2002, a study by the U.S. National Heart, Lung, and Blood Institute, part of the WHI huge research program, suggested that HRT in pill form, which has to go through the liver, should not be recommended for long-term use; in fact, the results were so alarming, the study was halted before its completion date. It was found that Prempro, a combination of estrogen and progestin that was a "standard issue" HRT formulation for postmenopausal women, increased the risk of invasive breast cancer, heart disease, stroke, and pulmonary embolisms (blood clots). However, Prempro did reduce the incidence of bone fractures from osteoporosis and colon cancer. The study participants were informed in a letter that they should stop taking their pills. Among women in good health, without thyroid disease, HRT in the short term to relieve menopausal symptoms is still considered a good option, and there was no evidence to suggest that short term use of HRT (one to five years) was harmful. The study only has implications for women on oral HRT for long-term use—something that was recommended to millions of women over that past twenty years because of perceived protection against heart disease.

In 1998, an earlier trial known as the Heart and Estrogen/Progestin Replacement Study (HERS) looked at whether HRT was reduced in women who already had heart disease. HRT was not found to have any beneficial effect. Women who were at risk for breast cancer were never advised to go on HRT; similarly, women who had suffered a stroke or were considered at risk for blood clots were also never considered good candidates for HRT. It had long been known that breast cancer was a risk of long-term HRT, as well as stroke and blood clots. However, many women made the HRT decision based on the perceived heart disease protection. Today, the only thing the experts can agree on is that the HRT decision is highly individual and must be an informed decision, where all of the possible risks and benefits of taking—or not taking—HRT are disclosed.

The Components of HRT

Hormone replacement therapy (HRT) refers to estrogen and progestin, which is a factory-made progesterone, given to women after menopause who still have their uterus to prevent the lining from overgrowing and becoming cancerous (known as endometrial hyperplasia). Estrogen replacement therapy (ERT), sometimes called ET, refers to estrogen only, which is given to women who no longer have a uterus after surgical menopause. Both HRT and ERT are designed to replace the estrogen lost after menopause, and hence:

1. Prevent or even reverse the long-term consequences of estrogen loss. The only proven long-term benefit of HRT is that it can help to prevent bone loss and reduce the incidence of fractures. Until July 2002, it was believed that HRT protected women from cardiovascular disease, but this is no longer considered true. In women who are at higher risk of breast cancer, HRT was always believed to be risky; now it is believed that it may trigger breast cancer in low-risk women.
2. Treat the short-term discomforts of menopause such as hot flashes and vaginal dryness. This is still true for women in otherwise good health. You must discuss with your doctor

whether this would be beneficial for you, if your blood sugar is well-controlled.

You can take estrogen in a number of ways. The most common estrogen product uses a synthesis of various estrogens that are derived from the urine of pregnant horses. That way the estrogen mimics nature more accurately. Estrogen replacement comes in pills, trans-dermal patches, or vaginal creams. Other common synthetic forms of estrogen include micronized estradiol, ethinyl estradiol, esterified estro-gen, and quinestrol. Progestins are taken in separate tablets along with estrogen. Together, the estrogen and progestin you take is called HRT.

If you are suffering from great discomfort during perimenopause, and your thyroid hormone levels are normal (again, women in peri-menopause frequently need to increase their thyroid hormone dosage), discuss with your health-care provider whether short-term HRT is an option. If you suffered from cardiovascular effects as a result of untreated hypo- or hyperthyroidism (or thyrotoxicosis), HRT may be more risky for you, in light of the 2002 study results.

There are also numerous natural methods to control symptoms. For example, many women are using soy, a type of plant estrogen (or phytoestrogen), in place of conventional HRT. It's critical to note that if you're on thyroid hormone, soy supplements can decrease the absorp-tion of thyroid hormone, and you may need to increase your dosages while on soy. Sometimes, taking your soy at night and your thyroid hormone pill in the morning may lessen the absorption problem, but it's important to request regular thyroid function tests (see Chapter 11) while you're on soy. For more information about natural approaches to HRT, consult my book *The Natural Woman's Guide to HRT.*

Osteoporosis

Postmenopausal women are at highest risk of developing osteoporosis (bone loss), which can be aggravated by thyrotoxicosis or hyperthy-roidism. Eighty percent of all osteoporosis sufferers are women as a direct result of estrogen loss. Maintaining bone mass and good bone health is your best defense against osteoporosis. Although osteoporosis can be disfiguring, it is a relatively silent disease in that there are often no immediate symptoms, pain, or suffering that occur with it. The problem is not osteoporosis itself, but the risk of fractures. One out of two women over fifty will have an osteoporosis-related fracture in her lifetime. If you have osteoporosis and fall down, a fracture can dramatically affect the quality of life you currently enjoy, and can continue to enjoy for years to come. If you've ever experienced reduced mobility, or being dependent on someone else to prepare meals, shop, or run errands, you may have some idea as to how debilitating being bedridden can be. A full 70 percent of all hip fractures are a direct result of osteoporosis. Roughly 20 to 25 percent of those suffering hip fractures will die; 50 percent will be disabled. In fact, more women die each year as a result of osteoporosis-related fractures than from breast and ovarian cancer combined.

Osteoporosis literally means "porous bones." Normally, in the life of a healthy, unremarkable woman, by her late thirties and forties her bones become less dense. By the time she reaches her fifties, she may begin to experience bone loss in her teeth and become more susceptible to wrist fractures. Gradually, the bones in her spine weaken, fracture, and compress, causing upper back curvature and loss of height, known as *kyphosis*, or sometimes, *dowager's hump*. If you've ever been stopped at a traffic light and watched an elderly woman cross, stooped over and struggling to get across the street in time, you've seen osteoporosis in full flare. You don't have to become such a sight; there are many ways to maintain bone mass after menopause and prevent the disfiguring effects of bone loss.

Osteoporosis is unfortunately more common in women because when a woman's skeletal growth is completed, she typically has 15 percent lower bone mineral density and 30 percent less bone mass than a man of the same age. Studies also show that women lose trabecular bone (the inner, spongy part making up the internal support of the bone) at a higher rate than men.

There are three types of osteoporosis women are prone to: postmenopausal, senile, and secondary. *Postmenopausal osteoporosis* usually develops roughly ten to fifteen years after the onset of menopause. In this case, estrogen loss interferes with calcium absorption, and you begin to lose trabecular bone at three times faster than the normal rate. You will also begin to lose parts of your cortical bone (the outer shell of the bone), but not as quickly as the trabecular bone.

Senile osteoporosis affects both men and women. Here, you lose cortical and trabecular bone because of a decrease in bone cell activity that results from aging. Hip fractures are seen most often with this kind of osteoporosis. The decrease in bone cell activity affects your capacity to rebuild bone in the first place, but is also aggravated by low calcium intake.

Secondary osteoporosis means that there is an underlying condition that has caused bone loss. These conditions include chronic renal disease, hypogonadism (an overstimulation of the sex glands, or gonads), thyrotoxicosis or hyperthyroidism, some forms of cancer, and the use of anticonvulsants.

What Causes Bone Loss Anyway?

Our bones are always regenerating (known as *remodeling*). This process helps to maintain a constant level of calcium in the blood, essential for a healthy heart, blood circulation, and blood clotting. About 99 percent of all the body's calcium is in the bones and teeth; when blood calcium drops below a certain level, the body will take calcium from the bones to replenish it. But by the time we reach our late thirties, our bones lose calcium faster than it can be replaced. The pace of bone calcium loss speeds up for newly postmenopausal women, those who are three to seven years beyond menopause. But bones start absorbing calcium again when this "bone-pause" is past. And consumption of calcium-rich foods, combined with moderate exercise, can help to reverse osteoporosis.

The pace of bone loss then slows once again, but as we age, the body is less able to absorb calcium from food. One of the most influential factors on bone loss is estrogen; it slows or even halts the loss of bone mass by improving our absorption of calcium from the intestinal tract, which allows us to maintain a higher level of calcium in our blood. And, the higher the calcium levels in the blood, the less chance you have of losing calcium from your bones to replenish your calcium blood levels. Testosterone does the same thing for men regarding calcium absorption, but unlike women, men never reach a particular age when their testes stop producing testosterone. If they did, they would be just as prone to osteoporosis as women.

There is a long list of other factors that affect bone loss. One of the most obvious contributing factors is calcium in our diet. Calcium is regularly lost to urine, feces, and dead skin. We need to continuously account for this loss in our diet. In fact, the less calcium we ingest, the more we force our body into taking it out of our bones. Exercise also greatly affects bone density; the more we exercise, the stronger we make our bones. In fact, the bone mass we have in our late twenties and early thirties will affect our bone mass at menopause.

Finally, there are several physical conditions and external factors that help to weaken our bones, contributing to bone loss later in life. These include:

- Heavy caffeine and alcohol intake. Because caffeine and alcohol are diuretics, they cause you to lose more calcium in your urine. Heavy drinkers tend to suffer from more hip fractures. Since alcohol can damage the liver, which could impair its ability to metabolize vitamin D, it can aggravate bone loss.
- Smoking. Research shows that smokers tend to go into earlier menopause, while older smokers have 20 to 30 percent less bone mass than nonsmokers. Several studies have shown that women who smoke have a greater risk of fractures than women who do not.
- Women in surgical menopause who are not on HRT or ERT—losing estrogen earlier than you would have naturally increases your bone loss.
- Diseases of the small intestine, liver, and pancreas—which prevent the body from absorbing adequate amounts of calcium from the intestine.
- Untreated hyperthyroidism or thyrotoxicosis.
- Lymphoma, leukemia, and multiple myeloma.
- Chronic diarrhea from ulcerative colitis or Crohn's disease— this causes calcium loss through feces.
- Surgical removal of part of the stomach or small intestine— this affects absorption.
- Hypercalciuria, a condition where one loses too much calcium in the urine.

- Early menopause (before age forty-five)—the earlier you stop producing estrogen, the more likely you are to lose calcium.
- Lighter complexions. Women with darker pigments have roughly 10 percent more bone mass than fairer women because they produce more calcitonin, the hormone that strengthens bones.
- Low weight. Women with less body fat store less estrogen, which makes the bones less dense to begin with and more vulnerable to calcium loss.
- Women with eating disorders (yo-yo dieting, starvation diets, binge/purge eaters). When there isn't enough calcium in the bloodstream through our diet, the body will go to the bones to get what it needs. These women also have the risk associated with lower weight.
- A family history of osteoporosis. Studies show that women born to mothers with spinal fractures have lower bone mineral density in the spine, neck, and midshaft.
- High-protein diet. This contributes to a loss of calcium in urine.
- Women who have never been pregnant. They haven't experienced the same bursts of estrogen in their bodies as women who have been pregnant.
- Lactose intolerance. Since so much calcium is in dairy foods, this allergy is a significant risk factor.
- History of teenage pregnancy. When a woman is pregnant in her teens, her bones are not yet fully developed and she can lose as much as 10 percent of her bone mass unless she has an adequate calcium intake of roughly 2,000 milligrams per day during the pregnancy and 2,200 while breast-feeding.
- Scoliosis.

Fractures

One in four women over fifty has osteoporosis, and as the 1960s generation begins turning fifty in record numbers, we'll be facing a "fractured generation" of sorts—the most debilitating of which are hip fractures. Your risk of a hip fracture is equal to your combined risk of breast, uterine, and ovarian cancer.

In general, all bones are vulnerable to fractures, including the ribs, ankles, and pelvis. Osteoporosis-related fractures are categorized as wrist fractures, vertebral fractures, and the most serious of all, hip fractures (fractures of the proximal femur).

Wrist Fractures

Wrist fractures start to occur in women fifty and over, and the incidence rises until age sixty-five, and then flattens out. You break your wrist usually by trying to break a fall (especially if you live in an icy area). These tend to heal fairly easily and don't lead to serious disability in the same way as hip fractures. But your wrist will still be stiff or sore, and if you use a computer or work with your hands, it will obviously cause discomfort and lost time.

Vertebral Fractures

Vertebral fractures are common within the first twenty postmenopausal years. Meaning, if your last period was at fifty-three, you can be vulnerable to these fractures until well into your seventies. This is when you may fall on the ice and fracture your tailbone. Women with bone loss in the teeth, or who have already suffered from fractures of the wrist, which contains trabecular bone, are most at risk for vertebral fractures.

Hip Fractures

North American women have the highest rates of hip fractures. At fifty-five, you have a 17 percent chance of sustaining a hip fracture, which compares to only 6 percent in men of the same age. And women who have had one hip fracture are four times more likely to have a second one than women without a history of fractures. Why are hip fractures so serious? Currently, about 20 to 25 percent of people with hip fractures die from complications, such as pneumonia. The problem begins with being bedridden. You're lying in bed, in pain, on a lot of pain medications. You just get sicker and sicker until one thing leads to another—actually the fate of many long-term, chronic illness sufferers. Fifteen to twenty percent of those who suffer hip fractures are still in long-term care institutions a year after the injury.

Most hip fractures occur in Caucasian or Asian women who are in their seventies and eighties. White women sixty-five or older have twice the incidence of fractures as African-American women. But by "boning up" on calcium now (see the "Preventing Bone Loss" section), you can help to prevent this very debilitating fate. Researchers aren't sure whether the high rate of hip fractures in the seventy- to eighty-year-olds is due to poor nutrition in younger years. The difference between you and your mother is huge from a nutritional standpoint. Mom grew up during the Depression; you grew up during abundant times in the 1950s. That said, your mother probably wasn't much of a dieter. Anyone coming of age in the sixties has been exposed to the Twiggy-like thinness that has remained in vogue (and in *Vogue*) ever since. And, your mother may not have smoked and may not—ulti-

Eight Ways to Avoid a Fall

If you have suffered some bone loss, here are eight tips to fall-proof your home:

1. Don't leave loose wires, cords, or slippery throw rugs lying around.
2. Make sure you have a nonslip mat in the shower or bathtub.
3. Install night-lights to avoid tripping in the middle of the night.
4. Clean up spills on the floors to avoid slipping.
5. Install treads, rails, or carpeting on wooden stairs.
6. Start wearing comfortable, sturdy shoes with rubber soles.
7. Avoid activity when taking medications that can make you drowsy.
8. Cut down on alcohol: you can become klutzy and fall more easily when you're under the influence of alcohol.

mately—have been as sedentary as you may be. So the fracture statistics may "stick" for other reasons.

Risky Movements

If you have more severe bone loss, everyday movements can cause fractures. Watch out for the following:

- Lifting heavy objects (such as groceries) or excessive bending.
- Forceful sneezing or coughing.
- Reaching above your shoulders (as in reaching for something in closets or cupboards).
- A sudden twist or turn, which you may do when driving.
- Getting in and out of beds or chairs; stiffness can be quite severe if you have osteoporosis; sitting or lying down in one position for too long can make the normal movements of getting up hazardous. Go slow. To lessen stiffness, use a pillow for back support and avoid cold drafts.

Preventing Bone Loss

There are a few routes you can take to prevent bone loss. The ever-popular "diet and lifestyle changes" is the most natural route, and a route many women feel most comfortable with. There are also bone-building drugs (discussed further on in this chapter). According to the National Institutes of Health Consensus Panel on Osteoporosis, pre-menopausal women require roughly 1,000 milligrams of calcium a day; perimenopausal or postmenopausal women already on HRT or ERT, 1,000 milligrams; and peri- and postmenopausal women not taking estrogen, roughly 1,500 milligrams per day. For women who have already been diagnosed with osteoporosis, the Panel recommends 2,500 milligrams of calcium a day. Foods that are rich in calcium include all dairy products (an eight-ounce glass of milk contains 300 milligrams calcium), fish, shellfish, oysters, shrimp, sardines, salmon, soybeans, tofu, broccoli, dark green vegetables (except spinach, which contains oxalic acid, preventing calcium absorption). It's crucial to determine how much calcium you're getting in your diet *before* you start any calcium supplements; too much calcium can cause kidney stones in people who are at risk for them. In addition, not all supplements have been tested for absorbency. It's crucial to remember that a calcium supplement is a supplement and should not replace a high-calcium diet. So the dosage of your supplement would only need to be roughly 400 to 600 milligrams per day, while your diet should account for the remainder of your 1,000 to 1,500 milligrams' daily intake of calcium. Calcium supplements can also affect the absorption of thyroid hormone, so you should discuss with your doctor whether you need to adjust your thyroid hormone dosage accordingly or time your calcium and thyroid hormone at different intervals to maximize the absorbency.

The most accurate way to measure your risk of osteoporosis is through bone densitometry (or DEXA), which measures bone mass and provides you with a fracture risk estimate. This test involves low-dose x-rays and takes about thirty minutes.

Selective Estrogen Receptor Modulators (SERMs)

A new class of drugs originally designed to help treat estrogen-dependent breast cancers, selective estrogen receptor modulators were instead shown to help prevent bone loss—particularly around the spine and hips, and even increase bone mass. The first drug from this family, approved for use in 1998, is raloxifene (Evista). Women who took raloxifene for three years reduced their risk of fractures by about 50 percent. Even better, raloxifene may help protect you from heart disease. Raloxifene also helps lower LDL ("bad") cholesterol. Some studies also suggest that raloxifene may also reduce the incidence of breast cancer in some women. Raloxifene and HRT are equally effective in protecting your bones. And of course, you can continue to take calcium and/or vitamin D with raloxifene.

The bad news is that raloxifene has some estrogenlike side effects, including hot flashes and the risk of blood clots. However, it doesn't cause breast tenderness or bloating. And unlike HRT, raloxifene does not help with the signs of menopause, and may even aggravate them. You cannot take raloxifene unless you are postmenopausal, meaning that you have been free from periods for at least one year. The drug has not been tested in women still having periods. If you are taking any type of blood thinner, such as warfarin, you may also not be able to take this drug, and should discuss it with your doctor.

Ideal raloxifene users are postmenopausal women at risk for osteoporosis and heart disease who are not taking HRT, or postmenopausal women at risk for osteoporosis and at high-risk for breast cancer. Women who should not take raloxifene include:

- Premenopausal women
- Pregnant women or women who are breast-feeding
- Women with a history of blood clots or leg cramps (signs of possible blood clots)
- Women on any form of estrogen or progestin therapy that comes as a pill, patch, or injection
- Women taking cholestyramine or colestipol
- Women with liver problems

SERMs have been studied on women taking thyroid hormone and have weaker effects on thyroid function, meaning that many women on SERMS will not need to adjust their thyroid hormone dosages.

Bisphosphonates: Bone-Building Drugs

Osteoblasts are the cells responsible for building bone, while *osteoclasts* are cells that remove old bone so the new bone can be laid. Bisphosphonates stop or slow down the osteoclasts, without interfering with osteoblasts, the bone-forming cells, so you wind up with greater bone density. In the past, these drugs were approved only for treating severe bone diseases, such as Paget's disease. Two bisphosphonates—etidronate (Didrocal/Didronel) and alendronate (Fosamax)—have been approved for use in women who are not on HRT, but who are at risk of osteoporosis. However, bisphosphonates do not relieve any menopausal signs, such as hot flashes, and offer no protection against heart disease.

Bisphosphonates are equally effective in reducing the risk of fractures as HRT and raloxifene (the rate is reduced by about 50 percent in women taking the drug for about three years). If you're taking bisphosphonates, however, you cannot take calcium supplements at the same time, because calcium prevents the body from absorbing the bisphosphonate.

If you're taking alendronate, you'll need to wait thirty minutes after taking it before you have food or take a calcium supplement. If you're taking etidronate, you'll need to take the drug in a cycle, which your doctor will discuss with you, so you can take calcium supplements. In general, alendronate is a more potent, more effective bisphosphonate.

The side effects of etidronate and alendronate may include nausea, abdominal pain, or loose bowel movements. In rare instances, some people develop skin rashes or esophageal ulcers.

Parathyroid Hormone (PTH)

There is also a new drug that can build bone density back to its original peak and sometimes can even surpass it in the form of recombinant parathyroid hormone; the drug is simply known as PTH, or parathyroid hormone, and the FDA approved one form of PTH, PTH-(1-34), known as Forteo, in 2003. There may be newer versions or brands of PTH, which your doctor can advise you about.

Thyroid Disease and Osteoporosis

One of the most common questions that women taking thyroid hormone ask is, What is the link between thyroid disease and osteoporosis? Contrary to what most women think, the link has nothing to do with calcitonin, which the thyroid also produces (discussed in Chapter 1).

Again, thyroid hormone is something our body uses literally from head to toe. In general, anyone with too much thyroid hormone in her system is vulnerable to bone loss. That is because thyroid hormone will speed up or slow down bone cells just as it will speed or slow other processes in our bodies, such as our metabolism. When you are hyperthyroid or thyrotoxic, osteoclasts (the cells that remove old bone) get overstimulated; in short, they go nuts. They begin to remove bone faster than it can be replaced by the osteoblasts, which are not affected by the excess thyroid hormone. The result? You wind up with too much bone removed and subsequent bone loss.

Once your thyroid hormone levels are restored to normal, the risk is gone. But, as discussed in Chapter 11, finding the right dosage can be tricky. Women who have had a thyroidectomy to treat thyroid cancer or for other reasons need to be on a slightly higher dosage of thyroid hormone to suppress all thyroid-stimulating hormone (TSH) activity. So they may live in a state of mild thyrotoxicosis. Essentially, postmenopausal women on thyroid hormone should have their levels checked every year so that they can adjust their dosages accordingly.

To prevent osteoporosis, consider some of the prevention strategies discussed earlier. If you are interested in going on HRT to prevent osteoporosis, discuss your risks with your doctor and weigh them against other prevention strategies. If you are not considered at risk for heart disease or breast cancer, studies do confirm that HRT does halt bone loss, and it is not clear yet whether some women may stand to benefit more from HRT than a bone-building drug if their risk of fracture is significant. Remember, too: calcium *can* be eaten and exercise will build bone mass. (See Chapter 8 for more information on diet.)

Staying Alert About Heart Disease

If you are past menopause, you must educate yourselves about the signs and symptoms of heart disease, since you are at higher risk. Other risk factors, such as smoking, obesity, high blood pressure, and high cholesterol, can be reduced with lifestyle changes. For example, women who are physically active have a 60 to 75 percent lower risk of heart disease than inactive women.

Heart disease is currently the number one cause of death in postmenopausal women; more women die of heart disease than lung cancer or breast cancer. Half of all North Americans who die from heart attacks each year are women.

One of the reasons for such high death rates from heart attacks among women is medical ignorance: most studies examining heart disease have excluded women, which led to a myth that more men than women die of heart disease. The truth is, more men die of heart attacks before age fifty, while more women die of heart attacks *after* age fifty. It remains unclear whether estrogen loss increases the risk, or whether the risk is more broadly linked to aging. We do know that women are under unique stresses due to their social position (see Chapter 3). Another problem is that women have different symptoms than men when it comes to heart disease, and so the "typical" warning signs we know about in men—angina, or chest pains—are often never present in women. In fact, chest pains in women are almost never related to heart disease. For women, the symptoms of heart disease, and even an actual heart attack, can be much more vague and seemingly unrelated to heart problems. Signs of heart disease in women include surprising symptoms, some of which may be masked by thyroid problems. A woman experiencing some of these symptoms may be worried she is having a heart attack, when in fact it is purely thyroid related. So, please review the following list of signs of heart disease in women carefully.

- Shortness of breath and/or fatigue
- Jaw pain (often masked by arthritis and joint pain)
- Pain in the back of the neck (often masked by arthritis or joint pain)
- Pain down the right or left arm
- Back pain (often masked by arthritis and joint pain)
- Sweating—have your thyroid checked; this is a classic sign of an overactive thyroid gland; also test your blood sugar—it may be low
- Fainting
- Palpitations—again, have your thyroid checked; this is also a classic symptom of an overactive thyroid
- Bloating (after menopause, would you believe this is a sign of coronary artery blockage?)
- Heartburn, belching, or other gastrointestinal pain (this is often a sign of an actual heart attack in women)
- Chest "heaviness" between the breasts (this is how women experience chest pain; some describe it as a "sinking feeling" or burning sensation). Also described as an "aching, throbbing, or squeezing sensation"; "hot poker jab between the breasts"; or feeling like your heart jumps into your throat.
- Sudden swings in blood sugar
- Vomiting
- Confusion

Clearly, there are many other causes for the symptoms on this list. But it is important that your doctor includes heart disease as a possible cause, rather than dismissing it because your symptoms are not "male" (which your doctor may refer to as "typical").

Diagnostic tests that can confirm heart disease in women include a physical exam (doctor examining you with a stethoscope); an electrocardiogram; an exercise stress test; an echocardiogram; and a myriad of imaging tests that may use radioactive substances to take pictures of the heart.

If you are diagnosed with heart disease, the "cure" is prevention through diet (see Chapter 8), exercise, and medications that may lower blood pressure or cholesterol. Of course, untreated hypothyroidism, hyperthyroidism, or thyrotoxicosis will aggravate any preexisting risk for heart disease as well.

7

Women and Thyroid Eye Disease

THIS CHAPTER IS devoted to a frustrating symptom associated with thyroid disorders: thyroid eye disease (TED), which can be disfiguring and demoralizing for women in particular. The typical scenario is to notice eye problems or changes with your eyes, only to realize there is little or no information available about what's going on, what it has to do with your thyroid, what you can do to relieve your symptoms, and how you can treat the condition. And as women, we are naturally concerned with how TED affects our appearance and what we can do to downplay those effects. Unfortunately, even feminists are not immune to societal expectations about body image and appearance. In this chapter, symptoms and treatment for TED are covered thoroughly, as well as self-help tips for relieving symptoms. This chapter also explores the more general problem of dry eye syndrome, which affects roughly eleven million North Americans.

What Is Thyroid Eye Disease?

As if hyperthyroidism was not miserable enough, a sister disease tends to strike people with Graves'-related hyperthyroidism and sometimes even those suffering from Hashimoto's disease. This sister disease is known as *thyroid eye disease (TED)*. In clinical circles, TED is known by several different names: *Graves' ophthalmopathy*, *thyroid-associated ophthalmopathy*, and, infrequently, *dysthyroid orbito-pathy*. (The prefix *ophthalmo* means "eyes," while *pathy* means "disease.") It is this disease that leads to the expression *thyroid eyes*—bulging, watery eyes—a condition known as *exophthalmos* (pronounced "exothalmus").

A common symptom of excessive thyroid hormone is lid retraction. Here, your upper eyelids can retract slightly and expose more of the whites of your eyes. The lid retraction creates a rather dramatic "staring" look, an exaggerated expression. Usually the eyes improve when the hyperthyroidism is treated. But this is not always the case, as many people also have bulging of their eyeballs from underlying TED, which may maintain a similar appearance.

When TED is associated with the hyperthyroidism of Graves' disease, the eye problems can be far more severe. At least 50 percent of all Graves' disease patients suffer from obvious TED. At one time, only

TED Alert

When you notice one or more of these eight signs of TED, request a thyroid function test. These symptoms usually appear at least a year before hyperthyroid or hypothyroid symptoms.

1. Gritty, itching, and watery eyes
2. Aching discomfort behind the eyes, especially when you look up or to the side
3. Sensitivity to light or sun
4. Congestion in the eyelids (this may be mistaken for an infection)
5. Dry eyes
6. Lid lag (where the upper lids are slow to follow when you look down)
7. Bulging eyes or a staring look (the first is caused by inflammation, the second by lid retraction)
8. Double vision, particularly when looking to the side

Figure 7.1 A typical Graves' disease patient with a goiter and thyroid eye disease (TED).

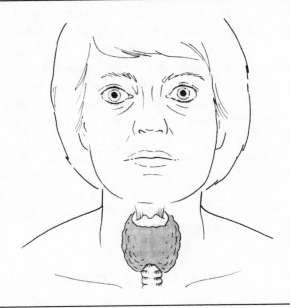

those with noticeable changes to the eyes were considered to have TED, but more sophisticated methods of diagnosis reveal that eye changes are present in almost all Graves' disease patients, even though symptoms may not be noticeable. (See Figure 7.1.)

The most common eye changes are bulginess and double vision. Generally, the changes to the eyes reach a "burnout" period within a two-year time frame and then stop. There are severe cases which can progress to blindness, even with proper intervention, but this is rare. Sometimes the eyes get better by themselves, but often, after the burnout period, the eyes remain changed but do not get any worse. The severity of the eye changes can be measured by an opthalmologist (an eye disease specialist) with an instrument called an *exophthalmometer*. This instrument measures the degree to which the eyes protrude out from the skull.

The Stages of TED

In 80 percent of cases of Graves'-associated eye disease, symptoms of TED appear about a year or more before the symptoms of Graves' disease. This, of course, can be very frustrating, and may throw your doctor off the scent of thyroid disease altogether. (See the sidebar "TED Alert" for the early symptoms of TED and request a thyroid function test if you suffer from symptoms.) When symptoms first appear, TED is said to be in its active, or initial, phase. This can last anywhere from eighteen to twenty-four months. During the active phase, you will experience the most dramatic eye changes, and it may not be necessary to treat the condition beyond symptom relief until the eyes reach their burnout phase. This means the eye problem will reach a maximum change point, where they will probably remain changed but not worsen. On the other hand, a few people have a rapid worsening which requires steroid treatments or surgery or both.

What Causes TED?

TED continues to fascinate thyroid specialists and researchers. Right now, it is believed that TED is caused by the autoimmune antibodies that develop in Graves' disease. For some reason, the same proteins in both your thyroid cells and your eye muscle cells react to the antithyroid antibodies that occur with Graves' disease. This is known as cross-reactivity. Since the treatment for the hyperthyroidism of Graves' disease involves reducing the ability of the thyyroid gland to make thyroid hormone, but doesn't alter the production of antibodies, treatment of the thyroid does not usually help the eyes. This continues to frustrate TED sufferers.

The fact that TED can occur in the absence of hyperthyroidism is what makes this a bit confusing. Probably some antibodies stick to eye muscles better than they stick to the thyroid gland. Environment and lifestyle seem to affect TED, however. Smokers are far more likely to suffer from severe TED than nonsmokers, while stress seems to aggravate the condition, too.

What Causes the Bulging?

Our eyeballs are encased in pear-shaped sockets known as *orbits*. The orbits of the eye are lined with pads of protective fat, connective tissue, blood vessels, muscles, nerves, and the lacrimal glands that are responsible for making tears. When the muscles that move the eyes enlarge and the fatty connective tissue within the orbits becomes inflamed, the eyeballs bulge forward, causing the classic bulging eyes for which TED is infamous.

Who Gets TED?

You are more likely to suffer from TED if you are:

- Diagnosed with Graves' disease (see Chapter 9)
- Middle-aged
- Under stress or work in a stressful environment (see Chapter 3)
- A smoker (see "Smoking and TED" later in this chapter)

The Symptoms of TED

Typical TED symptoms are caused by inflammation of the eye tissues: the eyes become painful, red, and watery with a gritty feeling. Sensitivity to light, wind, or sun are also common. The grittiness and light sensitivity worsen with lid retraction: when your eyes are less protected by the eyelids from dust, wind, and infection, you really feel it.

Other symptoms include discomfort when looking up or to the side. And while some Graves' disease patients suffer from excessive watering of the eyes, many will also suffer from excessive dryness. In rare and extreme cases, vision deteriorates as a result of too much pressure being placed on the optic nerve.

The covering of the eye is also inflamed and swollen. The lids and tissues around the eyes are swollen with fluid, and the eyeballs tend to bulge out of their sockets. Because of eye muscle damage or thickening, the eyes cannot move normally, resulting in blurred or double vision.

During what's called the *hot phase*, the initial active phase of TED, inflammation and swelling around and behind the eye are common. This phase lasts about six months, followed by the *cold phase*, where the inflammation subsides and you then notice more of the vision changes.

In severe cases, swelling may be so bad that you will find it difficult to move your eyes, and you may even develop ulcers on the cornea.
In most cases, both eyes are affected, but one may be worse than the
other. You may also experience a phenomenon called *lid lag*, when
your upper lids are slow to move when you're looking down.

Lid lag results from the effects of too much thyroid hormone and
will go away if thyroid hormone levels are lowered or you are treated
with a beta-blocker medication.

What You See in the Mirror

Not all of the symptoms of TED are visible in the mirror, but some of
them are. Your eyes may look puffy, have bags under them, and look
bloodshot at the corners. People may wonder why you seem to look
"stunned" or amazed all the time. This will be due to your lids being
retracted, thus giving you a more dramatic appearance. You may also
be able to observe that the whites of your eyes are visible between the
iris and lower lid and/or above the iris and upper lid.

Getting a Diagnosis

TED is frequently misdiagnosed as an allergy or pinkeye (also called
conjunctivitis). One easy way to confirm TED is to request that your
thyroid be checked and also to request a thyroid antibody test. If you
have noticed vision problems, you should also request screening for
type 2 diabetes. Diabetes-related eye disease is also a common problem for women over age forty-five, in particular. Imaging tests such as
CT (computerized tomography), ultrasound, or MRI (magnetic reso-
nance imaging) may be used to view the orbit or eye tissues.

Interestingly, some people will notice that TED symptoms worsen
when their thyroid hormone levels are lower than normal. Because
hypothyroidism causes bloating and fluid retention, this can exacerbate inflammation of the eyes, triggering TED symptoms of dryness
and grit. Many thyroid patients have ongoing disputes with their physicians over whether their TED flare-up is related to their thyroid condition. It may be. And since much is unknown about the relationship
between TED and thyroid hormone levels, you do not have to accept

your doctor's word upon being informed that you are imagining the connection.

Smoking and TED

The link between smoking and TED is so strong that thyroid specialists believe smokers with Graves' disease can probably count on developing TED. TED is much less common in nonsmokers. No one knows exactly why smokers are more vulnerable to TED. What we do know is that smokers are more vulnerable to many diseases and health problems than nonsmokers. Clearly, TED is one of them. However, it is certainly not surprising that an environment where you're surrounded by cigarette smoke (your own or others') would aggravate—or even help trigger—TED. In people with type 2 diabetes, diabetes-related eye disease is also more common and more severe among smokers because smoking restricts the small blood vessels.

In fact, one of the reasons that nonsmokers are so uncomfortable in smoke-filled rooms is because the smoke irritates their eyes, causing them to be watery, itchy, and red! Quitting smoking may help to ease some of the symptoms of TED.

Women and Cigarettes

Many women turn to cigarettes to deal with stress. Smoking also satisfies "mouth hunger"—the need to have something in your mouth, which often occurs during stressful periods. Women who are afraid that their stress will drive them to overeat often turn to cigarettes instead. Stress (see Chapter 3) can also turn a social smoker into a much heavier smoker, or even a chain smoker. It becomes a bit of a no-win cycle when women try to cut down, because the withdrawal symptoms can drive women to overeat as well, which only makes them want to smoke more.

The idea of controlling weight with cigarettes emerged in the 1920s when a tobacco company wife was told by her doctor to smoke to "relax"; not only did smoking relax her, but it actually helped to curb her appetite. Thus the luring of women to cigarettes as a food replacement began. In fact, medical journals and the medical profession at that time actually recommended smoking to women as a way to calm them. Today, almost every woman who begins smoking does so for weight control.

You've no doubt been bombarded with information about the health consequences of smoking. But you probably don't realize this alarming, yet underreported fact: *the number one cause of disease in women is cigarettes and smoking.* Smoking-related diseases affect women more than any other health or social problem in this order: smoking-related lung cancer, smoking-related heart disease, smoking-related stroke, and smoking-related chronic lung diseases. And did you know that early menopause and osteoporosis are more common among smokers?

All studies show that women who smoke "get sicker quicker." They develop, and die from, smoking-related diseases at much younger ages than men. If you compare a man and a woman with similar smoking habits, the woman is twice as likely to die. Yet women are smoking in increasing numbers. More shocking, 20 to 25 percent of pregnant women continue to smoke during their pregnancies.

A single cigarette affects your body within seconds, increasing heart rate, blood pressure, and the demand for oxygen. The greater the demand for oxygen (because of constricted blood vessels and carbon monoxide, a by-product of cigarettes) the greater the risk of heart disease. Lesser-known long-term effects of smoking include a lowering of HDL, or "good" cholesterol, and damage to the lining of blood vessel walls, which paves the way for a host of stress-related illnesses. In addition to reducing TED symptoms, take a look at some of the things you'll gain by quitting smoking:

- Decreased risk of heart disease
- Decreased risk of cancer (that includes cancer of the lungs, esophagus, mouth, throat, pancreas, kidney, bladder, and cervix)
- Lower heart rate and blood pressure
- Decreased risk of lung disease (bronchitis, emphysema)
- Relaxation of blood vessels
- Improved sense of smell and taste
- Better teeth
- Fewer wrinkles

How Women Become Addicted

Without the awareness and decision-making powers of an informed adult, once a young girl buys into the marketing messages delivered by tobacco companies (smoking is glamorous, keeps you thin, and so on) and begins smoking, she's hooked. Here's why:

Nicotine produces a "controlled" response, enabling the smoker to either stimulate herself or calm herself. Small, shallow puffs on a cigarette enable a smoker to keep awake, alert, or active when she is fatigued, facilitating the "double duties" of women's social roles (see Chapter 3).

Deep drags from a cigarette give the smoker larger doses of nicotine, facilitating the release of endorphins, "feel good" chemicals the body makes. Endorphins are naturally released when we laugh, exercise, and do anything pleasurable, such as eat something tasty. Since the endorphins are coming from the body naturally, smokers find that they do, in fact, perform better, and are less stressed when they smoke more. On drugs such as amphetamines, heroin, or cocaine, the "high" is produced by the drug, not the body, so it feels completely different. Nicotine does not feel like a drug in the same way.

What is addictive is the control the cigarette gives a woman: shallow puffs act like a stimulant; deep drags lead to relaxation. All studies on women smokers reveal that the more stress a woman is under, the more she will smoke. Smoking can allow a woman to tolerate much more stress, in fact, which takes a real physical toll on the body. We already know stress is hard on the body; smoking is also hard on the body, producing a "double whammy" physically.

Within seven to ten seconds of inhaling a cigarette, a concentrated dose of nicotine goes directly to the brain, producing a "rush," which in turn stimulates the release of a number of neurotransmitters, including dopamine and noradrenaline, a stress hormone.

When a woman tries to quit smoking, dopamine and noradrenaline levels drop, which produces a strong urge to smoke in addition to withdrawal symptoms such as anxiety, depression, irritability, insomnia, difficulty concentrating, increased appetite, gastrointestinal discomfort, headaches, and lightheadedness. These withdrawal symptoms can actually worsen over a week, rather than lessen. The cravings can last for months. Most women begin to smoke again to relieve the suffering—especially during high periods of stress.

What About "Light" Cigarettes?

In the 1960s, when health warnings about smoking were first issued, the tobacco industry introduced "light" or "low tar" cigarettes, which women bought in record numbers.

Women who wanted to quit smoking, or wanted to smoke without the health risks, bought the lie that a "lighter" cigarette is less harmful, and therefore "healthier." *This is completely false.* All cigarettes are made to deliver enough nicotine to keep you addicted. A light cigarette may be altered in that it smells different or appears less dense, but all research on light cigarettes since the 1980s has found that when smokers switch to a light cigarette, they actually get the same dose of nicotine by taking deeper drags on the cigarette and holding the smoke in their lungs longer. In short, women who smoke light cigarettes wind up smoking *more* rather than less. More recent research has linked some forms of cancer to women who smoke light cigarettes.

Quitting Smoking

Therapists who specialize in smoking cessation programs for women report that women refer to cigarettes as their "best friend" and will mourn the loss of the cigarettes when they try to quit. The cigarette is a reward for women. The smoking break is seen as "earned" by hard work or stress. Replacing the reward with something else that fills the woman's psychological and spiritual needs is imperative before women can successfully quit. When women seek out specific smoking cessation counseling while trying to quit, the success rate triples. (There are currently legal initiatives in motion to have tobacco companies pay for smoking cessation programs and counseling!)

The following smoking cessation programs are available:

- *Behavioral counseling.* Behavioral counseling, either group or individual, can raise the rate of abstinence to 20 to 25 percent. This approach to smoking cessation aims to change the mental processes of smokers, reinforce the benefits of not smoking, and teach skills to help the smoker avoid the urge to smoke.
- *Nicotine gum.* Nicotine gum (Nicorette) is now available over the counter. It helps you quit smoking by reducing nicotine cravings

and withdrawal symptoms. Nicotine gum helps you wean yourself from nicotine by allowing you to gradually decrease the dosage until you stop using it altogether, a process that usually takes about twelve weeks. The only disadvantage with this method is that it caters to the oral and addictive aspects of smoking (rewarding the "urge" to smoke with a dose of nicotine).

- *Nicotine patch.* Transdermal nicotine, or "the patch" (Habitrol, NicoDerm, Nicotrol), doubles abstinence rates in former smokers. Most brands are now available over the counter. Each morning, a new patch is applied to a different area of dry, clean, hairless skin and left on for the day. Some patches are designed to be worn a full twenty-four hours. However, the constant supply of nicotine to the bloodstream sometimes causes very vivid or disturbing dreams. You can also expect to feel a mild itching, burning, or tingling at the site of the patch when it is first applied. The nicotine patch works best when it is worn for at least seven to twelve weeks, with a gradual decrease in strength (the amount of nicotine administered). Many smokers find it effective because it allows them to tackle the psychological addiction to smoking before they are forced to deal with physical symptoms of withdrawal.

- *Nicotine inhaler.* The nicotine inhaler (Nicotrol Inhaler) delivers nicotine via inhalation from a plastic tube. Its success rate is about 28 percent, similar to that of nicotine gum. It's available by prescription only in the United States (and has yet to make its debut in Canada). Like nicotine gum, the inhaler mimics smoking behavior by responding to each craving or "urge" to smoke, a feature that has both advantages and disadvantages to the smoker who wants to get over the physical symptoms of withdrawal. The nicotine inhaler should be used for a period of twelve weeks.

- *Nicotine nasal spray.* Like nicotine gum and the nicotine patch, the nasal spray reduces craving and withdrawal symptoms, allowing smokers to cut back gradually on nicotine. One squirt delivers about 1 milligram of nicotine. In three clinical trials involving 730 patients, 31 to 35 percent were not smoking at six months. This compares to an average of 12 to 15 percent of smokers who were able to quit unaided. The nasal spray has a couple of advantages over the gum and the patch: nicotine is rapidly absorbed across the nasal membranes, providing a kick that is more like the real thing, and the prompt onset of action, plus a flexible dosing schedule, benefits heavier smokers. A disadvantage is that, because the nicotine reaches your bloodstream so quickly, nasal sprays do have a greater potential for addiction than the slower-acting gum and patch. (Nasal sprays are not yet available for use in Canada.)

• *Alternative therapies.* Hypnosis, meditation and acupuncture, and herbal smoking cessation aids have helped some smokers quit. In the case of hypnosis and meditation, sessions may be private or part of a group smoking-cessation program.

Smoking-Cessation Drugs

The drug bupropion (Zyban) is an option for people who have been unsuccessful using nicotine replacement. Formerly prescribed as an antidepressant, bupropion was discovered as a smoking-cessation drug by accident: researchers knew that quitting smokers were often depressed, so they began experimenting with the drug as a means to fight depression, not addiction. Bupropion reduces the withdrawal symptoms associated with smoking cessation and can be used in conjunction with nicotine replacement therapy. Researchers suspect that bupropion works directly in the brain to disrupt the addictive power of nicotine by affecting the same chemical neurotransmitters (messengers) in the brain, such as dopamine, that nicotine does.

The pleasurable aspect of addictive drugs like nicotine and cocaine is triggered by the release of dopamine. Smoking floods the brain with dopamine. The *New England Journal of Medicine* published the results of a study of more than six hundred smokers taking bupropion. At the end of treatment, 44 percent of those who took the highest dose of the drug (300 milligrams) were not smoking, compared to 19 percent of the group who took a placebo. By the end of one year, 23 percent of the 300-milligram group and 12 percent of the placebo group were still smoke-free. Using Zyban with nicotine replacement therapy seems to improve the quit rate a bit further. Four-week quit rates from the study were 23 percent for placebo; 36 percent for the patch; 49 percent for Zyban; and 58 percent for the combination of Zyban and the patch.

Battling the Bulge: Treating TED

Before specific treatments for TED begin, the thyroid condition is treated first. In some cases, when the hyperthyroidism is treated, the eyes tend to get better—even before burnout occurs. For example, TED in the absence of hyperthyroidism tends to be much easier to treat. In this case, you will probably suffer from irritation and some wateriness. Discomfort, redness, and intolerance of light can also be present. Sometimes, if hyperthyroidism is treated with radioactive iodine, it may seem to worsen TED.

Drug Treatments

Often the first step in treating TED is to use artificial tears during the day and lubricating ointment at bedtime. If TED becomes worse, the next step is to offer a steroid drug, prednisone, which will reduce the swelling and inflammation causing the more severe TED symptoms. Steroids have numerous side effects, however, and you'll need to balance the side effects against TED symptoms. The other problem with steroids is that once you go off of them, TED symptoms can resume, and may even get worse.

Side Effects of Prednisone

When you're on this drug, you'll have a lower resistance to infections and may develop harder-to-treat infections. It is also associated with mood changes and insomnia that can exacerbate symptoms of thyroid disease. There is a long list of other less common side effects associated with this drug, which you'll need to discuss with your doctor prior to consenting to this treatment. If you're pregnant, breast-feeding, or planning to get pregnant, you must not be on this drug, period.

Diuretics

Some doctors will prescribe diuretics that cause you to urinate more frequently, thereby eliminating excess fluid. This can sometimes help to reduce swelling. Unfortunately, women at risk for osteoporosis will want to be careful that they do not eliminate calcium in their urine and will need to increase calcium intake while on diuretics.

Radiation

If you choose not to go on steroids, external beam radiation therapy is another option. This procedure consists of x-ray, CT scans, and a simulation procedure in which careful measurements are taken in order to aim the x-ray beam properly; the x-ray is targeted at the muscles at the back of the eyes behind the lens—which may conceivably reduce the eye inflammation. The measurement is done using three laser light beams. Many of these treatments are successful, and the x-ray treatment is sometimes a way to avoid surgery

Corrective Surgery

A procedure known as *orbital decompression surgery* can remove bone from the eye socket and expand the area alongside the eyeball so that swollen tissue can move into it. It's best to wait until the burnout period before attempting surgery so the eyes do not get any worse.

There are other plastic surgery procedures that can help to reconstruct the eye area and correct the disfigurement. Before you undergo corrective surgery, it's best to consult with a surgeon who specializes in orbital surgery, facial surgery, and neurosurgery (you may need to see three different surgeons). An ear, nose, and throat specialist may also need to be consulted.

Generally, depending on your symptoms, surgery for TED can involve any of the following:

- Adjusting the position of your eyelids
- Correcting swelling around the eye
- Realigning eye muscles
- Orbital decompression

Finding Symptom Relief

To relieve irritation and inflammation, eyedrops or artificial tears are recommended, but it's important to ask your doctor for an appropriate brand. Double vision can be remedied by wearing plastic prism lenses that can be inserted inside your regular glasses, or operations that use similar techniques to those that correct squinting in childhood (strabismus) can be done at a later stage. Injecting botulinum toxin type A (Botox Cosmetic) can also help correct double vision. Botulinum toxin type A is a protein produced by the bacterium *Clostridium botulinum*. Small doses of the sterile, purified toxin are injected into the affected muscles and block the release of the chemical acetylcholine that would otherwise signal the muscle to contract.

The following self-help tips have been compiled from TED sufferers:

- Stop smoking and/or avoid secondhand smoke.
- Use artificial tears to help moisten the eyes.
- Sleep with the head of your bed raised (put some books under the legs) or prop yourself up on pillows to drain away excess fluid and reduce puffiness and swelling around the eyes.
- Cover your eyes when you sleep.
- Wear wraparound dark glasses outdoors during the day.
- Turn ceiling fans off before you go to bed.
- Avoid strong sunlight.
- Do not wear contact lenses.
- Try to help relieve swelling by drinking more fluids.
- Use cooling eye masks and gels.
- Wear a patch over one eye to help with double vision.

See the next section for more useful self-help tips.

Appearance Matters

Women suffering from TED may also suffer from body image problems as a result of the disfiguring symptoms. This is not unlike what cancer patients who lose their hair go through. When a disease has affected your appearance, there may be some benefit from counseling.

Book time with a makeup artist to show you brands of hypoallergenic eye makeup that do not contain perfume. (Perfumes used on other parts of the face or in your hair may also irritate your eyes, so it's best to avoid these.) A good makeup artist will show you techniques to downplay the eyes or to create the impression of less swelling with good brushes and shadows. Until you can acquire hypoallergenic products, you would be well advised to stop wearing eye makeup—mainly because what you are using may be harmful.

A good approach is to accentuate your lips (there are tricks for this, too, which a good makeup artist can show you) and get a good haircut. Highlights or color may also work to downplay the eyes. Having your eyebrows professionally shaped can also do wonders. Wearing fashionable wraparound sunglasses will enable you to attend outdoor events and activities. You can also pick up fashionable eyeglass frames that will downplay the eyes as well. (These can have nonprescription "lenses" if you don't normally need glasses.) Scarves and necklaces will divert attention away from the eyes, too.

Dry Eye Syndrome

Some symptoms of TED are not unique to women suffering from thyroid disease. Dry eyes are so common that a new syndrome has been recognized in general medical practice, known as *dry eye syndrome*. It's estimated that roughly eleven million North Americans suffer from dry eyes, meaning that tear production is inadequate or the tears evaporate so quickly that your eyes are left gritty and irritated with every blink.

What is unique about dry eyes these days is that they are now observed in much younger people. In the past, dry eyes were observed in people over age sixty-five; today they are common in thirty-year-olds.

Common causes of dry eyes (which could aggravate TED) include the following:

- Waking up (tear production decreases when we sleep)
- Wind, sun, and pollution
- Smoke
- Airplanes
- Hotels (with "canned air")
- Overly dry places or air-conditioning
- Chlorine from pools

- Saltwater
- Cycling without goggles
- Contact lenses
- Side effects to medications

Dry eyes can also result from focusing too long on display screens such as television or computer screens, which is one reason why experts think it's becoming increasingly common in young people.

Easy-fix solutions include using humidifiers at night and humidifying the air in winter (when furnaces can dry out the air). If your dryness is related to medication that you are taking, switching to a different brand can sometimes solve the problem, too.

Wetting Your Windows

If the eyes are the "windows to the soul," here are some ways to keep those windows moist:

- When you're involved in an outdoor sport, choose protective eyewear to preserve moisture and shield you from the wind.
- Always point car air vents away from your eyes.
- When you're working on the computer or watching television, don't forget to blink.
- Avoid prolonged use of hair dryers.

The Trouble with Eyedrops

Using the wrong eyedrops can aggravate, rather than relieve, dry eyes because they can contain irritating preservatives. Even antibiotic or antiallergenic drops can cause problems. The best solution (pardon the pun) is to ask your eye doctor to recommend a lubricating eyedrop that is free of such ingredients. Usually the eyedrops will be a methyl cellulose solution.

In severe cases, you can have silicone plugs surgically inserted into the drainage ducts leading out of the eyes, which will help you retain artificial tears or jellies. This will reduce the number of times you need to use eyedrops.

A Woman's Tears

Dry eyes are often a woman's problem since so many autoimmune diseases, which plague women in particular, are associated with dry eyes. Aside from Graves' disease, other autoimmune diseases causing dry eyes include Sjögren's syndrome (this impairs lacrimal gland function and the formation of watery tears; 90 percent of Sjögren's syndrome sufferers are women), rheumatoid arthritis, lupus, and type 1 diabetes.

Hormonal changes during pregnancy and menopause can also cause dry eyes, while asthma, glaucoma, blepharitis (chronic inflammation of the eyelids), cornea surgery, and corrective surgery for nearsightedness are other causes.

Women are also more likely to develop dry eyes because of side effects to medications. These include antidepressants (women tend to suffer from depression more frequently than men—see Chapter 3), decongestants, antihistamines, blood pressure drugs, hormones, oral contraceptives, diuretics, ulcer medications, and tranquilizers.

Aging, traditionally the reason why dry eyes were most often observed in older women, is also a cause. As we age, there is a decrease in tear production in both men and women.

Self-Education About TED

TED is such a complex problem, this chapter offers only a brief overview. I encourage all readers suffering from TED, also known as Graves' ophthalmopathy (GO) to turn to a much more detailed and thorough patient resource on this disease, *Thyroid Eye Disease: Understanding Graves' Ophthalmopathy* by Elaine Moore. This is the only book on this subject for patients as of this writing, and is available online (www.thyroid-eye-disease.com) or by calling toll free (866-752-6820). See Appendix A for more TED-related links.

8

The Weight and Diet Connection

WHEN WOMEN THINK "thyroid problem," they usually think "weight problem." Weight is a complex topic for women that has as much to do with our social conditioning about body size, and what we perceive to be an acceptable weight, as it does with actual calorie intake. At the same time, we are in the midst of an epidemic of obesity that is now as great a threat to public health as smoking. This chapter discusses how your thyroid problem can affect your weight and how it can aggravate a preexisting weight problem, which is usually the more serious consequence of a thyroid condition for most women. This chapter gives you the "skinny" on dieting, and the right diet to follow. For information on the low iodine diet used in preparation for scans that check for the presence of thyroid cancer, see Chapter 11.

Thyroid Disease and Obesity

Obesity refers to a body size that is too fat for good health. Obese people have greater incidences of type 2 diabetes, heart attacks, strokes, peripheral vascular disease (circulation problems that lead to many other health problems), and certain types of cancers. Hypothyroidism can aggravate obesity and complications from obesity. Hyperthyroidism or thyrotoxicosis, however, may assist with weight loss, but could aggravate other conditions that may be linked to obesity, such as heart disease or type 2 diabetes.

When obesity is due to hypothyroidism, most women will find that they return to their normal weight once their hypothyroidism is treated. Much of the weight gain in hypothyroidism is due to bloating. Nevertheless, many women who are overweight may indeed be suffering from untreated hypothyroidism. Therefore, if you are reading this chapter and wondering whether your weight problem is due to a thyroid problem, request a thyroid function test (see Chapter 11).

Feeling tired and low in energy, symptoms of hypothyroidism, may cause you to crave carbohydrates and quick-energy foods, which are higher in fat and calories. When you are hypothyroid, your activity levels will decrease as a result of your fatigue, which can also lead to weight gain. The craving for carbohydrates is caused by a desire for energy. Consuming carbohydrates produces an initial rush of energy, but then it is followed by a crash, which is sometimes known as *post-prandial depression* (or postmeal depression), exacerbating or contributing to hypothyroid-induced depression. Even in women with normal thyroid function, depression can cause cravings for simple carbohydrates such as sugars and sweets. Many women will notice that they are not craving food at all but are still gaining weight. Some of the weight gain is bloating from constipation. Increasing fluid intake and fiber will help the problem. See the section "The Hypothyroid Diet" for more details.

Obviously, cutting down on fat (see the section "Lowering Fat and Healthy Eating") will also help. But the problem for most women who are battling both obesity and hypothyroidism is that the weight problem often predates the thyroid problem, indicating that there are other factors involved in their weight gain. Stack a thyroid problem on top of that, and it may exacerbate all kinds of other behaviors that led to the initial weight gain, as well as aggravate risks associated with obesity in general.

Defining Obesity

At one time, being defined as clinically obese applied to anyone who weighed 20 percent more than the ideal weight for their age and height.

But this is not as accurate an indicator as the Body Mass Index (BMI), which is now the best measurement of obesity. The BMI is calculated by dividing your weight (in kilograms) by your height (in meters) squared. (The formula used is: BMI = kg/m^2 if you're doing this on your calculator.) BMI charts abound on the Internet, the backs of cereal boxes, and in numerous health magazines. Most people can now easily find BMI converters on the Net, where you simply type in your weight in pounds and your height to arrive at your BMI. As of this writing, a good BMI calculator can be found at www.consumer.gov/weightloss/bmi.htm. (There are many, however, when you type in the key word "BMI Chart" on your search engine. A good chart will calculate BMI by gender and sometimes age ranges.)

Currently, a BMI of 18.5 or less indicates that you are underweight. A BMI between 18.5 and 24.9 is normal. The most recent clinical guidelines define people with a BMI between 25 and 29.9 as overweight, and those with a BMI between 30 and 34.9 as obese (mild to moderate). A BMI between 35 and 39.9 would indicate severely obese; people with a BMI of 40 or greater are considered morbidly obese. (Using these BMI guidelines to calculate obesity matches new clinical guidelines for defining obesity as of 1998. Roughly 72 million more North Americans are now considered obese, who were not considered obese prior to 1998. The guidelines for what constitutes type 2 diabetes, similarly, changed in 1998 and again in 2003, which also meant that many more people were told they had diabetes who would not have been diagnosed prior to the guideline changes. This has also helped the diet industry and some food lobbies to sell people on particular types of diets, leading to more confusion than ever.)

Obesity itself is not an eating disorder, but can be the result of compulsive overeating, known as *binge eating disorder*, or *BED*. Roughly 20 to 46 percent of obese people suffer from BED.

Obesity rates in children and teens are calculated through BMIs that are at or above sex- and age-specific weights within the 95th percentiles. This is a more conservative approach to account for growing spurts.

The North American lifestyle is considered by obesity experts to be the single largest contributing factor to obesity. Although social, behavioral, metabolic, cellular, and molecular factors all contribute to obesity, obesity genes were found to be "turned on" only when they were exposed to an environment conducive to weight gain, such as the North American environment.

North Americans have the highest obesity rates in the world. More than half of North American adults and about 25 percent of North American children are now obese. These figures reflect a doubling of adult obesity rates since the 1960s, and a doubling of the childhood obesity rate since the late 1970s—a staggering increase when you think about it in raw numbers. Obese children will most likely grow up to become obese adults, according to the most recent research.

Waist circumference is another factor in calculating obesity—particularly abdominal obesity. Men with a waist circumference of 40 inches or more are at increased risk of obesity-related health problems, while women with a waist circumference of 35 inches or more are at an increased risk of obesity-related health problems.

The Impact of "Low-Fat" Products

Since the late 1970s, North Americans have been deluged with low-fat products. In 1990, the United States government launched Healthy People 2000, a campaign to urge manufacturers to double their output of low-fat products by the year 2000. Since 1990, more than one thousand new fat-free or low-fat products have been introduced into North American supermarkets annually.

Most of these low-fat products, however, actually encourage us to eat more. For example, if a bag of regular chips has nine grams of fat per serving (one serving usually equals five or six chips, or one handful), you will more likely stick to that one handful. However, if you find a low-fat brand of chips that boasts 50 percent less fat per serving, you're more likely to eat the whole bag (feeling good about eating "low-fat" chips), which can easily triple your fat intake. The result is that as a population we weigh more today than in 1980, despite the fact that roughly ten thousand more low-fat foods are available to us now than in 1980.

Low-fat or fat-free foods trick our bodies with ingredients that mimic the functions of fat in foods (discussed more under "Fat Replacers" later in this chapter). There's no question that low-fat foods are designed to give you more freedom of choice with your diet, supposedly allowing you to cut your fat without compromising your taste buds. Researchers at the University of Toronto suggest that these products essentially allow us to increase our calories even though we are reducing our overall fat intake. For example, in one study, women who consumed a low-fat breakfast food ate more during the day than women who consumed a higher-fat food at breakfast.

Studies and surveys show that we are actually eating about 500 calories more each day than we did in the 1970s; we're up from 3,300 to 3,800 calories per day per person. The addition of frequent snacking due to the development and marketing of more innovative and tempting snack foods by the food industry has been cited as one of the most apparent changes in our eating patterns over the last thirty years. In fact, the practice of snacking doubled from the mid-1980s to the mid-1990s. The fast-food invasion, of course, has contributed to the increase as well.

Biological Causes of Obesity

The physiological cause of obesity is eating more calories than you burn. People gain weight for two reasons: they may eat excessively (often excessive amounts of nutritious foods), which results in daily consumption of too many calories; or they may eat moderately, but simply be too inactive for the calories they *do* ingest. Genetic makeup can predispose some body types to obesity earlier in life because of "thrifty genes." But in general, experts in nutrition agree that genetics plays only a small role in the sharp increase in obesity. Since genetic changes take place over centuries, and our obesity rate has at least doubled since the 1960s, it's fairly obvious that lifestyle factors are the chief culprit. Furthermore, as we age, our metabolism slows down, which means that unless we decrease our calories or increase activity levels to compensate, we will probably gain weight. Other hormonal problems can also contribute to obesity, such as hypothyroidism.

Thrifty Genes

Genetics play a role in obesity in aboriginal and other minority groups, due to what some researchers call the "thrifty gene." This is the gene thought to be responsible for the higher rates of obesity and obesity-related conditions in aboriginal and non-European populations. This means that the more recently your culture has lived indigenously or nomadically (that is, living off the land you came from and eating seasonally or indigenously), the more efficient your metabolism is. Unfortunately, it is also more sensitive to nutrient excess. If you're an aboriginal North American, only about one hundred years have passed since your ancestors lived indigenously. This is an exceedingly short amount of time to ask thousands of years of hunter-gatherer genes to adjust to the terrible convenience-food diet that prevails in North America. If you're of African descent, you haven't lived here any longer than about four hundred years; prior to that, your ancestors were living a tribal, nomadic lifestyle. Again, four hundred years is not a long time.

As for Hispanic populations or other immigrant populations, many come from families who have spent generations in poverty. Their metabolisms adjusted to long periods of famine, and are often overloaded by our abundance of high-caloric foods.

Asian populations generally have the lowest rates of obesity, but that is also because they are frequently able to maintain their dietary habits when they emigrate to North America. In fact, European North Americans tend to benefit when they adopt the same diets. Thrifty genes are evident when you look at the obesity patterns in the United States. There, obesity is more prevalent in African-Americans, Latinos, Native Americans, Native Hawaiians, and American Samoans; these groups have higher incidences of diabetes and cardiovascular disease as well. For example, almost 63 percent of Native Hawaiian women are obese, and between 61and 75 percent of Yaqui Indians are overweight. Among Hispanics, Mexicans have the highest rates of obesity (48.2 percent), followed by Puerto Ricans (40.2 percent).

Diets of poverty may also be a factor; these diets typically rely on calories from high-fat, low-nutrient foods instead of fresher foods such as fruits and vegetables. Aboriginal, African, and Hispanic populations tend to have much lower incomes, and are therefore eating lower-quality food, which, when combined with the "thrifty gene," can lead to obesity and obesity-related health problems. When epidemiologists look at these same "thrifty gene" groups in higher income levels, the obesity rates are lower.

Leptin and Other Hormones

The most promising antiobesity treatment once involved the "anti-fat hormone" leptin; its discovery led to a surge of obesity drug research. Leptin, discovered in 1994, seemed promising because it was the first anti-fat hormone that surfaced. The leptin hormone receptor was discovered in 1997. Leptin was discovered when a mutant strain of extremely obese mice (lacking the gene to make leptin) were able to shed their weight when given leptin. On leptin, the mice's appetite decreased, while their metabolic rates increased. Although it led researchers to wonder whether all obese people would lose weight on leptin, this did not occur. It turns out that like the mutant obese mice, there are only a few rare cases of human obesity caused by leptin deficiency. Everyone else becomes obese by eating too much and being too sedentary. Some rare cases of human obesity are caused by defects in leptin production. The leptin discovery led to a successful treatment for rare and terribly sad cases of obesity in leptin-deficient individuals, however, who in the past would not have been able to lose weight.

Most people who are obese actually have higher than normal blood levels of leptin, which is produced by fat cells, but are resistant to its actions. In fact, obesity researchers now believe that leptin has more to do with protecting against weight loss in times of famine, than protecting against weight gain in times of plenty. When fat stores increase, so does leptin; when fat stores shrink, so does leptin. Appetite increases and metabolism decreases when leptin levels shrink, but the opposite does not occur when leptin levels rise: appetite is not suppressed when leptin increases, nor is metabolism increased. Leptin, it seems, is one of those evolutionary hormones designed to keep our species alive, and protect us from starvation. Finding leptin has led obesity researchers into finding out more about how appetite, fat stores, and "famine-protection" mechanisms work in the body.

Drug Treatment for Obesity

Throughout the 1950s, 1960s, and even 1970s, women, in particular, were prescribed thyroid hormone as a weight-loss drug. This practice has long been abandoned by physicians as people became thyrotoxic, but there are currently supplements still being sold with active thyroid hormone that are dangerous. Amphetamines or "speed" were often widely peddled to women by doctors, but these drugs, too, are dangerous, and can put your health at risk.

One of the most controversial antiobesity therapies was the use of fenfluramine and phentermine (fen-phen). Both drugs were approved for use individually more than twenty years ago, but in 1992, doctors began to prescribe them together for long-term management of obesity. In 1996, U.S. doctors wrote a total of 18 million monthly prescriptions for fen-phen, and many of the prescriptions were issued to people who were not obese. This practice is known as "off-label" prescribing. In July 1997, the U.S. Food and Drug Administration and researchers at the Mayo Clinic and the Mayo Foundation made a joint announcement warning doctors that fen-phen can cause heart disease. On September 15, 1997, fenfluramine was taken off the market. More bad news has since surfaced about fen-phen wreaking havoc on serotonin levels. The fen-phen lesson: diet and lifestyle modification are still the best pathways to wellness.

Approved Antiobesity Pills

In 2000, an antiobesity pill that blocks the absorption of almost one-third of the fat people eat was approved. One of the side effects of this new prescription drug, called *orlistat* (Xenical), causes rather embarrassing diarrhea when the fat content in your meal exceeds 20 percent. To avoid the drug's side effects, simply avoid having too much fat! The pill can also decrease absorption of vitamin D and other important nutrients, however.

Orlistat is the first drug to fight obesity through the intestine instead of the brain. Taken with each meal, it binds to certain pancreatic enzymes to block the digestion of 30 percent of the fat you ingest. When they combined it with a sensible diet, people on orlistat lost more weight than those not on orlistat. This drug is not intended for people who need to lose a few pounds; it is designed for medically obese people. The safety of orlistat for people with diabetes is under debate. Although in studies orlistat was found to lower cholesterol, blood pressure, and blood sugar levels (as a result of weight loss), it can lead to pancreatitis and inflammation of the gallbladder.

Another obesity drug, sibutramine, was approved for use in 2001. Sibutramine is meant for people whose body mass index (BMI) registers at 27 or higher. This is generally people who weigh more than 20 percent above their ideal weight. (To calculate your BMI, you can visit www.4meridia.com.)

If you're taking medications for depression, thyroid problems, seizures, glaucoma, osteoporosis, gallbladder disease, liver disease, heart disease or stroke prevention, kidney disease, migraines, or Parkinson's disease, you are also cautioned against taking sibutramine and should discuss with your doctor whether the drug is safe. Also, many nutritional supplements, such as tryptophan, are not recommended with sibutramine, so please disclose to your doctor all nonprescription, over-the-counter medications as well as all herbal and nutritional substances you're taking if you're considering sibutramine.

Lowering Fat and Healthy Eating

Dietary guidelines from nutrition experts, government nutrition advisories and panels, and registered dietitians have not changed in fifty years. A good diet is a balanced diet representing all food groups, based largely on plant-based foods such as fruits, vegetables, legumes, and grains (carbohydrates), with a balance of calories from animal-based foods, such as meats (red meats and poultry), fish, and dairy products (protein and fat). Nutrition research spanning the last fifty years has only confirmed these facts. What has changed in fifty years is the terminology used to define a good diet, and the bombardment of information we receive about which foods affect which physiological processes in the body, such as cholesterol levels, blood fats (triglycerides), blood sugar levels (blood glucose or glycemic load), and insulin. There are also different kinds of fats and carbohydrates, which has made eating seem so technical and scientific, ordinary North Americans feel more like chemists when trying to plan for healthy meals and diets.

Confusing information about "low fat" versus "low carb" has further distorted our perceptions about diet. But no matter how many properties in foods are dissected, what kind of diet program you buy into, healthy eating comes down to a balanced diet—something that, by the way, actually means "balanced way of life"; the root word of *diet*, *diatta*, literally means "way of life."

Understanding Fat

Fat is technically known as *fatty acids*, which are crucial nutrients for our cells. We cannot live without fatty acids. Fat is therefore a good thing—in moderation. But like all good things, most of us want too much of it. Excess dietary fat is by far the most damaging element in the Western diet. A gram of fat contains twice the calories of the same amount of protein or carbohydrate. Decreasing the fat in your diet and replacing it with more grain products, vegetables, and fruits is the best way to lower your risk of cardiovascular problems and many other diseases. Fat in the diet comes from meats, dairy products, and vegetable oils. Other sources of fat include coconuts (60 percent fat), peanuts (78 percent fat), and avocados (82 percent fat). There are different kinds of fatty acids in these sources of fats: saturated, unsaturated, and trans-fatty acids (also called *trans fat*), which is like a saturated fat in disguise. Some fats are harmful while others are considered beneficial to your health. The terms "good fats" and "bad fats" began to crystallize when diets higher in monounsaturated fats were closely observed, and these fats were found, in spite of being "fats," to raise good cholesterol, or HDL, which protects against heart disease.

Saturated Fat

Saturated fat is solid at room temperature and stimulates cholesterol production in your body. Foods high in saturated fat include processed meats, fatty meats, lard, butter, margarine, solid vegetable shortening, chocolate, and tropical oils such as coconut and palm oil (coconut oil is more than 90 percent saturated). Saturated fat should be consumed only in very low amounts.

Unsaturated Fat

Unsaturated fat is partially solid or liquid at room temperature. This group of fats includes monounsaturated fats, polyunsaturated fats, and omega-3 oils (fish oil), which protect you against heart disease. Sources of unsaturated fats include vegetable oils (canola, safflower, sunflower, and corn oil) and seeds and nuts. To make it easy to remember, unsaturated fats, with the exception of tropical oils, such as coconut, come from plants. The more liquid the fat, the more polyunsaturated it is, which, in fact, *lowers* your cholesterol levels. However, if you have familial hyperlipidemia (high cholesterol), which often occurs alongside diabetes, unsaturated fat may not make a difference in your cholesterol levels.

In Mediterranean diets, for example, which are considered among the healthiest diets, olive oil, herbs, and spices are routinely used in place of butter as spreads or dips for breads. Olive oil has been found to contain a host of protective factors and "catalyst" ingredients that allow phytochemicals from plant-based foods to work their magic in the body. The virtues of a Mediterranean diet with its "good fats" became the basis for a revolution in dietary fat guidelines, which now recognize that healthy diets should have some monounsaturated fats, the best of which is olive oil. Other monounsaturated oils are canola, peanut, sesame, soybean, corn, cottonseed, and safflower, but olive oil is 74 percent monounsaturated, while the next best oil, canola, is only 59 percent monounsaturated.

Trans-Fatty Acids (Hydrogenated Oils)

These are harmful fats that not only raise the level of bad cholesterol (LDL) in your bloodstream, but lower the amount of good cholesterol (HDL) that's already there. Trans-fatty acids are what you get when you make a liquid oil, such as corn oil, into a more solid or spreadable substance, such as margarine. Trans-fatty acids, you might say, are the "road to hell, paved with good intentions." Someone, way back when, thought that if you could take the good fat—unsaturated fat—and solidify it so it could double as butter or lard, you could eat the same things without missing the spreadable fat. That sounds like a great idea. Unfortunately, to make an unsaturated liquid fat more solid, you have to add hydrogen to its molecules. This is known as *hydrogenation*, the process that converts liquid fat to semisolid fat. That ever-popular chocolate bar ingredient, hydrogenated palm oil, is a classic example of a trans-fatty acid. Hydrogenation also prolongs the shelf life of fats, such as polyunsaturated fats, which can oxidize when exposed to air, causing rancid odors or flavors. Deep-frying oils used in the restaurant trade are generally hydrogenated.

The magic word you're looking on labels for is *hydrogenated*. If the product lists a variety of unsaturated fats (monounsaturated X oil, polyunsaturated Y oil, and so on), keep reading. If the word *hydrogenated* appears, the product contains trans-fatty acids—and you can count that product as a saturated fat; your body will! Trans-fatty acids are also now listed on most packaged food labels.

Fish Fat (Omega-3 Oils)

The fats naturally present in fish that swim in cold waters, known as omega-3 fatty acids or fish oils, are all polyunsaturated. Omega-3 fatty acids are crucial for brain tissue. They also lower your cholesterol levels and protect against heart disease. Cold-water fish have a layer of fat to keep them warm. Mackerel, albacore tuna, salmon, sardines, and lake trout are all rich in omega-3 fatty acids. Whale meat and seal meat are enormous sources of omega-3 fatty acids, and were once the staples of the Inuit diet, and protected that population from heart disease.

Fat Replacers

Fat replacers are found in many low-fat foods. Fat replacement is often achieved by using modified fats that are only partially metabolized, if at all. While some foods have the fat reduced simply by removing the fat (skim milk, lean cuts of meat), most low-fat foods require a variety of "fat copycats" to preserve the taste and texture of the food. Water, for example, is often combined with carbohydrates and protein to mimic a particular texture or taste, as is the case with a variety of baked goods or cake mixes. In general, though, the low-fat "copycats" are carbohydrate-based, protein-based, or fat-based.

Carbohydrate-based ingredients are starches and gums that are often used as thickening agents to create the texture of fat. You'll find them in abundance in low-fat salad dressings, sauces, gravies, frozen desserts, and baked goods. Compared to natural fats, which yield about 9 calories per gram, carbohydrate-based ingredients run anywhere from 0 to 4 calories per gram.

Protein-based low-fat ingredients are created by doing things to the proteins that make them behave differently. For example, by taking proteins such as whey or egg white and heating them or blending them at high speeds, you can create the look and feel of "creamy." Soy and corn proteins are often used in these cases. You'll find these ingredients in low-fat cheese, butter, mayonnaise, salad dressings, frozen dairy desserts, sour cream, and baked goods. They run between 1 and 4 calories per gram. The calorie-free fat substitute olestra is a fat-based fat replacer. It was approved for use in the United States by the FDA, and was developed by Procter and Gamble. But olestra is a potentially dangerous ingredient that most experts feel can do more harm than good. Canada has not yet approved it.

Critics of olestra argue that people will make the mistake of thinking "no fat" is healthy and choose olestra-containing Twinkies over fruits and think they're eating well. Olestra is currently being used in snack foods only, but potential uses for olestra could include restaurant foods touted as "fat-free": french fries, fried chicken, fish and chips, or onion rings. At home, olestra could be used as a cooking oil for sautés, as a butter substitute for baking, or in fat-free cheese. Potentially, we could be facing a future of eating "polyester foods" such as these. The FDA approved olestra (Olean) under the proviso that a warning label about olestra's health consequences be carried with each product containing it. (Current warnings about the product, when eaten in large amounts, causing "fecal leakage" are affixed to all Olean products.)

Low-Fat Versus Low-Carb Diets

A diet is considered "low fat" when it restricts calories from fat to below 30 percent of total calories daily. There are dozens of established low-fat diets on the market, but they vary from extremely low-fat diets, which restrict calories from fat to about 10 percent, to more moderate low-fat diets, which restrict calories from fat to 15 to 30 percent. *Very low-fat diets* (restricting calories from fat to 7 to 10 percent) are modeled after the originators of the very low-fat diet as we know it today—Nathan Pritikin, who popularized low-fat eating in the 1950s, and Dean Ornish, who reframed the original Pritikin diet in the late

Types of Fat Replacers Available

Carbohydrate-Based Fat Replacers
- Maltodextrins: baked goods
- Starches: baked goods, margarines, salad dressing, frozen desserts
- Cellulose: frozen desserts, sauces, salad dressings
- Guar, xanthan, or other gums: salad dressings
- Polydextrose: baked goods, cake mixes, puddings, frostings
- Oatrim: milk

Protein-Based Fat Replacers
- Protein concentrate (whey, egg white, soy): frozen desserts, reduced-fat dairy products, and salad dressings

Fat-Based Fat Replacers
- Caprenin: chocolate
- Salatrim: chocolate
- Olestra: snack chips, crackers

1970s. Ornish- and Pritikin-styled diets remain the most well-known and most effective diets for people who are extremely obese and at high risk of dying from an obesity-related health problem (but they are generally too restrictive for people with type 2 diabetes). The Center for Science in the Public Interest rated a number of diets for the masses in 2000. Very low-fat diets such as Pritikin's and Ornish's were actually found to be acceptable, but were found to restrict some healthy foods, such as seafood, low-fat poultry, and calcium. For people with high triglycerides, it was suggested to cut out some carbohydrates and replace them with unsaturated fats.

The main problem with very low-fat diets (7 to 10 percent calories from fat) is that they are too restrictive for the general public because they are extremely difficult to stick to unless you are very knowledgeable about low-fat cuisine and a creative chef. Also, the new information about the benefits of monounsaturated fats and omega-3 fatty acids (the "good fats") has caused nutritionists to rethink the rules governing fat in the diet. In the 1970s and 1980s, the limitations of the very low-fat diet (never intended for the masses, but as a heart disease therapy) led people to gorge on "bad carbs" (meaning carbohydrates high on the glycemic index, or simple sugars and starches) because they were led to believe that so long as a food was "fat free" it was healthy. Also, too few calories from fat left people hungry and craving food. Unfortunately, the gorging on carbs which peaked in the 1980s and early 1990s led to a sharp increase in insulin resistance from carbohydrate overload in the diet.

Then came the diet backlash: the low carb diet, or Atkins diet. Low carbohydrate diets are the opposite of low-fat diets; they restrict carbohydrates (which a healthy diet ought to be based on) to about 5 percent, and encourage mostly high-fat foods—the more saturated fat, the better. These diets are also known as high-protein diets, and in clinical circles, *ketogenic diets* because they trigger ketosis, a condition in which the insulin hormone is shut down, forcing the liver to produce ketone bodies. People can certainly lose weight while in ketosis, but living in a state of ketosis is not exactly what nature intended for a healthy human body. *When you have thyroid disease, living in a state of ketosis is potentially dangerous because ketosis can aggravate hypothyroidism, thyrotoxicosis, or hyperthyroidism.*

In addition to the dangers of ketosis, the Atkins diet can cause terrible constipation in the first phase, badly aggravating hypothyroidism, while consuming high levels of saturated fat spells disaster for people with hypothyroidism, especially for those with high levels of LDL. In addition, many people have a genetic condition that causes high triglycerides, which cannot be controlled through diet alone; in these people, the Atkins diet can be life-threatening (while a very low-fat diet has been shown, since the 1950s, to be lifesaving). Other groups who are warned against the Atkins diet are those who suffer from any disease that puts a strain on the kidneys: hypertension, cardiovascular disease, and bladder infections or conditions. Of course, anyone who is pregnant should absolutely stay away from this diet.

The Center for Science in the Public Interest rates the low carbohydrate diets, such as Atkins, Protein Power, and Sugar Busters, unacceptable in the nondiabetic population because of the high quantities of saturated fat and low quantities of fiber and essential nutrients. People become constipated. They may burn fat due to ketosis, but at the same time, they are depriving their bodies of essential nutrients, many of which are known to decrease incidences of diseases such as certain cancers. People who are also loading their bodies with saturated fats known to be associated with higher rates of cancers are obviously putting themselves at risk for certain cancers.

Sound nutritional experts maintain that carbohydrates do not make us fat; it is overindulgence in carbohydrates or protein or fat that makes us fat. Eating fewer carbs and less protein and fat—in other words, *eating everything in moderation, and expending more energy than is eaten, is the key to weight loss*. Eating whole-grain breads, pasta, rice, potatoes, vegetables, whole-grain cereals, beans, and fruit and vegetables does not make us fat; eating candy, chocolate, cookies, biscuits, sweets, and cakes—all of which are refined carbohydrates—makes us fat. And that is discouraged on any balanced diet that does not force your body into ketosis. In short, any balanced diet will result in weight loss with the added benefit of no health risks. Even an extreme Ornish- or Pritikin-style diet is fine for everyone, when followed correctly, and there are no health consequences other than improved health.

The Right Carbs

It's important to understand what is meant by *carbohydrates*. The diet lingo can often confuse us. Carbohydrates—meaning starchy stuff, such as rice, pasta, breads, or potatoes—can be stored as fat when eaten in excess.

Carbohydrates can be simple or complex. Simple carbohydrates are found in any food that has natural sugar (honey, fruits, juices, vegetables, milk) and anything that contains table sugar. These are the carbs that are high on the glycemic index, which should be minimized, as they can increase your blood sugar too rapidly, causing the "sugar crashes."

Complex carbohydrates are more sophisticated foods that are made up of larger molecules, such as grain foods, starches, and foods high in fiber. These are carbs that are low on the glycemic index and should be maximized, as they are higher in nutrients and take much longer to convert into glucose.

Normally, all carbs convert into glucose when you eat them. Glucose is the baseline ingredient of all naturally occurring sugars, which include:

- Sucrose: table or white sugar, naturally found in sugar cane and sugar beets
- Fructose: the natural sugar in fruits and vegetables
- Lactose: the natural sugar in all milk products
- Maltose: the natural sugar in grains (flours and cereals)

Factory-Added Sugars

What you have to watch out for is *added sugar*; these are sugars that manufacturers add to foods during processing or packaging. Foods containing fruit juice concentrates, invert sugar, regular corn syrup, honey or molasses, hydrolyzed lactose syrup, or high fructose corn syrup (made out of highly concentrated fructose through the hydrolysis of starch) all have added sugars. Many people don't realize, however, that pure, *unsweetened* fruit juice is still a potent source of sugar, even when it contains no added sugar. Extra lactose (naturally occurring sugar in milk products), dextrose ("pure glucose"), and maltose (naturally occurring sugar in grains) are also contained in many processed foods. In other words, the products may have naturally occurring sugars anyway, and then *more* sugar is thrown in to enhance consistency, taste, and so on. The best way to know how much sugar is in a product is to look at the nutritional label under "carbohydrates."

The Hypothyroid Diet

Since everything slows down when you're hypothyroid, you need to know how to eat and what to eat in order to compensate for your body's slowness during this time, as well as avoid complications of hypothyroidism. A high-fiber diet that is low in saturated fat and richer in unsaturated fat can help improve constipation and bloat, fatigue, and weight gain. In essence, this is a diet that will help you feel better while combating periods of hypothyroidism when you're not properly

The Glycemic Index at a Glance

This glycemic index, developed at the University of Toronto, measures the rate at which various foods convert to glucose, which is assigned a value of 100. Higher numbers indicate a more rapid absorption of glucose. This is not an exhaustive list and should be used as a sample only. This is not an index of food energy values or calories; some low GI foods are high in fat, while some high GI foods are low in fat. Keep in mind, too, that these values differ depending on what else you're eating with that food and how the food is prepared.

Sugars

Glucose	100
Honey	87
Table sugar	59
Fructose	20

Sample Snacks

Mars bar	68
Potato chips	51
Sponge cake	46
Peanuts	13

Cereals

Cornflakes	80
Shredded wheat	67
Muesli	66
All-Bran	51
Oatmeal	49

Fruit

Raisins	64
Banana	62
Orange juice	46

Orange	40
Apple	39

Dairy Products

Ice cream	36
Yogurt	36
Milk	34
Skim milk	32

Root Vegetables

Parsnips	97
Carrots	92
Instant mashed potatoes	80
New boiled potato	70
Beets	64
Yam	51
Sweet potato	48

Pasta and Rice

White rice	72
Brown rice	66
Spaghetti (white)	50
Spaghetti (whole-wheat)	42

Legumes

Frozen peas	51
Baked beans	40
Chickpeas	36
Lima beans	36
Butter beans	36
Black-eyed peas	33
Green beans	31
Kidney beans	29
Lentils	29
Dried soybeans	15

balanced on medication, while helping to prevent cardiovascular problems and colon health problems. It will also complement your thyroid medication, if you are balanced right now. And finally, it will help you combat a preexisting weight problem, which may be aggravated by your hypothyroidism.

Battling the Bloat

Feeling bloated and constipated is a classic hypothyroid ailment. Much of the bloat is actually caused by constipation; much of the bloat is also caused by not drinking enough water. But few people understand that when you increase fiber, you have to increase water intake. So here's what you need to know about fiber and water. You can take fiber supplements and stool softeners while hypothyroid, which will help you when your fiber intake is low. But these supplements can be added to a high-fiber diet as well, discussed here. It's important to note that fiber can interfere with the absorption of your thyroid hormone, so you should take them as far apart as possible (for example, fiber at night, and your thyroid hormone pill first thing in the morning).

Fiber is the part of a plant your body can't digest, which comes in the form of both water-soluble fiber (which dissolves in water) and water-insoluble fiber (which does not dissolve in water but instead, absorbs water); this is what's meant by *soluble* and *insoluble* fiber. Soluble and insoluble fiber do differ, but they are equally beneficial.

Soluble fiber—somehow—lowers the "bad" cholesterol, or low-density lipids (LDL), in your body. Experts aren't entirely sure how soluble fiber works its magic, but one popular theory is that it gets mixed into the bile the liver secretes and forms a type of gel that traps the building blocks of cholesterol, thus lowering your LDL levels. It's akin to a spider web trapping smaller insects

Insoluble fiber doesn't affect your cholesterol levels at all, but it regulates your bowel movements. How does it do this? As the insoluble fiber moves through your digestive tract, it absorbs water like a sponge and helps to form your waste into a solid form faster, making the stools larger, softer, and easier to pass. Without insoluble fiber, your solid waste just gets pushed down to the colon or lower intestine as always, where it is stored and dried out until you're ready to have a bowel movement. High-starch foods are associated with drier stools. This is exacerbated when you ignore the urge to have a bowel movement, as the colon will dehydrate the waste even more until it becomes harder and difficult to pass, a condition known as *constipation*. Insoluble fiber will help to regulate your bowel movements by speeding things along. Insoluble fiber decreases the "transit time" by increasing colon motility and limiting the time dietary toxins "hang around" the intestinal wall. This is why it can dramatically decrease your risk of colon cancer.

Good sources of soluble fiber include oats or oat bran, legumes (dried beans and peas), some seeds, carrots, oranges, bananas, and other fruits. Soybeans are also a good source of soluble fiber. Studies show that people with very high cholesterol have the most to gain by eating soybeans. Soybean is also a *phytoestrogen* (plant estrogen) that is believed to lower the risks of estrogen-related cancers (for example, breast cancer), as well as lower the incidence of estrogen-loss symptoms associated with menopause.

Good sources of insoluble fiber are wheat bran and whole grains, skins from various fruits and vegetables, seeds, leafy greens, and cruciferous vegetables (cauliflower, broccoli, and brussels sprouts). The problem is understanding what is truly whole-grain. For example, there is an assumption that because bread is dark or brown, it's more nutritious; this isn't so. In fact, many brown breads are simply enriched white breads dyed with molasses. (*Enriched* means that nutrients lost during processing have been replaced.) High-fiber pita breads and bagels are available, but you have to search for them. A good rule is to simply look for the phrase *whole-wheat*, which means that the wheat is, indeed, whole.

What's in a Grain?

Most of us will turn to grains and cereals to boost our fiber intake, which experts recommend should be at about 25 to 35 grams per day. Use the following list to help gauge whether you're getting enough insoluble fiber. If you're a little under par, an easy way to boost your fiber intake is to simply add pure wheat bran to your foods. Wheat bran is available in health food stores or supermarkets in a sort of "sawdust" form. Three tablespoons of wheat bran is equal to 4.4 grams of fiber. Sprinkle one or two tablespoons onto cereals, rice, pasta, or meat dishes. You can also sprinkle it into orange juice or low-fat yogurt. It has virtually no calories, but it's important to drink a glass of water with your wheat bran.

Cereals	Grams of Fiber *(based on ½ cup unless otherwise specified)*
Fiber First	15.0
Fiber One	12.8
All Bran	10.0
Oatmeal (1 cup)	5.0
Raisin Bran (¾ cup)	4.6
Bran Flakes (1 cup)	4.4
Cheerios (1 cup)	2.2
Cornflakes (1¼ cups)	0.8
Special K (1¼ cups)	0.4
Rice Krispies (1¼ cups)	0.3

Breads	Grams of Fiber *(based on 1 slice)*
Rye	2.0
Pumpernickel	2.0
12-grain	1.7

100-percent whole wheat	1.3
Raisin	1.0
Cracked wheat	1.0
White	0

Keep in mind that some of the newer high-fiber breads on the market today have up to 7 grams of fiber per slice. This chart is based on what is normally found in typical grocery stores.

Fruits and Veggies

Another easy way of boosting fiber content is to know how much fiber your fruits and vegetables pack per serving. All fruits, beans (also known as *legumes*), and vegetables listed here show measurements for insoluble fiber.

Fruit	Grams of Fiber
Raspberries (¾ cup)	6.4
Strawberries (1 cup)	4.0
Blackberries (½ cup)	3.9
Orange (1)	3.0
Apple (1)	2.0
Pear (½ medium)	2.0
Grapefruit (½ cup)	1.1
Kiwi (1)	1.0

Beans	Grams of Fiber *(based on ½ cup unless otherwise specified)*
Green beans (1 cup)	4.0
White beans	3.6
Kidney beans	3.3
Pinto beans	3.3
Lima beans	3.2

Vegetables	Grams of Fiber *(based on ½ cup unless otherwise specified)*
Baked potato with skin (1 large)	4.0
Acorn squash	3.8
Peas	3.0
Creamed, canned corn	2.7
Brussels sprouts	2.3
Asparagus (¾ cup)	2.3
Corn kernels	2.1
Zucchini	1.4
Carrots (cooked)	1.2
Broccoli	1.1

Drinking Water with Fiber

It's important to drink water with fiber. Water means *water*. Milk, coffee, tea, soft drinks, or juice are not a substitute for water. Unless you drink water with your fiber, the fiber will not bulk up in your colon to create the nice, soft bowel movements you so desire. Think of fiber as a sponge. Obviously, a dry sponge won't work. You must soak it with water in order for it to be useful. Same thing here. Fiber without water is as useful as a dry sponge. *You gotta soak your fiber!* So drink a glass of water with fiber.

Avoiding Alcohol

Alcohol is poorly metabolized in people who are hypothyroid because the liver is slowed down. It is also fattening, delivering about 7 calories per gram or 150 calories per drink. A glass of dry red or white wine has calories but no sugar. The same thing goes for cognac, brandy, and dry sherry that contains no sugar.

On the other hand, a sweet wine means that it contains 3 grams of sugar per 100 milliliters or 3.5-ounce portion. Dessert wines or ice wines are really sweet; they contain about 15 percent sugar or 10 grams of sugar for a 2-ounce serving. Sweet liqueurs are 35 percent sugar.

A glass of dry wine with your meal adds about 100 calories. Half soda water and half wine (a spritzer) contains half the calories. When you cook with wine, the alcohol evaporates, leaving only the flavor.

If you're a beer drinker, that's about 150 calories per bottle; a light beer has fewer calories but contains at least 100 calories per bottle.

The stiffer the drink, the higher in calories it gets. Hard liquors such as Scotch, rye, gin, and rum are made out of cereal grains; vodka, the Russian staple, is made out of potatoes. In this case, the grains or potatoes ferment into alcohol. Hard liquor averages about 40 percent alcohol, but has no sugar. Nevertheless, you're looking at about 100 calories per small shot glass, so long as you don't add fruit juice, tomato or clamato juice, or sugary soft drinks. The bottom line: while hypothyroid, avoid or limit alcohol intake as much as possible.

Putting It All Together

When you look at all the government food guidelines, and the sound diet programs, they all say the same thing: eat largely plant-based foods because they're low in calories but high in vitamins, minerals, fiber, and phytochemicals. Cut down on saturated fat (or foods of animal origin); use unsaturated or fish fats instead, and cut down on refined sugars. The most important component to any diet, however, is activity: using more energy (calories) than you ingest will maintain your body weight or lead to weight loss. This is what dietitians of the 1950s and 1960s called a sensible or balanced diet. By 1990, it was called a low-fat diet. *But it's the same diet.*

Original food guidelines and serving suggestions were designed in the early twentieth century to prevent malnutrition from vitamin deficiencies. By 1950, the problem of overnutrition began to be evident, which is what led to a rise in obesity-related diseases such as type 2 diabetes. In a 1959 book on heart disease, *Eat Well and Stay Well*, which was written by a physician, Ancel Keys, and his wife, Margaret Keys, the guidelines for a healthy heart were almost identical to today's dietary guidelines: maintaining normal body weight; restricting saturated fats and red meat; using polyunsaturated fats instead to a maximum of 30 percent of daily calories; plenty of fresh fruits and vegetables and non-fat milk products; avoidance of overly salted foods and refined sugar. The Keys's guidelines even stressed exercise, stopping smoking, and stress reduction!

Most people's diets do not even come close to balanced. Many North Americans eat nothing *but* the types of foods that have always been discouraged: saturated fats (thanks to fast food), sugar (thanks to the soft drink industry), refined carbohydrates (thanks to snack foods), and not enough fiber.

Again, losing weight means eating fewer calories and/or expending more calories than you eat. Fat has more calories per gram than carbohydrates (9 calories per gram versus 4 calories per gram). Saturated fats are the building blocks of clogged arteries and cardiovascular problems; unsaturated fats are heart-protective. We can therefore choose the right type of fat over the wrong type of fat. But overall weight loss, *by simply eating less*, will have more of an impact on reducing obesity and obesity-related health problems than "splitting fats" at the end of the day. Programs such as Weight Watchers, for example, which are based on calorie-counting, are considered terrific starting points for people who need to lose weight. In general, you can judge a good diet based on these four simple questions:

1. Are all food groups included: plant-based; grains and complex carbs; proteins (lean meats); fats? If not, stay away.
2. Are you encouraged to have the least number of calories from fats, and discouraged from junk foods and refined sugars? If so, this is sensible.
3. Is weight loss promised averaging about one to two pounds per week, or is weight loss promised ten or more pounds per week? Anything more than one to two pounds a week is suspicious and likely faddish. Gradual weight loss is sustainable for life; speedy weight loss leads to yo-yo effects, where you gain as much back as you lost.
4. Is it a diet that offers enough variety that you would feel good eating this way for life, and feeding your whole family with the foods encouraged? People on the Atkins diet, for example, have stated that they "can't take it" beyond a certain point, and cannot feed their children with the diet.

How to Get More Fruits and Vegetables

Here are some ways to add fruits and vegetables to your diet:

- Go for one or two fruits at breakfast, one fruit and two vegetables at lunch and dinner, and a fruit or vegetable snack between meals.
- Consume many differently colored fruits and vegetables to get all the different vitamins. For color variety, select at least three differently colored fruits and vegetables daily.
- Put fruit and sliced veggies in an easy-to-use, easy-to-reach place (sliced vegetables in the fridge; fruit out on the table).
- Keep frozen and canned fruit and vegetables on hand to add to soups, salads, or rice dishes.

The Hyperthyroid Diet

Most women concerned about thyroid and weight will be suffering from hypothyroidism, which may have resulted from treatment for hyperthyroidism. If you are currently in the throes of hyperthyroidism and are thyrotoxic, it's important to note that your thyroid helps to control food absorption, gastric emptying, secretion of digestive juices, and motility of the digestive tract. When you're thyrotoxic, despite a voracious appetite, you might lose weight, have hyperdefecation (frequent bowel movements), develop mild anemia, and suffer bone loss as calcium is taken out of the blood and excreted in the urine.

The calcium loss can exacerbate risk factors for osteoporosis. Generally, premenopausal women need 1,000 milligrams of calcium per day, while a postmenopausal woman needs 1,200 to 1,500 milligrams of calcium daily. But you can help ease the unpleasantness by choosing what you eat. Increase your calcium intake by having more dairy products. The dairy product highest in calcium is live-culture yogurt. (Choose yogurt made from milk without hormone and antibiotic residues.) Yogurt also strengthens the digestive system, boosts the immune system, eases the nervous system, and helps prevent vaginal infections. Yogurt is much lower in fat than other dairy products. In fact, 25 percent (350 to 400 milligrams) of your 1,500 milligram daily calcium requirement can come from 1 cup (250 milligrams) of yogurt, which is equal to 1 cup of milk, 1 ounce (30 grams) hard cheese, or ½ cup (115 grams) ricotta cheese.

Dairy products containing fat will also help to keep your weight up. Peanut butter, mayonnaise, and animal fat can help prevent weight loss as well. To reduce diarrhea, cut down on fruit juices and fresh fruits. Peanut butter is also good for binding. Sometimes, hyperthyroid people will develop sudden lactose intolerance. This can lead to gas and other unpleasantries. Eliminate all milk products in this case, and take a calcium supplement (discussed in the section "Preventing Bone Loss" in Chapter 6) while getting your fat from the nondairy foods mentioned above. In addition, consider the following excellent sources of calcium:

- Almond milk
- Soy milk
- Broccoli, kale, turnip greens, or mustard greens

- Cooked collards, wild onions, lamb's-quarter, or amaranth greens
- Tahini
- Soy or tofu (not all tofu contains calcium; check labels)
- Oats, oatmeal
- Seaweed
- Sardines
- Yogurt
- Nettles
- Dandelion leaves
- Dried fruit
- Corn tortillas (because these are made with lime, they are high in calcium)

You may want to take vitamin supplements as well. (Vitamins A, D, and E are stored in body fat and can be lost through excretion if you are hyperthyroid.) When you are in balance again, you will need to cut down on your fat and calcium intake.

Iodine Foods and the Thyroid

If you have a normal functioning thyroid gland but are concerned that you are at risk for a thyroid problem, is there a "thyroid disease prevention diet" you can follow?

Well . . . it will depend on where you live. We know, for example, that a lack of iodine can cause the thyroid gland to enlarge (see Chapter 1). By the same token, too much iodine is believed to be responsible for triggering goiters and thyroid disorders, too. That's one reason taking kelp (seaweed) is not recommended. If you live in North America, you're getting enough iodine in your diet from your food. Taking kelp in the belief that it will prevent a thyroid problem is simply bad practice. Not only will it not prevent a thyroid problem, it could trigger one. Other than recommending against taking kelp, North American physicians do not generally warn people at risk for a thyroid disorder about avoiding iodine-containing food because those foods offer important nutrients. A healthy thyroid gland will take what it needs from your daily diet.

Your thyroid gland uses about a milligram of iodine per week (or 90 micrograms per day) to make thyroid hormone; that is a tiny amount, so it is easy to understand that a balanced diet provides more than enough iodine for the average thyroid gland. A healthy thyroid gland can store enough iodine to last for three months. How much food do you need to eat to reach 90 micrograms? Well, one small carton of yogurt contains 125 grams of iodine, or 125,000,000 micrograms.

According to some sources, a diet too high in fiber may prevent your gut from absorbing enough iodine, while a strict sodium-free or salt-free diet may not provide enough iodine. Given that iodine is present in so many foods, however, it's unlikely that you're suffering from iodine deficiency in North America.

It is also important to note that low-iodine diets are necessary for thyroid cancer patients undergoing thyroid scans. (See Chapter 11 for more information.)

Goitrogens

Goitrogens are chemicals that block, or interfere with, iodine absorption. Known goitrogens include vegetables from the Brassica family (cabbage, turnips, kohlrabi, bean sprouts, cauliflower), almonds, sweet corn, and some dairy products (it depends on whether the cow was dining on goitrogenic veggies). But unless your diet contains only goitrogens (which it does not), there is no need to worry about having these foods, as they are excellent sources of fiber, important vitamins, and cancer-fighting agents.

Some women with Graves' disease have investigated a goitrogenic diet over conventional treatment, such as radioactive iodine or antithyroid medication (see Chapter 11). The attraction is that it is "natural." Such a diet could theoretically work to block the effects of thyroid hormone, but you'd have to eat such large quantities of goitrogenic foods (for example twenty pounds of raw cabbage) and, in addition, follow a strict low-iodine diet each day. Also, a goitrogenic diet cannot cure the underlying autoimmune disease that is causing thyrotoxicosis.

9

Autoimmune
Thyroid Disease

TWO OF THE most common thyroid diseases, Hashimoto's disease and Graves' disease, are autoimmune diseases, meaning that the body attacks its own tissues. Women are more prone to autoimmune diseases and disorders for reasons that remain a mystery to medical investigators. Some evidence indicates that autoimmune disorders are triggered by stress, and we also know that women are more prone to stress in our culture. (See the section "What Is a Woman's Stress?" in Chapter 3.)

What Is an Autoimmune Disorder?

The word *autoimmune* means "self-attacking." But before you can really grasp what this means, it's important to understand how your body normally fights off infection or disease.

Whenever an invading virus or cell is detected, your body produces specific "armies" called *antibodies*, which attack the foreign intruders, which are known as *antigens*. Antibodies are special proteins made by one type of white blood cell (called *lymphocytes*), and each antibody is designed for a specific virus, bacteria, or toxin (the antigen) in the same way that a key is designed for a specific lock. The antibody acts as the key, while the antigen, or "intruder," is the lock. For example, if you contract chicken pox as a child, you do not contract it again; your body is armed with the antibody that kills the chicken pox virus. But the specific chicken pox antibody is useless against all other viruses, such as the mumps or measles. The importance of this can be seen when the immune system is impaired, such as in AIDS from the HIV virus; impaired antibody production permits many of these diseases to come back. Also, an impaired immune system leaves the body vulnerable to opportunistic infections.

Often, our doctors give us vaccines to prevent the development of a particular virus, such as polio, for example. Vaccines work like this: the serum contains a small amount of a particular virus in a deadened, noncontagious form. Essentially, the vaccine shows your body a sample of the virus. The vaccine serum stimulates your immune system to produce a specific antibody to combat the unwanted virus. Later, if you catch the virus, your body will destroy it before it can do any damage. That's why you don't necessarily need to get chicken pox to be protected from it; you can be vaccinated against it instead. However, creating a vaccine is a painstaking, complicated process, and it can take years for scientists to develop vaccines to combat specific viruses. Polio struck at epidemic proportions throughout the 1940s and 1950s until a vaccine was discovered.

With an autoimmune disorder, your body's immune system makes some mistakes when it tries to distinguish foreign intruders from normal tissue. It confuses the two and perceives specific healthy organs as foreign. Your body then winds up attacking its own organ. Some doctors describe it as a sort of allergy, where your body is in fact allergic to itself. So in the same way that the body develops specific antibodies to fight specific infections, in this case the body develops specific antibodies to attack specific organs. These are known as *autoantibodies*. Many kinds of illnesses are in fact autoimmune disorders; Graves' disease and Hashimoto's disease are two of them. In other examples, antibodies against joints cause rheumatoid arthritis; antibodies against muscles cause myasthenia gravis; while antibodies against DNA cause lupus.

Who Is Vulnerable?

Generally, anyone can develop an autoimmune disorder. Many autoimmune disorders are hereditary, while some disorders—although not directly hereditary—run strongly in families. This is referred to as a *genetic tendency* or *inherited predisposition*.

There is a great deal of evidence, though, to suggest that stress is a major factor in triggering an autoimmune disorder. When you are under unusual or extreme stress, depression or exhaustion can set in, which will weaken your immune system. What is labeled "unusual" or "extreme"? A death or a tragedy in the family is considered to be extremely stressful. Starting a new job, moving, or relocating is also very stressful; getting married or having a new baby is stressful. Generally, any major change in our daily routine—whether positive or negative—is stressful, but people cope with change differently. What one person finds stressful may not bother another person at all.

Women who either are pregnant or have just given birth, however, are particularly vulnerable to autoimmune disorders (see Chapter 5).

Hashimoto's Disease

The most common autoimmune thyroid disease is Hashimoto's thyroiditis, also known as Hashimoto's disease. It is important to note, however, that there are other forms of thyroiditis which are not autoimmune disorders (discussed in Chapter 2). In medical circles, Hashimoto's disease is referred to as *chronic lymphocytic thyroiditis* because of the involvement of self-attacking lymphocytes. This disease is named after Hakaru Hashimoto, the Japanese physician who first described the condition in 1912.

Like Graves' disease (discussed later in this chapter), a tendency for Hashimoto's disease is also inherited, but much of the time Hashimoto's disease strikes women over age thirty (though many younger women have also been diagnosed with it). Statistically, two in ten women will develop Hashimoto's disease in their lifetime.

Hashimoto's disease is caused by abnormal autoantibodies and white blood cells attacking and damaging thyroid cells. Eventually, this constant attack destroys many of the thyroid cells; the absence of sufficient thyroid cells causes hypothyroidism. In most cases a goiter develops because of the inflammation and overstimulation of the residual thyroid cells, though sometimes the thyroid gland can actually shrink.

If you develop Hashimoto's disease, you probably will not notice any symptoms. Sometimes there is a mild pressure in the thyroid gland

and fatigue can set in, but unless you are on the lookout for thyroid disease, Hashimoto's disease can go undetected for years. Only when the thyroid cells are damaged to the point that the thyroid gland functions inadequately will you begin to experience the symptoms of hypothyroidism, described in Chapter 2.

In rare instances, thyroid eye disease can set in as well (see Chapter 7). In many ways, Hashimoto's disease is the same as Graves' disease except that the antibodies don't stimulate the thyroid to make thyroid hormone. As discussed later in this chapter, the antibodies produced in Hashimoto's disease most likely also attack the proteins in the eye muscle. Treating eye problems associated with Hashimoto's disease involves treating the initial hypothyroidism first. If eye problems persist, the same treatment pattern outlined for Graves' disease will be necessary.

Rarer still, some people with Hashimoto's disease experience thyrotoxicosis as well as hypothyroidism. This combination sometimes occurs due to two phases of the disease. First, the attack of the antibodies causes the stores of thyroid hormone to suddenly leak out and raises the thyroid hormone level in the blood too high. This condition has been termed *Hashitoxicosis*. Anyone suffering from this somewhat paradoxical condition would first experience all the symptoms of Graves' disease. After a month or two, the antibodies attacking the thyroid cells cause them to stop working and the leaking stored hormones are depleted, causing the hyperthyroidism to cure itself. Then, as Hashimoto's disease progresses, you would eventually become hypothyroid unless a replacement hormone was prescribed.

Diagnosis and Treatment of Hashimoto's Disease

The signs of Hashimoto's disease are not at all obvious. In its early stages, a goiter can develop as a result of inflammation in the thyroid gland. The goiter is usually firm but in rare cases can be tender. The goiter's tenderness can suggest Hashimoto's disease, but it is usually suspected because of the onset of sudden hypothyroidism or the age of a hypothyroid patient, given that it is common in women over age forty. Hashimoto's disease is frequently missed as a diagnosis, however. Often, symptoms of hypothyroidism are attributed to age—particularly in women entering menopause. This results in failing to relieve hypothyroid symptoms, otherwise easily treatable with thyroid hormone.

Hashimoto's disease is easily diagnosed through a blood test that indicates high levels of antibodies in the blood. The specific antibodies are called TPO (thyroid peroxidase) autoantibodies and antithyroglobulin (TG) antibodies. Another method of confirming diagnosis is through a needle biopsy. Here, a needle is inserted into the thyroid gland to remove some cells. The cells are then smeared onto a glass slide which, in the case of Hashimoto's disease, would reveal abnormal white blood cells. This procedure is usually not necessary, except when making sure that a thyroid nodule is due to Hashimoto's rather than thyroid cancer.

The treatment is simple: thyroid replacement hormone is prescribed as soon as the diagnosis is made—even if there are no symptoms. There are three reasons why this is done. First, the synthetic thyroid hormone suppresses production of thyroid-stimulating hormone (TSH) by the pituitary gland, which, in turn, shrinks any goiter that may have developed or is about to develop. Second, because Hashimoto's disease often progresses to the point where hypothyroidism sets in, the thyroid hormone nips hypothyroidism in the bud and prevents the Hashimoto's patient from suffering the unpleasant symptoms of hypothyroidism. Finally, for some reason, synthetic thyroid hormone seems to interfere with the autoimmune response by reducing TSH-stimulated release of thyroid antigens.

If you have developed a goiter as a result of Hashimoto's disease, the goiter usually persists unless thyroid hormone is prescribed. In rare cases, the goiter shrinks on its own. Once thyroid hormone treatment begins, it takes from six to twelve months for the goiter to shrink as much as it can, provided that TSH levels are normal. (Remember, a goiter is simply an enlarged thyroid gland; when the thyroid gland shrivels up, it no longer functions.) In rare instances, goiters can persist—despite synthetic thyroxine—for years.

Graves' Disease

Graves' disease is the next most common autoimmune thyroid disease. It is named after Robert Graves, the nineteenth-century Irish physician who first recognized the condition (in some countries it is called Base-dow's disease, named after a German physician who did the same thing). Graves' disease occurs in both sexes, but tends to affect younger and middle-aged women—usually between ages twenty to forty and during their childbearing years. It is also not unheard of for someone in her fifties or sixties to develop Graves' disease, or for young girls to get it.

Graves' disease occurs much more frequently in women than men. Roughly 1 percent of the population has Graves' disease, which includes former U.S. President George Herbert Walker Bush, former First Lady Barbara Bush, and their dog. The late John F. Kennedy Jr. suffered from Graves' disease as well as Addison's disease like his father, the late President John F. Kennedy. (Addison's disease is also an autoimmune disorder, discussed later in this chapter.) At one time, the Bushes' Graves' disease was considered a mutual and medically fantastic coincidence, but some data have suggested that there may be an infectious agent at work that is associated with Graves' disease. Some investigators wonder whether German measles (rubella) may also trigger autoimmune thyroid disease. This may explain why there seem to be families of Graves' patients. At a 1994 Graves' disease convention I attended, one endocrinologist talked about testing the Bushes for this infectious agent (they tested positive, and George apparently warned, "Don't get any blood on the carpet or Barbara will kill you."). To date, the infection theory is still just that—a theory. Much more study is needed before there's a clear-cut answer. Indeed, it will be interesting to see whether any of the Bushes' offspring, including George W. Bush or Jeb Bush, develop Graves' disease in the future.

Although there is strong evidence for the hereditary nature of Graves' disease, some doctors prefer to classify it as a disorder that "runs strongly in families." That's because no specific gene responsible for Graves' disease has been isolated.

What Happens in Graves' Disease?

In Graves' disease, an abnormal antibody is produced, called *TSA (thyroid-stimulating antibody)*, also known as *TSI (thyroid-stimulating immunoglobulin)*. TSA stimulates the thyroid gland to vastly overproduce thyroid hormone (this is hyperthyroidism). Normally controlled by the pituitary gland, the thyroid's triggers are tricked into being stimulated by abnormal antibodies. The result is thyrotoxicosis, and a goiter almost always develops. Yet sometimes the goiter is so slight that your doctor cannot feel it.

A study that surveyed Graves' patients and non-Graves' patients found that more Graves' disease patients were under stress before they developed Graves'. Some experts believe that once the stressful period is over and the weakened immune system bounces back to normal function, it may bounce back too aggressively and attack normal tissue. It's much like the watch dog example earlier in the book: a dog that has been cooped up all day, once released from its crate, will go crazy and jump all over you, perhaps even biting you because it is not exercising much self-control. (See Chapter 3 for more on the stress connection.)

Diagnosing and Treating Graves' Disease

Again, the signs of Graves' disease are often obvious: you may develop a goiter and display all the classic signs of thyrotoxicosis. Or you may just develop thyroid eye disease symptoms, which are usually telltale signs of Graves' disease. When the signs are obvious, your doctor simply confirms the diagnosis with blood tests that check your thyroid function and check for the presence of thyroid antibodies in the blood.

If you're not showing any blatant signs of hyperthyroidism but suspect Graves' disease because it runs in your family or you're experiencing more subtle symptoms, Graves' disease is again detected through blood tests that check thyroid function. If your thyroid function tests confirm hyperthyroidism, your doctor will then test for the presence of thyroid antibodies in your blood. Since Graves' disease is responsible for 80 percent of all hyperthyroid cases, most doctors routinely screen for it when hyperthyroidism is diagnosed. If the Graves' disease is not obvious, or there is a lumpy gland, a radioactive iodine thyroid scan may be needed to make the diagnosis.

There is no way to treat the root cause of Graves' disease—the autoimmune disorder itself. Therefore, treating Graves' disease involves treating the hyperthyroid situation. To treat hyperthyroidism, the thyroid gland is usually rendered inactive with radioactive iodine or antithyroid drugs or is removed by surgery.

To deaden the thyroid gland, radioactive iodine is the most common treatment. Radioactive iodine is simply iodine in radioactive form.

Since the thyroid naturally takes in iodine to function, when the iodine is made radioactive, the malfunctioning thyroid gland greedily absorbs it and, if a high enough dose is given, basically destroys itself in the process. (There is sometimes some residual thyroid function left.) Although this seems a rather drastic description, the procedure isn't dangerous, and there are usually no side effects other than some minor swelling or irritation to the throat, although it appears as though Graves' patients receiving radioactive iodine tend to develop thyroid eye disease, or a worsening of these symptoms (see Chapter 7). The only time radioactive iodine isn't used is when patients are very young children or pregnant. In over fifty-five years of active use, radioactive iodine has not yet proved harmful when given for this purpose. Taken either in capsule form or dissolved in water, radioactive iodine effectively destroys the thyroid gland. (See Chapter 11 for a detailed discussion of radioactive iodine treatment.) There is usually a waiting period after the radioactive iodine treatment is administered to determine if the thyroid's function has lowered. Usually the doctor will wait until you are hypothyroid before prescribing thyroid replacement hormone to replace the output of a functioning thyroid. If you remain hyperthyroid for at least five months after the first radioactive iodine treatment, a second dose will be administered. Sometimes three or more doses have to be applied.

Another treatment is either a partial or total thyroidectomy (surgical removal of the thyroid gland). A thyroidectomy might be performed when there is either a goiter causing obstruction in the neck or concern that a thyroid nodule is suspicious for cancer. This major surgery involves a general anesthetic and postsurgical stay in the hospital of at least one to two days. A waiting period again is involved as well. Sometimes, small pieces of thyroid tissue are left behind that could potentially reactivate Graves' disease. If this happens, radioactive iodine is used to kill the remaining bits of tissue. When you become hypothyroid, thyroid replacement hormone will be prescribed.

Sometimes, doctors prefer to treat Graves' disease with antithyroid drugs. These drugs prevent the thyroid from manufacturing thyroid hormone. Then, as the production of hormone decreases, the hyperthyroidism will disappear. Usually, antithyroid drugs are used if patients are under age twenty, but some doctors prefer to use them at any age. Patients themselves may opt to try antithyroid drugs before more drastic measures are taken. Graves' disease, in virtually all patients, can be easily controlled with antithyroid medication. This means that the hyperthyroid symptoms caused by Graves' disease subside with antithyroid medication. However, when patients are taken off the drugs, only about 20–30 percent of them experience true remission, while the majority will experience a recurrence of Graves' disease. Why even bother with antithyroid medication then? Because many doctors feel that Graves' disease patients should have a chance at remission initially before more drastic therapies are used. It takes about six to eight weeks on the medication for the thyroid hormone levels to reach a normal range, but patients are usually kept on them for six to twelve months to see if a true remission will occur. In the end, many of the patients on antithyroid drugs wind up having either a thyroidectomy or radioactive iodine treatment. There is an upside to antithyroid drugs, however. Patients with eye problems will experience more improvement in their eyes while on antithyroid medication than with other forms of treatment. The downside of antithyroid drugs is a small (around 1 percent) risk of destroying the bone marrow (causing aplastic anemia, when you do not make blood cells) or the liver (requiring a liver transplant).

A final note on treatment of Graves' disease: occasionally, after radioactive iodine treatment or surgery, just enough of the thyroid gland remains to function normally on its own. This means that thyroid replacement hormone is not necessary. This is not the norm, however. If you have Graves' disease, it's far more realistic to assume that after treatment you'll need to be put on thyroid replacement hormone for life. There is data that radioactive iodine therapy doesn't work as well on Graves' disease patients who were treated with the antithyroid medication propylthioruracil (PTU) first. If you're having radioactive iodine therapy after pretreatment with antithyroid medication, the current literature suggests a need for higher doses of radioactive iodine. The general recommendation is to avoid antithyroid medication if a doctor knows for certain that you'll be having radioactive iodine therapy. Instead, beta-blockers are used to control some symptoms of hyperthyroidism until the thyroid hormone level is restored to the normal range.

Other Autoimmune Disorders

If you have one autoimmune disease, you are more likely to start a collection of them. Graves' disease and Hashimoto's disease are associated with other conditions, just as Hashimoto's disease is associated with myasthenia gravis. The most common autoimmune disorders thyroid sufferers are at risk for include the following.

Addison's Disease

Addison's disease is caused by your adrenal glands failing to make cortisone and steroid hormones—the adrenal products your body needs to function properly. This is rare among thyroid patients, but it tends to occur frequently in people with pernicious anemia, discussed in the following section, which is commonly found in thyroid patients.

Anemia

When you're anemic, there's a decrease in the number of red blood cells carrying oxygen to various body tissues. Often, people who are hypothyroid are mildly anemic because of the body's tendency to slow its functions. There are usually no specific symptoms associated with mild anemia, and it corrects itself when hypothyroidism is treated. A more serious type of anemia—*pernicious* (meaning serious) *anemia*—tends to occur in older people who either have or have had Grave's disease or Hashimoto's disease. Pernicious anemia is caused by a deficiency of vitamin B_{12}, the vitamin essential for producing red blood cells. When your thyroid is functioning normally, cells lining the stomach produce *intrinsic factor*, which enables the body to absorb vitamin B_{12} from food. Self-attacking antibodies to intrinsic factor occur in pernicious anemia. Thus, they can be considered an associated autoimmune disease genetically related to Graves' or Hashimoto's disease (like thyroid eye disease). The interference can prevent the body from absorbing the vitamin B_{12} it needs to manufacture sufficient quantities of red blood cells. When vitamin B_{12} levels drop, anemia can set in.

Symptoms of pernicious anemia include numbness and tingling in the hands and feet (this happens because vitamin B_{12} also nourishes the nervous system), loss of balance, and leg weakness. Studies suggest that 5 percent of those diagnosed with Graves' disease and 10 percent of those diagnosed with Hashimoto's disease may develop pernicious anemia. However, because this type of anemia usually develops in patients over age sixty, younger patients with either Graves' or Hashimoto's disease are probably not at risk. But if you're sixty or older and have ever been diagnosed with Graves' or Hashimoto's disease, ask your doctor to specifically measure vitamin B_{12} levels in your blood. If the levels are low or borderline, request an additional test, known as the Schilling test, which can detect if you're having difficulty absorbing vitamin B_{12} from food. If you do have pernicious anemia, it is easily corrected with an intramuscular injection of vitamin B_{12}. Usually the treatment is once monthly, but it will vary depending on the severity of the condition.

Arthritis

Some people with Graves' or Hashimoto's disease experience tendon and joint inflammation. Painful tendonitis and bursitis of the shoulder, for example, was reported in about 7 percent of Graves' and Hashimoto's patients, compared to only 1.7 percent of the general population.

On the other hand, rheumatoid arthritis, a more serious disease, appears to be only slightly more common among thyroid patients than the general population. It can cause inflammation of many joints in the body including knuckles, wrists, and elbows. Stiffness tends to be more severe in the morning. If you are either hyper- or hypothyroid and have noticed this kind of pain or stiffness, ask your doctor to recommend appropriate medication for arthritic symptoms. Sometimes, pain and stiffness will improve when the thyroid condition is corrected.

Diabetes

There is an increased incidence of type 1 diabetes (formerly known as juvenile diabetes or insulin-dependent diabetes) in families where Graves' or Hashimoto's disease has been diagnosed.

If you do happen to have both conditions, an overactive thyroid will often make the diabetes worse and more difficult to control with insulin. Once your thyroid condition is treated, though, you will find it easier to regain control over the diabetes.

Inflammatory Bowel Disease (IBD)

Inflammatory bowel disease is an umbrella term that comprises Crohn's disease as well as colitis. IBD is a miserable condition where the lower intestine becomes inflamed, causing abdominal cramping, pain, fever, and mucousy, bloody diarrhea. IBD may occur more often in thyroid disease patients and can generally be controlled through diet and medications. If you have IBD, it's best to ask to be referred to a gastroenterologist (also known as a G.I. specialist), who is the specialist to manage it. This is not to be confused with irritable bowel syndrome (IBS), a stress-related disorder that often masks hyperthyroid symptoms.

Lupus

Lupus is a frightening condition that imitates many other diseases. For years, lupus patients went undiagnosed, similar to many thyroid patients. This is an autoimmune condition that affects many body tissues causing arthritic symptoms, skin rashes, and kidney, lung, and heart problems. Lupus patients often test positive for antithyroid antibodies. What's interesting about lupus is that it is rare among thyroid sufferers even though lupus sufferers often have thyroid problems. If you know someone with lupus, a thyroid function test is a good idea, so any thyroid-related symptoms can be discovered and treated.

Myasthenia Gravis

Myasthenia gravis is a rare autoimmune disorder of the muscles that affects only about thirty people per million, but it's ten times more common in Graves' disease patients. Symptoms include muscle weakness, double vision, and difficulty swallowing—some of which can be present in both Graves' and thyroid eye disease. Ask to be tested for myasthenia gravis when you have these symptoms. They may not be caused solely by Graves' disease.

Other Stress-Related Disorders

Women suffering from thyroid disease are not immune to other stress-related disorders that can aggravate or mask thyroid symptoms. Common stress-related disorders in women include irritable bowel syndrome (IBS) and interstitial cystitis (IC). There is also some debate over the role of stress in chronic fatigue syndrome and fibromyalgia, both discussed in Chapter 3.

10

Thyroid Lumps
and Thyroid Cancer

IF YOU'RE NERVOUS about a lump in your neck, or think you may be at risk for thyroid cancer, this is the chapter to read. Thyroid lumps, called *nodules*, are usually benign and not signs of cancer. Thyroid cancer still remains a rare cancer, accounting for just about 2 percent of all cancers. Nevertheless, at the 2003 American Thyroid Association conference, thyroid cancer was ranked as the fastest rising cancer in women, topping lung and breast cancers. Women outnumber men in developing thyroid cancer by three to one. Put another way, women account for 77 percent of all new cases of thyroid cancer, and 61 percent of all deaths from thyroid cancer occur in women. In 2001, only 4,600 men developed thyroid cancer, compared to 15,000 women; 500 deaths from thyroid cancer occurred in men, and 800 deaths occurred in women. This statistical imbalance illustrates the fact that thyroid problems are seen much more frequently in women, the reason why I've devoted this book to the topic of women and thyroid disease. Other than environmental exposures (discussed later in this chapter) it is currently not known why thyroid cancer is diagnosed so much more frequently in women. That said, it has also been observed that women who have had thyroid cancer are at an increased risk of developing breast cancer, which is why doing breast self-exam and regular mammography is important. (See Chapter 1.)

Thyroid Self-Exam (TSE)

Every year, thousands of women find breast cancer lumps by doing breast self-exam (BSE). Self-exams have also been introduced as a tool to find early testicular cancers, skin cancers, and a host of others. This simple lump-finding tool was introduced into the thyroid world in the mid-1990s. The thyroid self-exam is also known as the "neck check" and works along the same principles of BSE. The neck check was developed by the American Association of Clinical Endocrinologists. To do a neck check, you'll need a glass of water and a handheld mirror. Here are the standard steps:

1. Hold the mirror in your hand, focusing on the area of your neck just below the Adam's apple (which is the thyroid cartilage) and immediately above the collarbone, where the thyroid gland is located.
2. While focusing on this area in the mirror, tip your head back slightly.
3. Take a drink of water and swallow. Normally, as you swallow, your windpipe rises and then goes back to its normal position.
4. As you swallow, look at your neck. Check for any bulges or a protrusion in this area when you swallow. Repeat this a few times to be sure you're "all clear."

Over and above the standard TSE:

• Place your fingers at the back of your neck, at the top of your spine, and then knead your neck tissue toward the front like a piece of raw dough, feeling all around to the front of your throat. Work the right side of your neck from back to front center, and then the left side from back to front center. You're looking for a painless lump, anywhere from the size of a pea to the size of a golf ball.

• Feel all around the area just above the collarbone, or "pocket." If you notice any bulges or lumps in these areas, see your doctor as soon as possible to have the lump investigated. If you have swollen lymph nodes in your neck or under your ears that persist for longer than one month, get them evaluated by a doctor. Your doctor can tell you if the lump is in the thyroid or not, possibly with the aid of ultrasound.

Signs of Thyroid Cancer

It's important to recognize the signs of thyroid cancer, particularly if your thyroid has been exposed to radiation. Often the signs are not that obvious, but they can include the following:

- A hard and painless lump (nodule) anywhere on your neck.
- A thyroid nodule that continues to enlarge.
- Difficulty swallowing food or liquids.
- Change in your voice or hoarseness (this may indicate that the cancer is spreading beyond the thyroid gland).
- Pain in your neck tissues, jawbone, or ear (this is a very uncommon sign of thyroid cancer but has been reported).
- A diagnosis of sleep apnea, which has come on suddenly (this is a sleep disorder characterized by interrupted breathing). This is very rare, but there have been cases where thyroid cancer patients have been falsely diagnosed with sleep apnea when, in fact, a growing thyroid tumor was present. In these cases, difficulties with breathing were actually caused by a spreading thyroid tumor, which can block breathing passages!

In the great majority of people with thyroid cancer, the first sign of cancer is a non-tender lump in the neck that is found by themselves, a relative, or a doctor during a routine exam. The signs of two types of thyroid cancers, medullary thyroid cancer and anaplastic thyroid cancer, are somewhat different and are discussed briefly in the following sections. (These types of cancer are discussed in detail in *The Thyroid Cancer Book*.)

Investigating a Thyroid Nodule

A lump is called a *nodule*, which literally means "knot." Single thyroid nodules are usually one of three things: a growth that contains fluid (called a *cyst*); a growth that contains abnormal but non-cancerous cells (called a *benign tumor* or *adenoma*); or a growth that contains cancerous abnormal cells (called a *malignant tumor* or *carcinoma*). Cysts are frequently benign, and the majority of thyroid lumps are also benign.

Thyroid lumps are evaluated by the following types of doctors, listed in order of the least skilled in thyroid disease to the most skilled:

- Primary care doctors (family physicians, general practitioners, or internists).
- Endocrinologists (doctors specializing in the endocrine or hormone system, which includes the thyroid gland).
- Thyroidologists (endocrinologists who only specialize in treating thyroid disease).

Fine Needle Aspiration Biopsy

A diagnostic procedure known as *fine needle aspiration (FNA)* has changed the way thyroid lumps are diagnosed. If you walked into your doctor's office with a lump on your neck twenty years ago, you'd have had a thyroid scan and ultrasound, and you might have had the entire lump removed through a procedure known as *excisional biopsy*—a nasty little procedure that was used to diagnose my own thyroid cancer in 1983. You might have also been sent for an ultrasound to see if your lump was fluid-filled or solid or, with a scan, "hot" or "cold"— meaning that it's either sucking up iodine more than the other parts of the thyroid or relatively less. Well, these scans are rarely necessary today.

FNA, a twenty-minute procedure, is now basically considered the gold standard for evaluating a thyroid nodule. FNA is usually very accurate. It can be performed in a doctor's office, and is as simple as drawing a blood sample. The skin around your lump is cleansed with antiseptic before doing FNA. The needle (which is smaller than the standard needles used to sample blood) needs to be inserted three to six times to obtain a good sample. This is known as obtaining *passes*, where each nodule is aspirated in different areas and in different directions. If you have several nodules, they'll each need to be aspirated with the appropriate number of passes, with greater attention paid to larger nodules. FNA will suck out cells and/or fluid (if it's a cyst), which is sent off to a pathologist (a specialist who examines cells), who is then able to determine if the lump is benign or malignant. FNA is usually very accurate. If your lump is a cyst, this procedure can also drain the cyst and collapse it, taking care of the problem entirely. FNA outweighs other diagnostic procedures in terms of the benefits; it's cheap, easy, fast, reasonably accurate, and places far less stress on you, the patient. Studies show that because of FNA, cases of thyroid surgery have dropped by 50 percent. This means that many people can be spared "look-see surgery," which used to be done frequently when cancer was suspected. In some cases (such as when the lump can't be felt by the doctor), FNA is done using ultrasound to guide the needle.

Anytime you have FNA, it's a good idea to avoid medications that prolong blood clotting, such as aspirin. If you're on prescription medication, let your doctor know prior to the procedure. However, being on these medications doesn't mean you can't have this procedure done; abstaining from them prior to FNA just reduces risks of bleeding. Once it's done, you'll have a bandage on the puncture site and then go home. You may have some neck tenderness or mild swelling afterwards, but you'll be fine in twenty-four hours. If you develop a fever, notice the puncture site becoming black or blue, or begin bleeding, call your doctor. This may mean that you have a broken blood vessel or an infection at the puncture site.

FNA Accuracy

Like many diagnostic procedures used to detect cancer, including Pap smears (which detect cervical cancer) and mammograms (breast imaging tests), FNA is not 100 percent accurate. Any physician, including endocrinologists and internists, surgeons, pathologists, and radiologists, can perform FNAs if they're trained in the procedure. But FNA is not an exact science. Much depends on the skills of the doctor performing the FNA, his or her ability to obtain an adequate specimen of the right area, and the experience of the pathologist reading the slide that contains the smear. As a result, there are often inconclusive results, which occur about 10 to 15 percent of the time, or even unsatisfactory results, which occur 1 to 10 percent of the time. A result that's *inconclusive* means that there's no way for the pathologist to tell whether the lump is benign or malignant.

If your care has been managed by a family doctor or internist up to this point, you may want to seek out an endocrinologist for a consultation. Sometimes the slides are sent to another pathologist who has more experience in interpreting thyroid cells (known as a *cytopathologist*). He or she can review the slides as well as interpret them. Otherwise, the rule is to either wait and repeat the FNA, or even go directly to surgery, depending upon the size and characteristics of the lump. An *unsatisfactory* FNA result means that the FNA procedure was not successful in obtaining enough thyroid cells for the pathologist to make a diagnosis (in other words, not enough "stuff" was obtained from the lump). In this case, the FNA may need to be performed by a more experienced doctor, or with the aid of ultrasound for guidance.

The tissue samples obtained through FNA have to be reviewed by a pathologist, a doctor who specializes in interpreting tissue samples. The results of an FNA are often dependent upon how much experience the pathologist has in cytology (the review of cells). In recent years, many reports about the shortage of pathologists, particularly in Canada, and their overwork have surfaced. An overworked pathologist may make errors in the interpretation of a sample. This can mean that cancerous tissue may be overlooked or not classified correctly. Or, tissue that's benign may be mistakenly labeled cancerous, which can cause unnecessary stress and trauma. It is, therefore, resource shortages, rather than the FNA technology itself, which have created limitations to the accuracy of FNA. In smaller areas, many family doctors are not trained to do FNA, which also creates problems.

Common pathology errors include:

- Calling tissue malignant (meaning cancerous) when it's benign (noncancerous). This is called a *false positive*.
- Calling tissue benign when it's malignant. This is called a *false negative*.
- Identifying the malignant tumor correctly, but not classifying it as the right cell type or grade.

- Calling inadequate FNA samples benign because no cancer cells are seen. In order to be considered benign, the slides must contain sufficient numbers of noncancerous thyroid cells to show that an adequate sample was taken.

Common problems occur when there are simply not enough cells for the pathologist to sample to determine as much information as possible. And sometimes pathologists simply can't tell if the cells are malignant.

Confirming a Pathology Report

The only way to confirm a cancer diagnosis is through a biopsy of the tissue. If you receive news that your lump is (or might be) cancerous, you should get a second pathologist with more experience to review the biopsy slides and provide an independent, separate opinion. A qualified pathologist should be board certified in anatomic pathology and based in a university teaching hospital or major cancer center. At any one time, tissue samples are crisscrossing the country via FedEx for this very purpose!

If Your Doctor Can't Perform FNA

Not all doctors are trained to do FNA. First, try to find someone with lots of experience who can perform it. Contact the Thyroid Cancer Survivors Association (ThyCa) for a referral to a trained specialist in your area if you live in a remote or underserviced area. It's worth traveling the distance to find the right doctor to perform FNA.

Diagnostic Imaging Tests

An imaging test is used to evaluate lumps to determine a few things:

- Is the lump solid or fluid-filled?
- Does the rest of the thyroid gland look normal, or are there other lumps that can't be felt?
- Are these "hot" or "cold" nodules ("working" or "not working" nodules) on the thyroid (see next section)?

To distinguish hot and cold nodules, the best imaging test is a scan that involves a small dose of radioactive iodine, which normal thyroid cells absorb and the imager picks up. Normal functioning thyroids will absorb radioactive iodine; these are known as "hot" nodules. Most benign and malignant nodules will not absorb radioactive iodine and are "cold" nodules. Also, most benign nodules are "cold" on scanning. A radioactive iodine scan involves taking pictures of your thyroid gland twenty-four hours after you ingest a small dose of radioactive iodine (called a tracer), or you may be given a simple tracer technetium by injection, which only requires a two-hour wait before imaging. Since most "hot" nodules occur in people with elevated thyroid hormone levels, scans should not be done if elevated levels are not present.

Hot Versus Cold Nodules

A "hot" nodule is a lump on the thyroid gland made up of functioning thyroid cells. Therefore, these lumps absorb the radioactive iodine eagerly. Chances are, if the nodule is functioning or "hot," it's not cancerous. In these cases, the lump found is either one of the nodules making up a multinodular goiter or is a solitary toxic adenoma.

A "cold" nodule, on the other hand, is made up of cells that have diminished ability to absorb iodine. However, only 10 percent of all cold nodules found turn out to be malignant. A cold nodule simply means that the cells making up the nodule are abnormal in that they absorb less iodine than the rest of the thyroid gland. But the nature of these cells has yet to be determined—and that can only be done through an FNA biopsy. If your scan shows the presence of only hot nodules, your doctor will probably not bother to do a biopsy because cancerous cells are rarely hot. A cold nodule merely means that it's a suspicious nodule—not necessarily cancerous. A biopsy is needed to determine whether a cold nodule is cancerous.

For people with normal levels of thyroid hormone, only FNA biopsies, not scans, should be performed.

Ultrasound

Ultrasound may be used to check structure, too, and can help to evaluate whether the lump was a cyst or solid. But today, ordering an ultrasound to evaluate thyroid nodules wouldn't typically give as much information as an FNA *unless* there was a questionable result with FNA, or a lump was difficult to see and biopsy without the aid of an ultrasound.

Types of Lumps

Let's start with the good news: 85 percent of all thyroid lumps turn out to be benign. Lumps are often benign if you discover more than one of them, or if the rest of the thyroid gland itself is enlarged. Benign lumps also tend to be fleshier and softer, like the tip of your nose. Cancerous lumps tend to be hard, like the tip of your elbow. There are many kinds of benign lumps, which could be caused by inflammation of the thyroid (thyroiditis), discussed in Chapter 2; secretions from the thyroid gland could also cause the lump (known as a *colloid nodule*). The following are other kinds of benign thyroid conditions or lumps.

Multinodular Goiter

The term *multinodular* means "many nodules," as is the case with a multinodular goiter. What happens here is that normal functioning thyroid cells grow in places they don't belong, forming lumps outside the normal boundaries of where thyroid cells usually grow. The lumps can overproduce thyroid hormone, causing thyrotoxicosis.

Adenoma

This involves glandular cells, which usually clump together in a harmless, benign lump. Since the thyroid is a gland, any benign tumor that develops in the thyroid is called an *adenoma*. When abnormal cells grow in the thyroid gland, they vary in activity. Sometimes the cells are like bumps on a log; they're lazy, inactive, and are just there without a purpose. It's as though the cells develop and then lack the drive or capability to do anything else. They don't reproduce wildly, and they don't interfere with normal thyroid function; they simply exist. These cells live in a clump, and appear as a nodule in your thyroid. Since the FNA biopsy appearance of adenomas is similar to that of a type of thyroid cancer, most of these nodules require thyroid surgery to be properly classified.

Solitary Toxic Adenoma

There can be another kind of benign growth, known as a *solitary toxic adenoma*. This is when the growth itself works overtime and produces too much thyroid hormone regardless of levels of thyroid-stimulating hormone (see Introduction). The adenoma is *toxic* (not to be confused with malignant) in this case because it causes thyrotoxicosis. The adenoma hijacks the main function of the gland and assumes full production of thyroid hormone. The pituitary gland, which regulates thyroid-stimulating hormone, gets confused by the situation and turns off. What happens then is that there's no monitoring system in place and the adenoma makes too much thyroid hormone. A solitary toxic adenoma is a type of thyroid disorder and is not malignant. It's easily treated with radioactive iodine or antithyroid medications. Most of these nodules do not get biopsied because they produce "hot" nodules on thyroid scans.

Adenocarcinoma

About 10 percent of the time, the lump will be diagnosed as an adenocarcinoma. The word *carcinoma* refers to a malignant growth that involves the epithelial cells. But when a tumor in a glandular area is malignant and stems from these epithelial cells, it's referred to as an *adenocarcinoma*. This often applies to thyroid cancer; although adenocarcinoma doesn't describe what kind of thyroid cancer you have. Very rarely, the malignant tumor is not a thyroid tumor, but one that has spread from another organ, such as the lung, breast, or kidney.

Who Gets Thyroid Cancer?

By all accounts, thyroid cancer is still considered a rare cancer, accounting for 2 percent of all cancers. It was almost unheard of by the average person in the early 1980s. But actually, thyroid cancer is now the fastest growing cancer, according to studies tracking cancer incidence (based on the number of cases per 100,000 people per year). Thyroid cancer was seen to increase at a steady rate of 6.6 percent among women and 4.2 percent among men per year. In 2001, there were 19,500 new cases of thyroid cancer in the United States, and about

1,300 deaths, according to the latest statistics available from the American Cancer Society. In fact more people were diagnosed with thyroid cancer in 2001 than with liver or brain cancer, which demonstrates that thyroid cancer ought to be considered a common cancer today.

The Fallout Story

If you follow the wind patterns from nuclear testing fallout, nuclear facilities, or even buried nuclear waste (which we may not even know about), you'll find a trail of thyroid cancer. The most common known cause of thyroid cancer is exposure to radioactive iodine, which affects the cells of the thyroid gland, causing them to mutate. A fourteen-year National Cancer Institute study, published in 1997, looked at the health risks of radioactive fallout released at the Nevada Test Site from 1951 through 1958. The study concluded that people living in the Midwestern regions of North America were more at risk for thyroid cancer, particularly if they were children during the testing. Radioactive iodine is emitted whenever fallout from nuclear accidents, testing, and, of course, atomic bombs occurs. Most unfortunately, we're seeing a tremendous increase in childhood thyroid cancer in certain "hot" areas, such as parts of Russia, Belarus, and the Ukraine exposed to fallout from the 1986 Chernobyl nuclear reactor accident, which released 40 million curies of radioactive iodine into the atmosphere. That's a lot, considering that thyroid cancer patients typically receive at least if not more than 100 millicuries, discussed in Chapter 11.

Reports of high rates of thyroid cancer are also coming in from Hanford, Washington, where residents were exposed to fallout from the Hanford nuclear facility, which produced plutonium for nuclear weapons from 1944 through 1957.

Anyone living downwind from the Nevada Test Site (residents in southwestern Utah for example) between the years 1951 and 1962 is also vulnerable to thyroid cancer. Other areas affected by fallout are the Marshall Islands in the South Pacific, as a result of atomic bomb testing at Bikini Atoll in 1954. Here, thyroid cancer occurs one hundred times more frequently than in the general population.

In the aftermath of a very long cold war, more information is slowly becoming available about just how "hot" North America, Europe, and other parts of the world really are. The predictions are that thyroid cancer incidence will continue to rise in our lifetimes. But we're seeing this trend with a variety of other cancers, too. The Oak Ridge Health Agreement Steering Panel reported that young women born in 1952 who drank milk contaminated by test fallout were more likely to develop thyroid cancer in their lifetime than women born in the northeastern United States. The Energy Research Foundation in the United States concludes that thousands of North Americans may have ingested milk that was contaminated with this fallout, and, as a result, are at greater risk for thyroid cancer.

The nuclear accident at the Chernobyl atomic power station on April 26, 1986, exposed millions of people with healthy thyroid glands to excessive levels of radioactive iodine. People living within a thirty kilometer zone of the accident inhaled the radioactive iodine, while people living outside the thirty-kilometer zone ingested the radioactive iodine. For reasons not quite understood, potassium iodide tablets (thyroid-blocking agents) weren't distributed to the public by the appropriate government agencies, except in Poland. Now, there appears to be an eightyfold increase in the incidence of thyroid cancer in children, and an increase of thyroid cancer in adults in Belarus, Russia, and the Ukraine. For example, one study out of the Ukraine found that between 1981 and 1985, the number of new cases of thyroid cancer in children from birth to fourteen years old totaled 25. But between 1986 and 1994, the number of new cases of thyroid cancer in this age-group totaled 210, with peak periods in 1992 and 1993.

Without a doubt the most infamous nuclear reactor accident was Chernobyl in 1986. Since then, another major nuclear reactor accident took place on September 29, 1999, in Tokaimura, Japan. Residents in the area were told to stay indoors with windows and vents closed in order to minimize exposure to various radioactive gases that were released. In the case of Tokaimura, radioactive iodine was released in small quantities into the air for a full week before the reactor problem was detected. By October 8, 1999, the levels of radioactive iodine released into the air were twice the allowable levels.

The fallout story makes sense once you understand how the thyroid gland works and that it needs to extract iodine from various sources because iodine is the building block it needs to make thyroid hormone. Thyroid hormone is also the building block we need to function properly. So, the thyroid gland has a sort of fatal attraction to iodine and radioactive iodine, which has the unique ability to head straight for the thyroid gland. The bottom line is this: radioactive iodine causes changes in the DNA of your healthy thyroid cells. Ironically, radioactive iodine can also be used to target and kill cancerous thyroid cells as treatment for thyroid cancer, discussed in Chapter 11.

Preventing Thyroid Cancers Caused by Fallout

We can only prevent thyroid cancers that are directly caused by radioactive fallout. There's a blocking agent, potassium iodide, that can prevent radioactive iodine from being absorbed by the thyroid gland. This is the only specific way to protect against thyroid cancer triggered by radioactive iodine fallout; potassium iodide has no protective effect against any other kind of radiation.

In this age of terrorism, people are nervous about potential nuclear terrorism, and potassium iodide is available through pharmacies. However, if a nuclear attack occurred, thyroid cancer would, of course, be the least of your worries. To be effective, potassium iodide must be dispensed just prior to being exposed to radioactive iodine, and then continued for the duration of the exposure. This is pretty difficult to do unless an accident or incident is predicted in advance, or the air path of a specific accident is tracked and therefore anticipated. And potassium iodide is not designed as a long-term therapy because of side effects that occur with prolonged use. Complications include serious allergic reactions, skin rashes, and thyroid disorders (like hypothyroidism or hyperthyroidism).

In pregnant women, long-term use of potassium iodide can also cause the fetus to develop a goiter. For the last forty years, various government agencies around the world have monitored the amount of radioactive iodine in the air. And for many years, they've detected low levels of radioactive iodine fallout as a result of nuclear testing or reactor problems. Emergency plans for potassium iodide distribution in European countries require pills or tablets to be predistributed to households within three miles of nuclear plants, and possibly to households within six miles. Tablets also are to be stored at central locations, such as schools, factories, and town halls, for quick distribution within fifteen and a half miles of plants. Since 1982, households within about nine miles of four nuclear plants have received tablets. Every five years, regional authorities repeat the distribution, to approximately fifty thousand households, through the mail.

Distribution of potassium iodide in the United States remains controversial, but is being revisited in light of 9/11. To date, the Three Mile Island accident was the most serious nuclear reactor accident to have occurred in North America. Twenty years later, state and federal officials are still debating potassium iodide's costs and benefits. After the accident, a presidential commission strongly recommended stockpiling the drug near all U.S. reactor sites, but it was subsequently found that the average population exposure from radioactive iodine following Three Mile Island was very small—much less radiation than a chest x-ray, and thousands of times less than a routine diagnostic I-131 uptake test. Because of these findings, and the possible effects of radioactive iodine, both the American and Canadian Food and Drug Administrations haven't released potassium iodide as a drug for thyroid blocking, except to state/province and local governments who stockpile it for emergency use. Even then, access is limited. The U.S. Nuclear Regulatory Commission (NRC) at one point endorsed stockpiling potassium iodide for any state that wanted it, but then reversed this decision because of budget concerns. When the NRC approached the Federal Emergency Management Agency (FEMA) to cover the costs of stockpiling potassium iodide, FEMA would not. So, many residents are now living in states with no stockpiles (or access to) potassium iodide, which would protect them from thyroid cancer in the event of a nuclear accident. As of this writing, Tennessee, Alabama, Arizona, Maine, California, and Ohio have potassium iodide stashes for the areas around and downwind from nuclear power plants.

The X-Ray Story

In other cases, radiation to the head and neck area from high-dose x-rays (common from the 1940s through the 1970s) during childhood or adolescence can cause thyroid cancer to develop later in life. In the 1940s and 1950s, x-ray therapy was commonly used to treat infants with enlarged thymus glands (which were falsely believed to cause crib death) and children with enlarged adenoids and tonsils. X-ray therapy was also used to treat facial acne in teenagers, birthmarks, whooping cough, scalp ringworm, and sometimes as a means to improve hearing for the deaf.

The practice of using x-rays began in the 1920s, peaked in the 1940s and 1950s, and then slowly petered out by the 1960s. The treatment was administered in one of two ways. One way involved an x-ray machine (called *external beam radiation*); the other way involved placing radioactive material such as radium directly in or on the tissue to be treated. The immediate results were often promising. For example, acne improved, while acne scarring was reduced, and some forms of deafness were improved. (Enlarged lymph tissue would sometimes block the inner ear and cause deafness; radiation was used to shrink the lymph tissue and improve hearing.) However, the long-term consequences of x-ray treatment canceled out any short-term benefits. Unlike laser treatments, x-ray treatments weren't concentrated onto one small area but also irradiated surrounding areas.

Since the thyroid gland is located in the center of the neck, x-rays beamed at the face (to treat acne), chest (to treat asthma, pneumonia, and even hyperthyroidism), adenoids, tonsils, thymus gland, ears, or scalp were also targeting the thyroid gland. By the 1950s, doctors began to notice an increase in benign and malignant nodules on the thyroid glands of patients who had previously been treated with x-rays. Then, by the late 1950s and early 1960s, it was found that many victims of the atomic bomb in Hiroshima and Nagasaki were developing malignant tumors on their thyroid glands.

X-rays were also widely used in the 1930s and 1940s to determine fetal positions in prenatal care. This was known as *pelvimetry*, and unfortunately exposed the fetal tissue to radiation. Let's also not forget the radiation used to treat congenital heart problems, as well as those standard TB exams most employers demanded between 1920 and 1960. Much of the radiation therapy between the 1920s and 1960s was probably poorly documented, meaning that there was more exposure than was recorded.

Thyroid cancer is not the only cancer caused by exposure to x-rays. In his controversial book *Preventing Breast Cancer: The Story of a Major, Proven, Preventable Cause of This Disease*, John W. Gofman, M.D., Ph.D., concludes that about 75 percent of breast cancer cases are largely due to past medical-related radiation.

It's estimated that millions of people throughout North America, Europe, and the United Kingdom received these treatments in the past.

(In the United States alone, over two million people are estimated to have received them.) Generally, benign thyroid nodules and thyroid cancer have been discovered in people anywhere from ten to sixty years following x-ray therapy.

It's important to note that not all people exposed to radiation develop thyroid cancer. Thyroid cancer experts maintain that most people who are diagnosed with thyroid cancer have no known exposure to radiation. But my opinion is that all of us living in this toxic soup called Earth have been exposed to countless carcinogens (meaning cancer-causing agents) if we were born after 1945. The fact that some of these carcinogens trip our "cancer genes," or *oncogenes*, is how genetics may play a role in thyroid cancer.

The Gene Story

There is only one type of thyroid cancer that's sometimes known to be absolutely genetic in the absence of an external or environmental trigger: this is called *medullary thyroid cancer*. But there are also certain types of thyroid cancers that are believed to have a hereditary link. Thyroid cancer falls under the general category of endocrine cancers, and some researchers believe that people who come from a family where other endocrine cancers (such as ovarian or adrenal cancer) seem to strike may be particularly vulnerable to thyroid cancers. In addition some genetic syndromes associated with colon polyps also have papillary thyroid cancers, and new studies show family clusters of this cancer.

To date, we don't know of a "thyroid cancer gene" that absolutely predicts thyroid cancer, other than the gene causing inherited medullary thyroid cancer, which is quite distinct from the more common types of thyroid cancer. We are living in an age, however, where other types of cancer genes are being found, such as breast cancer genes and colon cancer genes. In these cases, finding a cancer gene is not necessarily meaningful information, since there's a wide range of varied effects of these genes in causing cancer. And frequently, there is nothing one can reasonably do to prevent the cancer for which the gene is a marker, although lifestyle changes can help to prevent certain cancers. For example, lung cancer, which tops the charts, would be almost completely eradicated if people stopped smoking—even if they were genetically wired for it. Additionally, many cancers are triggered by environmental factors, which turn on various genes. That's how it normally works.

But the gene for inherited medullary thyroid cancer is different. This is one of the few cases when having the gene almost guarantees that you will develop inherited medullary thyroid cancer. In this case, genetic screening can be a useful tool in predicting who may develop this type of thyroid cancer because it can also be used to prevent this type of cancer (someone who tests positive for the gene will have a total thyroidectomy, thus removing the threat). If you or someone in your family has had medullary thyroid cancer, it's recommended that the person being treated for thyroid cancer see a genetic counselor to discuss the benefits of screening for this disease to prevent cancer in the rest of the family.

Types of Thyroid Cancer

The majority of thyroid cancers are either papillary or follicular, or subtypes of each. The words *papillary* and *follicular* refer to both the physical shape and personality of the cancer cells, as well as the behavior of the cells. In general, papillary cancer is more likely to spread to lymph nodes in the neck, and follicular cancer is more aggressive with spread to distant sites, such as lung and bone. In other words, follicular is often a more dangerous kind of cancer. This kind of cancer is extremely treatable and has an excellent survival rate, however. The "standard issue" thyroid cancer is papillary cancer. For women under fifty and men under forty, the cure rate is quite high. In the worst-case scenario, this cancer has a much smaller chance of recurrence, and a history of only less than 5 percent death rate. This is why many people think of it as "the good cancer."

The "Good Cancer"

Since the 1940s, the most common types of thyroid cancer (papillary, follicular, or a mix of the two) have been completely treatable 95 percent of the time. The reason is that papillary and follicular thyroid cancers grow relatively slowly compared to other kinds of cancers, such as colon, prostate, or breast cancer. In essence, most types of thyroid cancers take a very long time to spread. In fact, you could conceivably walk around with undiagnosed thyroid cancer for a decade and still respond well to treatment.

Second, radioactive iodine (discovered in the 1940s) can often eradicate and/or control the growth of thyroid cancer. In a way, radioactive iodine is close to a "miracle cure" for thyroid cancer. So the first thing most people diagnosed with thyroid cancer hear is, "This is a good cancer." But because it's a "good cancer," there has been an assumption that thyroid cancer patients do not suffer and do not need the same level of psychosocial support as other cancer patients. Thyroid cancer patients go through a great deal of treatment to become and remain cancer free. So hearing that you've got a "good cancer" is not that comforting when you're struggling to fight cancer.

The "good cancer" line is also deceiving, especially when we know that some people do die from thyroid cancer, particularly those who are diagnosed with a rare form known as *anaplastic thyroid cancer*. Also, in some cases, "well-differentiated" (more treatable) thyroid cancers can become more aggressive or "poorly differentiated" with time.

The majority of the thyroid cancer stories go like this: the thyroid cancer is usually caught in a primary or secondary stage. In the primary stage, a malignant nodule or lump is found on the thyroid gland; in the secondary stage, a malignant nodule is found somewhere on the neck, invading surrounding tissues, or in a lymph node nearby, which is traced to the thyroid gland. Therefore, in a secondary stage, the thyroid cancer has already spread beyond the thyroid gland. Thyroid cancer can also spread into the lungs and bone, but this is unusual. Essentially, it's misleading to call thyroid cancer a "good cancer" when it's a type of cancer demonstrating the full range of behavior, from slow-growing, treatable cancers to one of the most aggressive types of cancers.

Common Types of Thyroid Cancers

Papillary tumors account for more than 75 percent of all thyroid cancers. The ten-year survival rate remains at 80 to 90 percent, meaning that ten years after this diagnosis, 80 to 90 percent of people diagnosed with papillary thyroid cancer are still alive.

Once you get papillary cancers under a microscope, things get a little more complicated because there are variations on types of papillary cancers. There are subtypes of thyroid cancer tumors—and some cell variants that can make the normally slow-growing papillary a little more aggressive. Having a *tall cell* variant of papillary thyroid cancer means you have a cancer that spreads more rapidly, and has a greater chance to lose the ability to suck up iodine.

Roughly 10 percent of all thyroid cancers are purely follicular. This type of thyroid cancer tends to strike people over forty more frequently than younger adults, and is not a type of thyroid cancer that commonly occurs as a direct result of radiation exposure. Age is the most important factor in figuring out how treatable follicular thyroid cancer is. If you are under forty, follicular thyroid cancer tends to be less aggressive than in people over forty; this is because it responds better to radioactive iodine therapy in younger people.

Hurthle cell thyroid cancer is a type of follicular thyroid cancer. This is an unusual type of tumor that's less common than follicular cancer, making up only 4 percent of all thyroid cancers.

Uncommon Types of Thyroid Cancers

As discussed earlier, there is a type of thyroid cancer called *medullary cancer*, a subtype of which is inherited. Medullary thyroid cancer accounts for less than one out of ten cases of thyroid cancer found in the United States each year. Roughly one-third of patients with medullary thyroid cancer have inherited a defective (mutant) gene which causes this cancer and may be passed on to other family members. The other people with this cancer develop medullary thyroid cancer without having this inherited gene.

Medullary thyroid cancer can often be very slow-growing, but is considered potentially very dangerous because there aren't any effective ways to treat this cancer if it spreads outside of the neck. Sometimes it can be more aggressive and grow more rapidly, spreading to many parts of the body. The *RET proto-oncogene test* has been extremely important in helping with this cancer. If you test positive for this inherited medullary thyroid cancer gene, the recommendation is to have what's called a *prophylactic thyroidectomy*, meaning a preventive removal of the entire thyroid gland.

Anaplastic thyroid cancer accounts for a paltry 1.6 percent of all thyroid cancers, which translates into about three hundred cases in the United States per year. However, it is an aggressive, wildly undifferentiated cancer that has no real cure. Indeed, thyroid cancer is unusual in that it represents both the "best" and "worst" kind of cancers in terms of treatability.

Different people can be diagnosed with the same kind of thyroid cancer, but their treatments will depend on the stage of the cancer. To complicate matters, we also know that some cancers, such as tall cell papillary, are more aggressive and may require more aggressive therapy. Most thyroid cancers have four stage classifications that basically answer the question, where has it spread?

General Treatment for Thyroid Cancer

Papillary thyroid cancers that are one centimeter or less in size (less than half an inch), exist as a single tumor within the thyroid gland, and show no evidence of any spread to the neck or elsewhere, can be treated with surgery alone (usually removal of half of the thyroid, a *lobectomy*). These small papillary cancers do not require radioactive iodine scans or treatments. Many physicians will have you take sufficient amounts of thyroid hormone (T4) to keep the TSH slightly less than normal, although some people may not be told to take any thyroid hormone at all.

All other papillary cancers and all follicular thyroid cancers of any size require a total (or near total) removal of the thyroid and removal of any lymph nodes in the neck likely to contain tumor cells.

This is followed by radioactive iodine (RAI) therapy, followed by nuclear medicine tests using small RAI doses to search for the recurrence of tumors with whole body scanning. Usually, by six months after the first RAI treatment, a whole body scan (see Chapter 11) and a blood test that checks for a specific protein, thyroglobulin, is done, to make sure that all evidence of thyroid cancer is gone. If so, then these assessments are repeated with longer and longer intervals between them.

If not, then the RAI treatment is repeated (no closer than five to six months apart) until all the tests show you to be free of tumors.

For medullary thyroid cancers, and for those papillary and follicular cancers that are persistent and unresponsive to RAI, there are no definitive treatments aside from surgery. In some situations, external beam radiotherapy can be used; however, tumors that have spread beyond the neck are rarely treatable with current methods. Anaplastic thyroid cancers are both rare and extremely dangerous, requiring immediate involvement of specialist physicians from the earliest moment that they are discovered. (Your doctor can telephone these specialists for a consultation.)

Further, more detailed information about the various types of thyroid cancer and their treatments can be found in *The Thyroid Cancer Book* (available online at www.thyroidcancerbook.com).

11

Thyroid Tests, Treatments, and Self-Care

UNDERSTANDING THE PURPOSE and meaning of the diagnostic tests that can evaluate your thyroid health, the treatment, and follow-up care is the key to managing your thyroid condition and staying healthy. In addition, there are numerous complementary and self-care strategies that can improve your well-being before, during, and after a thyroid problem has been resolved. This chapter outlines all of these issues.

What the Doctor Orders

What diagnostic tests and therapies can you expect to undergo to assess and treat your thyroid condition and monitor how well you have responded to therapy?

Blood Tests

If you are suffering from hyperthyroidism, often the signs are obvious, and a simple TSH test measuring thyroid-stimulating hormone levels in your blood will confirm the diagnosis. TSH levels will read below normal, while thyroid hormone levels are elevated. Sometimes, if a patient knows that thyroid disease runs in the family, the doctor will regularly check thyroid function via blood test and can detect hyper-thyroidism before any onset of blatant symptoms. But when the symptoms of hyperthyroidism are not recognized, and the patient notices only subtle differences such as irritability or fatigue, misdiagnosis can also occur.

The appropriate blood tests are those that check your free T4 (FT4, in lab-speak) levels and your TSH. The term *free* refers to unattached thyroid hormone that travels in your bloodstream. Every hormone in our body tends to be bound, or attached, to a chemical protein in our blood. The bound hormone is inactive, while the free hormone is active. That's why it's crucial to measure free and, hence, active hormone. If your doctor is ordering an older test called a *total T4* (TT4, in lab-speak), this should be combined with a T3 resin uptake test, which determines the ratio of free hormone. For the record, total T4 tests are considered obsolete and have been replaced with free T4 tests. Any doctor ordering a TT4 should be asked why. To confirm or rule out an autoimmune disease such as Graves' disease or Hashimoto's thyroiditis (discussed in Chapter 9), you will be tested for antithyroid antibodies, which are also called *thyroid-stimulating antibodies.*

If you are suffering from hypothyroidism, the TSH blood test can also determine low levels of thyroid hormone by rising as the result of even minimal reductions in thyroid hormone production. Another blood test, called *anti-TPO antibodies* (antithyroid peroxidase antibodies) can also detect the presence of antibodies in your bloodstream that point to an autoimmune disorder; this would be the test that could confirm Hashimoto's thyroiditis, for example.

Most people feel best when their TSH readings are between 1 and 3 (the normal range is 0.5 to 5). It is critical to note that many women who complain of persistent hypothyroid symptoms in spite of a "normal" TSH test are likely higher than 3. All thyroid experts who are up-to-date recognize that lower TSH targets are the key to quality of life for women dependent on thyroid hormone replacement. The original targets (the 0.5 to 5 range) are based on males in older studies (women until recently were banned from clinical studies as an ethical protection due to previous abuses). It is also postulated that some of the men were also subclinically hypothyroid, which drove up the range. So you should be requesting the lab results—in numbers—of your TSH test before you accept that it is "normal" and are sent home. If your TSH is 2 or under and you still feel "hypothyroid" it's clear that your symptoms are due to other factors, which could include depression or normal fatigue caused by sleep deprivation or stress (see Chapter 3).

A TSH of 5 or over will mean that you are probably suffering from hypothyroid symptoms, while a TSH of under 0.5 may mean that you are suffering from thyrotoxic symptoms. If you've had thyroid cancer, your TSH levels should be zero (0) to prevent a recurrence of the cancer (see "If You've Had Thyroid Cancer" subhead in the "Thyroid Hormone Replacement" section).

Radioactive Iodine Testing

Radioactive is the adjective used to describe elements containing unstable atoms—or atoms that are emitting energy and, hence, releasing radiation. A radioactive element is called an *isotope*. Radioactive iodine is used in thyroid testing, and is the standard form of treatment given exclusively to patients who are either hyperthyroid—from diseases such as Graves' disease (see Chapter 9)—or who are diagnosed with thyroid cancer (see Chapter 10). It is also used as a tracer for certain diagnostic tests.

The Uptake Test: Testing Function

A common test to check thyroid function is known as the *radioactive iodine uptake* test. This is reserved for hyperthyroid patients only and may help to pinpoint how abnormal the thyroid is. (Blood tests such as the TSH test, discussed above, are still the most accurate method for determining levels of hypothyroidism.) Abnormality is determined by reading how much radioactive iodine is absorbed by the thyroid. This is a twenty-four-hour test.

When you come to the hospital on the day prior to the test, you will be given a minuscule amount of radioactive iodine. It may be in the form of a capsule or waterlike liquid. You ingest the iodine and go home. You are usually (but not always) given instructions that tell how to reduce the risk of radiation exposure to others around you.

There is more than one isotope or recipe of radioactive iodine available, but isotopes with an atomic weight of either 123 or 131 (usually referred to as I-123 or I-131) are the ones most widely used. At any rate, the test is known as the *I-131 uptake test*. The next day, you return to the hospital and sit in front of a huge cameralike instrument. A conelike device is brought right up to your neck area, and the machine then measures the amount of radioactive iodine absorbed by your thyroid by counting the radioactive emissions. This instrument is known as a *scintillation*, or *counting probe* (see Figure 11.1).

If your thyrotoxicosis is caused by an overproduction of thyroid hormone (hyperthyroid), your uptake, or absorption, of the radioactive iodine is high (usually more than 30 percent in twenty-four hours). If you are thyrotoxic but your uptake is low, your thyrotoxicosis is probably caused by either an overdose of thyroid replacement hormone or some sort of inflammation in the thyroid.

If you are hypothyroid, this test is not appropriate. It usually shows nothing more than a blood test would, and so it is never used.

It's important to note that the medical philosophy regarding radioactive iodine uptake tests has shifted dramatically since the early

Figure 11.1 A radioactive iodine uptake test.

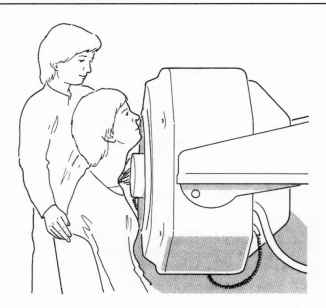

Reprinted from *Nichts Gutes im Schilde Krankheiten der Schiddruse.* Copyright 1994, Georg Thieme Publishing.

1990s. Many endocrinologists now believe that radioactive iodine uptake tests should be reserved only to determine why you have a goiter, why you have a lump on your thyroid gland, whether a lump on your thyroid gland is cancerous, and sometimes, to determine the cause of hyperthyroidism if you test negative for Graves' disease antibodies. To order this test to simply confirm hyperthyroidism or determine "how hyperthyroid you are" is considered a waste of time and money. If your free T4 readings are high and your TSH readings are low, you are hyperthyroid. Period.

The only time thyroid hormone readings are difficult to interpret is when you're pregnant, on oral contraceptives, or taking certain medications that may interfere with thyroid hormone readings.

The Imaging Test: Testing Structure

The *thyroid imaging test* is similar to the uptake test. The basic difference between an uptake test and an imaging test is that the uptake test measures thyroid performance, while the imaging test measures form. Also a twenty-four-hour test, the purpose of an imaging test is to check for "hot" or "cold" nodules of the thyroid or to show if the entire gland takes up radioactive iodine.

An imaging test is also done to check the success of a thyroidectomy procedure performed for thyroid cancer to verify how much (if any) thyroid tissue or thyroid cancer tissue is still left in your body. Again, you are given a "tracer" of radioactive iodine (I-131 or I-123). Usually a slightly higher dosage is required for this test. When you return to the hospital the day after ingesting the tracer, you will lie down under a large camera or imager that takes pictures of your entire body (known as a *whole body scan*). The iodine absorption is visible in the pictures, and your doctor can tell by the images where residual thyroid or thyroid cancer is present.

If you are being given this test as a follow-up to a thyroidectomy (usually performed only in the event of thyroid cancer), your doctor will take you off your thyroid replacement hormone. This is done to deliberately induce a hypothyroid state and trigger the release of thyroid-stimulating hormone (TSH) into your blood. TSH will stimulate cancerous tissue to absorb iodine, making the test far more sensitive. A similar thing is also done if you are being treated for thyroid cancer with radioactive iodine.

Depending on your condition and the hospital, TC pertechnetate, a more convenient tracer, may be used instead of I-131 or I-123 for both the uptake and imaging tests. When TC pertechnetate is used, your thyroid is exposed to less radiation than would occur with I-123, for example, and the tests can be performed only twenty minutes after the tracer is administered. This is not as specific for thyroid disease as is radioactive iodine; however, it is less expensive for diagnostic studies.

Ablating the Thyroid Gland

In cases such as Graves' disease, for example, radioactive iodine is used to *ablate* or "kill" the overactive thyroid gland—the source of your hyperthyroidism. A by-product of this treatment may well be hypothyroidism, because once your thyroid gland is destroyed, of course, it can no longer produce thyroid hormone. It's a "feast or famine" situation. This is very easily remedied, though. Once the gland no longer functions, you're immediately put on thyroid replacement hormone (to be taken daily) to bring you back to the *euthyroid*, or normal, state.

The treatment for Graves' disease is similar to the first stage of the diagnostic tests described earlier, only you're given a far more potent dose of radioactive iodine. A *curie* is the unit of measurement for radioactive substances. Doses of radioactive iodine are administered in either *millicuries* (one-thousandth of a curie) or *microcuries* (one-millionth of a curie).

A typical dose of radioactive iodine for treatment of Graves' disease would consist of anything between 3 to 20 millicuries, while a radioactive iodine tracer for an uptake test would consist of anything between 4 and 6 microcuries. A tracer for an imaging test (or scan) would range between 20 and 50 microcuries. A dosage over 30 millicuries often requires hospitalization, but dosages for treatment of Graves' disease rarely reach these levels of potency. You are usually sent home immediately after treatment but must observe the rules outlined to avoid exposing others around you to the radiation you have received.

For hyperthyroidism, usually just a single dose is required. And it's totally painless, regardless of whether you're given a capsule or liquid. Only in very high dosages (over 30 millicuries) would you feel any discomfort. With a higher dosage you might feel some tenderness in your neck. Sometimes a high dosage affects the salivary glands and causes your mouth to feel drier after the treatment. But that's really it. You're rechecked (through a blood test, usually) at six weeks, three months, nine months, and then annually.

This brings us to one of the most misunderstood aspects of radioactive treatment. Many thyroid patients believe (or are told by others) that when hypothyroidism sets in after treatment, it means you've had an "overdose" of radioactive iodine. This is just plain wrong! The *point* of radioactive iodine therapy is to ablate, or destroy, the thyroid gland. This will eliminate your hyperthyroidism permanently. So if you are hypothyroid after this treatment—good! That means it worked, and you will not have to repeat the therapy. To restore thyroid hormone, all you need to do is take a pill, something I discuss at great length in the next section.

Now, some doctors enjoy the challenge of administering just the right amount of radioactive iodine to cure the hyperthyroidism without making you hypothyroid. This is a hotly debated issue. Many doctors feel this approach is fruitless due to the nature of autoimmune thyroid disease. For most cases of Graves' disease, the thyroid gland will continue to overproduce thyroid hormone no matter how precise a radioactive dosage you have gotten. (Treatment for thyroid cancer has different goals, which are discussed in Chapter 10.)

It's also important to note that radioactive iodine does not go to work immediately on your hyperthyroidism. In other words, your symptoms are not going to disappear overnight. It takes at least four to six weeks, and often closer to three months, for the treatment to decrease the size of your thyroid gland as well as thyroid hormone secretion. Fifteen percent of all patients treated with radioactive iodine for hyperthyroidism will need a second dose, while 5 percent may even need a third helping. Ultimately, the majority of those who receive this treatment for hyperthyroidism will become hypothyroid (a sign that you are cured), and will then need to be on thyroid hormone replacement for life in order to return to a normal thyroid state. Generally, most people treated with radioactive iodine can expect to be hypothyroid in ten years. That's why it's very important to have regular thyroid function tests every six months or so.

Misinformation about the safety of radioactive iodine abounds. Patients who have received this therapy (including me, for thyroid cancer) have been followed since the 1950s and have not developed higher rates of cancer compared to the general population. If your doctor tells you otherwise, he or she is just not knowledgeable on the current literature. Earlier studies suggested that one could expect five cases of leukemia per thousand patients treated with 500 millicuries of radioactive iodine—an almost unheard of amount. Essentially, stating that you're likely to develop leukemia after a standard 100-millicurie dose of radioactive iodine is as logical as saying, "Your chances of being hit by lightning may increase after this therapy."

What is true, however, is that if you have had one endocrine cancer, you are statistically at increased risk for other endocrine cancers such as breast cancer. But this has nothing to do with radioactive iodine and probably more to do with your genes and family history.

The only other risk known at present is the effect of radioactive iodine therapy on the salivary glands. There seems to be an increase in salivary gland inflammation (called sialoadenitis) following this therapy. Some experts recommend sucking on lemons or sour candy following the therapy to get your salivary glands working and stimulated; however, no one has ever studied whether this is in fact helpful. Other options for treating Graves' disease are antithyroid drugs (see Chapter 9), and in mild cases with no symptoms, potentially allowing Graves' disease to run its course. For those with thyroid eye disease, use of steroids with RAI will prevent a worsening of TED after RAI therapy. Indeed, many Graves' patients who have received radioactive iodine were not given complete information or an opportunity to discuss the pros and cons of treatment options. As a result, a lot of misinformation surrounding potential, unestablished risks of radioactive iodine have amassed on the Internet by patients who regret their decision (for many unfounded reasons). For more information about radioactive iodine therapy for Graves' disease, see www.ngdr.com.

Killing Cancer Cells

For thyroid cancer treatment, much higher doses of RAI are required. A typical tracer dose of RAI is about 2 to 5 millicuries; a typical treatment dose of RAI for thyroid cancer ranges from 100 to 200 millicuries. The amount given depends on the aggressiveness of the thyroid cancer, its ability to take up iodine, and how much cancer was removed during surgery. It's important to note that not all thyroid experts agree about how much radioactive iodine is needed to destroy leftover thyroid tissue, or remnant tissue. Some people may receive a dose as low as 29 millicuries, which in the past was the maximum outpatient dose one could receive without requiring a stay in isolation in the hospital. Thyroid cancer experts now consider this too small a therapeutic dose. Rather than prescribe RAI doses to save hospitals the expense of isolation, the trend is to provide the most effective treatment, which means that most people ought to expect an RAI treatment dose exceeding 100 millicuries. And if tumors are discovered outside of the neck region, it's often appropriate to give very high RAI doses, often exceeding 200 millicuries. Administration of such high doses requires distinct expertise (which could necessitate traveling to specialized centers) and techniques of *dosimetry* that permit the physician to calculate the highest RAI dose that can be given safely.

After you receive a treatment dose of radioactive iodine, there's enough radioactivity coming off of your body, in the form of radioactive iodine in your sweat and saliva as well as x-ray energy, to be a potential source of exposure to others. Depending upon the local regulations of your hospital, dosages ranging from 30 to 150 millicuries may require you to be kept in an isolation room at your hospital. The main reason you're isolated is to comply with public policy regulations and reduce exposure of other people to unnecessary radiation, rather than prevent danger to your dog, cat, or husband. Most nuclear medicine specialists find the isolation rules, which you'll read further on, a bit overly restrictive because the actual risks are quite theoretical and unlikely to ever cause harm to others.

Radioactive iodine doesn't hang around too long in your body because most of it gets excreted through urine. It doesn't really "stick" to any part of the body aside from the thyroid cancer cells. The effective *half-life* is the time that it takes for one-half of the radioactivity to go away. It's a combination of the physical half-life (eight days for iodine-131) and the biological half-life (under two days for a person after a thyroidectomy). The effective half-life is usually two to three days, and sufficient radiation leaves your body to allow you to go home in one to three days, depending on the hospital's policies and the dosage given.

Side Effects

Although most people feel no real side effects after RAI therapy for thyroid cancer, the following side effects are reported:

- *Sore throat/hoarseness.* (Or swelling under the ears and jaw, which resembles mumps.) This is usually due to swollen salivary glands as a result of the radiation. Sucking on sour candy or lemons might help prevent this from occurring although this has never been directly tested or studied. The area around the remaining thyroid tissue can also become tender because of dying thyroid cells.
- *Nausea/vomiting.* This is usually caused by your own anxiety and stress over the RAI, which can even induce a panic attack. You can take medication to help with this, and see Chapter 3 for more information on dealing with anxiety and panic. If you vomit after having RAI, it will have to be cleaned up by a special radiation safety team.
- *Headache.* Could be caused by stress; probably not by RAI. Plain Tylenol without codeine is best.
- *Diarrhea.* Diarrhea can be caused by nerves and stress. The more frequently you move your bowels, and the looser they are, the more RAI will clear your system. Keep drinking to avoïd dehydration and don't attempt to treat your diarrhea until the RAI is cleared from your system (this takes about forty-eight hours). Also try the BRAT diet: bananas, rice, applesauce, and tea.
- *Constipation.* Constipation is not a good thing after RAI. And it may be the state of affairs if you're hypothyroid. If you haven't had a bowel movement after twelve hours, take a laxative (thyroid cancer experts recommend milk of magnesia during RAI treatment). An herbal laxative with cascara segrada is highly effective, and although it's a stimulant laxative, it's not as habit forming as others. Taking fiber is not advised.

Getting Clearance

Large doses, as mentioned previously, require you to be isolated in a private hospital room. No visitors should come without a really good reason; in that case, your hospital will have its own specific rules.

All meals, bedding, and towels will be provided; you may be asked to make your own bed to avoid exposing hospital staff. Some people find this time relaxing—especially if life is hectic. It's forced R & R. You should be advised to change into your hospital gear before the RAI is administered; that way you don't have to worry about your clothing being "hot" (exposed to radiation). Have someone bring you to the hospital, change in the room, and either hand your clothes to your support person or keep them in a closet in the room. When you're picked up, you can just remove the hospital gown, shower, and change into fresh clothes. The amount of time you spend in the hospital is based on the amount of RAI you were given.

While in the hospital, you may be required to urinate into a special container that fits like a "pottie" over the toilet bowl; alternatively, you may simply be required to use the bathroom in the room and flush twice. Men will be asked to sit down when they urinate to avoid splashes. In other hospitals, staff may check you with a handheld dosimeter or enter your room and check your urine with a Geiger counter to determine the amount of radioactivity released (based on how much RAI you were given). Once your levels of radiation are safe enough for others to be exposed to you, you're allowed to go home, so long as you practice your posttreatment precautions for the next ten days.

The reason for these precautions is to prevent the exposure of others through your saliva, sweat, mucus, urine, feces, or other bodily secretions, as well as x-rays coming from the RAI still in your body. You should minimize contact with pregnant women or small children because children, infants, and fetuses are more sensitive to radiation exposure. You should use nonporous dishes and cutlery, and wash them before others handle them. You should abstain from all sexual activity (including kissing), sleep alone, and wash your linens and clothing separately after use. After a typical laundry cycle, both the clothing and the washing machine are free of radioactivity. You should use a separate hairbrush, comb, towel, and facecloth, as well as a separate toilet-paper roll. Using a damp paper tissue, wipe the toilet seat and sink bowl after each use, flushing the tissue down the toilet.

After you use the toilet, you should wash your hands carefully and flush two to three times. If you use the telephone, you must wipe the mouthpiece with a damp tissue after use. Showering two or three times a day as well as washing your hair will help wash away radioactive perspiration. If you prepare food for others, wear rubber gloves to prevent your perspiration from getting in their food.

The Rules to Live by for Ten Days

- Minimize contact with small children or pregnant women.
- Use separate towels and sheets; wash separately.
- Wash your clothes and underwear separately.
- Flush toilet two or three times after use.
- If you're a man, sit to urinate like a woman.
- Do not share your bodily fluids in any way.

In some cases, external beam radiation therapy is used in thyroid cancer therapy following radioactive iodine therapy. (For more information about radioactive iodine and other treatments for thyroid cancer, consult *The Thyroid Cancer Book*, which can be obtained online at www.thyroidcancerbook.com.)

Whole Body Scans

A whole body scan is necessary after a thyroidectomy to check for remnants of thyroid cancer cells throughout your body, and to determine whether you need radioactive iodine therapy as a treatment. There's also a blood test known as the *thyroglobulin test* (*Tg test*), which is used to detect whether there are any remaining thyroid cancer cells; this blood test only works if you've had a total thyroidectomy and RAI treatment, and is even more sensitive if you're prepared to go off your thyroid hormone medication or are injected with artificial TSH (Thyrogen). If thyroglobulin is detectable, it's a sign of recurrence.

Preparing for follow-up scans after thyroid cancer involves going on a low iodine diet (LID), and either going off thyroid hormone replacement to increase the body's own natural thyroid-stimulating hormone (TSH) or taking artificially produced human TSH (Thyrogen) to stimulate RAI uptake in thyroid cancer cells without the necessity of becoming hypothyroid (see the following section, "Thyrogen Scans"). Typically, whole body scans involve going off thyroid hormone for four to six weeks to deliberately induce a hypothyroid state, causing your TSH levels to increase to more than 30 mIU per liter, which would stimulate any thyroid cancer cells left to "stand and be counted" by absorbing the radioactive iodine. This is known as the *withdrawal scan*. The same thing is done when you're given radioactive iodine (RAI) as a treatment for thyroid cancer.

Withdrawal scans are planned at least six weeks in advance. This is because it takes this length of time for the thyroid hormone levels to be totally depleted. The first four weeks are made tolerable by taking a short-acting form of thyroid hormone, liothyronine (Cytomel), twice daily. In the final two weeks, the low iodine diet is started and you're advised to avoid driving or similar skilled activities because you're quite slow and tired. A small radioactive iodine *scan dose* is then given and a nuclear scan performed from one to three days later. Should the scan show residual thyroid tissue or evidence of thyroid cancer anywhere in your body, you're already prepared to be treated with a treatment dose of radioactive iodine. Although it's uncomfortable to be hypothyroid since all bodily functions are slowed down, this allows the radioactive iodine to be taken up by any thyroid cancer cells. Following this, you resume your usual thyroid hormone dose and diet.

Thyrogen Scans

An alternative way of preparing for a thyroid scan after a thyroidectomy, for patients who are considered likely to be free of residual cancer, uses Thyrogen, a synthetic thyroid-stimulating hormone, to substitute for the natural TSH produced by withdrawal of thyroid hormone. This method is used for follow-up assessments after conventional withdrawal scans have been negative for evidence of cancer, and it's far more comfortable for you.

The Low-Iodine Diet

The low-iodine diet is a diet in which you avoid all of the iodine-containing foods discussed in Chapter 1. Low-iodine diets are usually started about two weeks prior to a scan or treatment with RAI. Iodine from food can interfere with the sensitivity and accuracy of RAI scans or treatment. By avoiding iodine prior to RAI scanning or treatment, you can maximize the results.

When Your Doctor Tells You to Take a Pill

When you are taking thyroid medication, you are either on thyroid replacement hormone for life to compensate for a hypothyroid condition (often the result of treatment for hyperthyroidism) or you are taking antithyroid medication to control hyperthyroidism. Depending on your condition, age, sex, weight, and lifestyle habits, your doctor will recommend one of these two forms of medication.

Thyroid Hormone Replacement

In the United States, more than fifteen million prescriptions of thyroid hormone per year are sold. Even if only part of your thyroid gland was surgically removed, thyroid hormone replacement may be prescribed.

Thyroid hormone has come a long way. In the 1890s, medical textbooks gave recipes for preparing animal thyroid glands as a treatment for thyroid patients. You were likely to have fried, minced thyroid, served with bread and currant jelly for breakfast. A few decades ago, the first form of thyroid replacement hormone used was desiccated thyroid hormone, which was composed of dried animal thyroid hormone. Unlike the synthetic hormone used today, dried animal thyroid hormone was a mixture of T4 and T3, and no two batches of desiccated thyroid hormone were alike, but were a bit of a "mixed bag" of compounds. For example, one pill may have contained more T3 than T4, while another contained the reverse. As a result, although desiccated thyroid hormone worked, it was not consistent.

Today's thyroid replacement hormone, or synthetic thyroid hormone, comes in colored tablet form. (A prescription costs anywhere from thirty to seventy dollars for a three-month supply, depending on the brand.) The generic name is *levothyroxine sodium*. Each color represents a different strength, depending on the brand. This is done to improve what pharmacists refer to as *patient compliance*. When each dosage comes in a different color, it's much easier for patients to say, "I'm taking the pink pill" than "112 micrograms," for example. Even more helpful, most name brand levothyroxine tablets (thyroid hormone) have the dosage strength printed on the tablet in micrograms.

If you have a rare problem with dyes used to color the pills, most brands offer their 50-microgram strength as a plain white pill, without dye. Pharmaceutical manufacturers recommend that you ask your doctor to prescribe your thyroid hormone replacement in increments of the white pill (such as 150 micrograms taken in three pills of 50 micrograms each) if you are experiencing a reaction to the dye.

(See "What Is in This Stuff, Anyway?" for more information on pill ingredients.)

If you are taking multivitamin pills or iron supplements such as ferrous sulphate, take your thyroid hormone pill at least five hours in advance. Iron appears to bind to thyroid hormone, thus making less of it available for absorption into your body.

The Right Dosage

If you are on too high a dosage of synthetic thyroid hormone, you will develop thyrotoxicosis and many of the classic symptoms discussed under "Fast Women: The Hyperalphabet Soup" in Chapter 2. If this happens, notify your doctor; your dosage will be adjusted accordingly. The correct dosage of levothyroxine sodium is determined by a normal TSH reading (according to the newer targets) and other blood tests.

After treatment for hyperthyroidism, the average dose is roughly 1.6 micrograms per kilogram of body weight. Most people will be able to find the right dose for them in the eleven dosage strengths that various brands offer, which range from 25 to 300 micrograms. The average daily dose after thyroid cancer is 2.0 micrograms per kilogram of body weight, but this is an average of a wide range. So, for example, the hypothyroid replacement dose for a 60-kilogram woman is 100 micrograms, and the same woman treated for thyroid cancer would need 125 micrograms each day.

As discussed previously, a normal TSH reading ranges from (0.5 to 5 mU/L), while most people feel best around 2 to 3. A reading greater than 5 mU/L suggests that you are hypothyroid, while a reading less than 0.5 mU/L suggests you are thyrotoxic. Free T4 readings may also be checked. The normal range is between 50 and 165 nmol/L, but most people feel best when the readings are above 110.

If You've Had Thyroid Cancer

The appropriate thyroid hormone replacement dosage is slightly different for thyroid cancer patients. That is because the goals of therapy are a little different. Any microscopic piece of thyroid cancer in your body will be stimulated by TSH. TSH may stimulate cancerous tissue enough to cause it to grow. In your case, the trick is to find a high

226 THE THYROID SOURCEBOOK FOR WOMEN

enough dosage to suppress your TSH, which means that your free T4 readings will be higher than in just "plain ol' hypothyroid" patients. But you need not suffer any hyperthyroid symptoms. TSH suppression can be accomplished with one of the precise doses offered by brand name thyroid hormone replacement pills.

One study found that patients on thyroid hormone specifically for TSH suppression were better off waiting one hour after taking their pill in the morning before having breakfast. It was suspected that the absorption of the medication was better on an empty stomach.

If You Are Elderly or Have Heart Disease

To avoid any risk of being *overreplaced* (overdosed to the point where you are thyrotoxic), dosages of thyroid hormone in your case may start fairly low, at around 50 micrograms. Dosages should be adjusted very, very slowly, in increments of 25 micrograms until you reach the proper thyroid level.

What Brand Should I Take?

The key phrase in a quality thyroid hormone replacement pill is *precise dosing*. This enables your doctor to prescribe the lowest, most effective dose without either overdoing it or underdoing it. It's also important to keep in mind that thyroid hormone brands are not interchangeable. Endocrinologists have seen significant differences in thyroid function after patients have switched brands. The right dose for you on Brand A may not be the right dose on Brand B.

That said, studies to date indicate no significant differences between the four most commonly dispensed brands of levothyroxine. In "clinical speak," they were found to be pharmacologically equivalent (absorbed in the blood in precisely the same way) and considered bioequivalent under current FDA guidelines. This means that the brands studied were found to be interchangeable in the majority of patients receiving thyroid hormone replacement therapy. But disagreement persists regarding bioequivalency among thyroid brands. This is because many thyroid experts believe that bioequivalence requires comparing TSH responses, rather than just T4 levels. Very simple changes in the manufacturing of levothyroxine tablets can make a big difference in performance. (One manufacturer had to recall some of its batches from the market because the batches were made from nonmicronized raw materials from another supplier; this meant that the drug was not being manufactured in a standardized way.) In addition, when the batch of thyroid pills that you receive from your pharmacist has been on the shelf for too long, or exposed to heat, the pills may not be as potent as they were when first shipped. Therefore, it's crucial to always ask when your pills expire. Experts also warn that a bottle of pills that expires in March 2010, which is dispensed in December 2009, should be rejected by the buyer as a batch that is not fresh.

The shortest route to maintaining thyroid hormone function with your thyroid pill is to:

1. Choose a brand of thyroid hormone pill that offers precise dosing. This is particularly important for women over age forty who may be approaching menopause, and anyone over age sixty as well as people with heart conditions.
2. Stay on that brand; don't switch around. Again, because you may require a different dose on Brand A than you do on Brand B, just stay on your present brand.
3. Watch for signs of thyrotoxicosis (see Chapter 2). These symptoms mean that you're on too high a dosage of thyroid hormone.
4. Watch for signs of hypothyroidism (see Chapter 2). These are signs that you're on too low a dosage of thyroid hormone.
5. Get a thyroid function test every three months for the first couple of years after you begin your pills; then graduate to every six months; then annually.
6. Always find out when the pills expire and how long they have been on the pharmacist's shelf.
7. If you miss a pill, don't worry; take two the next day. Thyroid hormone pills have a very long half-life, and missing a pill every now and then won't make any difference as long as you make up for it.
8. Take your pill on an empty stomach if you can. Don't take it at the same time as a multivitamin; take the vitamin at bedtime and the thyroid pill in the morning.

What Is in This Stuff, Anyway?

Thyroid hormone pills contain a number of excipients (substances added to a medicine that allow it to be formed into a shape having consistency). These include diluents, lubricants, binders, and disintegrants. The pills may contain acacia, lactose, magnesium stearate, povidone, confectioner's sugar (which has cornstarch), and talc. The lactose used in thyroid hormone pills is minimal; there is approximately one hundred times the amount of lactose in one-half cup of whole milk as in one tablet of Synthroid, for example. If you are highly lactose intolerant, you can take your thyroid hormone pill together with a lactose enzyme.

The T3 Issue

In recent years, it became in vogue for thyroid patients to request supplementation with a combination of T3 (Cytomel) and T4 (levothyroxine sodium). Patients' experiences (called *anecdotal reports*) with T3 abounded on the Internet, while certain books and articles about T3 supplementation reported that it helped with "brain fog," depression, and other apparent symptoms of hypothyroidism. A small preliminary study out of Lithuania, published in the February 11, 1999, issue of the *New England Journal of Medicine*, reported that subjects on combination T3/T4 performed slightly better on one type of psychological test. But the study was also based on a very small sample of patients (most were thyroid cancer patients and hence already slightly thyrotoxic), not representing the vast majority of hypothyroid patients. The results of this study caused many people (including me) to wrongly interpret it to mean that T3 improved "quality of life" for some hypothyroid patients. When flaws in the sample of patients were pointed out by others, these researchers reanalyzed their results, eliminating the thyroid cancer patients from the mix. Once this occurred, they were unable to find any benefit to T3/T4 therapy. It was concluded by other researchers that when the thyroid cancer patients in the 1999 study had their dosages of thyroid hormone slightly reduced during the clinical trial and were no longer thyrotoxic, they "felt better," which skewed the overall results. (Isn't research fascinating?)

Then, several subsequent, larger, well designed clinical trials investigating whether the T3/T4 combination offers any benefit to hypothyroid patients failed to verify that there is any value in the combination T3/T4 therapy. In fact, all the research now points to the fact that the original 1999 study was highly flawed, and that many were too quick to embrace the study as the solution for the hypothyroid masses. I have argued elsewhere that the T3/T4 combination therapy that many patients still embrace is fraught with ethical problems, since there are risks in taking the potent T3 hormone for several groups. Unfortunately, thyroid patient advocates and thyroid patients on Listservs continue to cling to the T3/T4 combination therapy as the answer to "living well" with hypothyroidism. The only patients who should be on the T3/T4 combination therapy are those patients who have just had a withdrawal scan that checks for thyroid cancer recurrence, and are temporarily climbing back up to normal levels of thyroid hormone. Otherwise, as of this writing, anyone that suggests to you that T3 should be added to your T4 is not up-to-date, or does not understand the medical literature adequately enough. It is analogous to a gynecologist suggesting to a menopausal woman that she should be on long-term HRT to protect her from heart disease, unaware of the new research that concludes that HRT offers no protection from heart disease, and in fact, could be harmful (see Chapter 6). Again, the T3/T4 combination therapy offers *no benefit* to thyroid patients, and in fact, may have risks for some groups.

Why Do I Still Feel Hypothyroid?

It's been suggested in some thyroid patient literature that some people fail to properly convert T4 into T3, which is why T3 is necessary, and further, why natural thyroid hormone (such as Armour thyroid) consisting of dried extracts of pig thyroid glands is better. Top thyroidologists assure me that this theory is highly flawed, and based on misunderstanding of concepts of basic biology. If you have normal levels of TSH, it is not possible that your T4 is not converting to T3, because it is T3 that shuts off TSH. If T4 were not converting to T3, you would have *high*, not normal, TSH levels. In the presence of normal TSH levels, saying that you're not properly converting T4 into T3 is a false statement.

Further research into the world of thyroid misinformation has yielded a file folder filled with incredibly fantastic and fictitious statements about thyroid biology, which thyroid patients with no medical education can easily buy into, found online or in books written by unknowledgeable practitioners (many of whom are not conventional M.D.s) claiming "inside" thyroid information or regurgitating long-debunked theories (such as those promoting basal body temperature tests for hypothyroidism). While space does not allow me to spend time on what's inaccurate, I invite you to consult the American Thyroid Association website (www.thyroid.org), which has responded to the especially harmful misinformation, such as "Wilson's Thyroid Syndrome" and other issues. (See Appendix A.)

You can continue to feel hypothyroid when you're not (meaning that your lab results show normal TSH levels according to the newer targets discussed earlier) because, as this book has demonstrated, all of the symptoms of hypothyroidism overlap with multiple causes not related to thyroid problems. For example, fatigue, depression, poor concentration, and poor digestion are common complaints among women even in the absence of a thyroid problem. Other potential causes of these ailments include physical and emotional stress, sleep deprivation, depression, fatigue (see Chapter 3), normal aging (including menopause), sedentary living (the older we get, the more active we need to be), poor diet, obesity or obesity-related diseases (for example cardiovascular disease), and other diseases we may be managing (such as diabetes). As much as we thyroid patients would like to, we simply can't blame all of our symptoms of poor health on our thyroid condition once it's under control.

Thyroid Replacement Hormone and Other Drugs

Because we either combine various medications from time to time or are taking other daily medications for different health conditions, it's important to be aware of how thyroid replacement hormone medication interacts with other prescription and nonprescription drugs.

• *Oral anticoagulants.* An anticoagulant, or blood thinner, helps prevent blood clotting and is prescribed for a variety of heart conditions. It is also prescribed during or after surgical procedures. When combined with thyroid hormone, some oral anticoagulants can become more potent—which could cause minor hemorrhaging. Your doctor may need to reduce the dosage. This occurs only when initiating thyroxine therapy, not when patients are taking it regularly. When an elderly patient is on these drugs, TSH levels should be tested every six months.

• *Estrogen.* This combination can increase your T4 (thyroxine) readings but doesn't do much to the free T4 level or the TSH. It's best to get your thyroid levels checked once a year if you are taking estrogen for any reason.

• *Insulin or oral hypoglycemics.* This combination lowers the effect of insulin, which means that your doctor may have to increase your insulin dosage. This occurs only when you begin taking thyroid hormone tablets. After both medications are adjusted, you should be fine. If you are diabetic, however, it's a good idea to get your TSH levels checked once a year.

• *Anticonvulsants.* Drugs such as Dilantin are prescribed for epilepsy; they help to prevent seizures. This combination lowers your T4 levels, and you should have your TSH levels checked more frequently.

• *High doses of calcium.* Thyroxine and high doses of calcium pills should be taken several hours apart to ensure better absorption of the thyroid medication.

• *Cholestyramine.* This drug is prescribed for people with high cholesterol levels. Cholestyramine lowers the absorption of thyroxine. Therefore, the two should not be taken together. A space of four to five hours between the two is recommended, with thyroxine being taken first.

• *Antidepressants.* If you start on thyroid replacement hormone while taking certain antidepressant drugs, the antidepressant dosage may need to be adjusted. These drugs include Elavil, Asendin, Etrafon, Limbitrol, Pamelor, Surmontil, Tofranil, Tofranil PM, Triavil, or Norpramin. It will only happen upon beginning your thyroid medication, however, and tapers off once your medications are balanced. Be certain to get your TSH levels checked every year, and inform whoever is managing your antidepressant medication that you are taking thyroid hormone.

• *Lithium.* Lithium is prescribed for bipolar disorder (formerly known as manic depression). Lithium can increase the effect of Hashimoto's disease in causing hypothyroidism. Between 8 and 19 percent of people on lithium become hypothyroid. Lithium has also been known to cause goiter. Insist that your TSH levels are checked every six months while you're on lithium.

• *Amiodarone.* This is a drug used to treat atrial fibrillation, which is a heart rhythm problem. This drug contains a lot of iodine, and it's been found to induce both hypo- and hyperthyroidism; in North America, where we have sufficient iodine, hypothyroidism is more common. It's also found to accelerate Hashimoto's disease but does not cause it in people who do not suffer from it initially. Hyperthyroidism is caused by this drug if you have a toxic multinodular goiter. If you are vulnerable to thyroid disease and you are taking this drug, request an antithyroid antibody test just in case. Since the drug is stored in body fat, it can induce a thyroid problem up to twelve months after it has been stopped. In some patients amiodarone can induce a destructive reaction in the thyroid that releases stored thyroid hormone causing severe hyperthyroidism.

Antithyroid Medication

The only time you will take antithyroid medication is if you are hyperthyroid. The most commonly used antithyroid drugs are propylthiouracil (PTU) and Tapazole (also known as methimazole). These drugs prevent the thyroid gland from manufacturing thyroid hormone, which causes the symptoms of hyperthyroid to subside. (As discussed in Chapter 9, these drugs cure Grave's disease less than 30 percent of the time.) You will probably begin to feel better within two weeks, will feel a difference by six weeks, and feel completely well again in ten to fourteen weeks. You will most likely be on antithyroid medication anywhere from six to twelve months. Your doctor will check at six months, nine months, and twelve months to see of you still need it. If your thyroid gland now functions normally off of this medicine, your family doctor will still check you periodically to be sure that your thyroid hormone level (free T4) remains within the normal range and the TSH is normal.

Drug Reactions

Some people develop various reactions to antithyroid medications. The reactions include rashes, itching, hives, joint pains, fever, sore throat, or aplastic anemia and hepatitis. If this happens, stop taking the drug and call your doctor right away. Although these reactions could occur for any number of reasons that may have nothing to do with antithyroid drugs, you don't want to risk them. At this point, your doctor will check your white blood cell count and make sure it's normal. If it is, your symptoms have nothing to do with the antithyroid drugs and your doctor will simply resume the antithyroid medication. If your white blood cell count is decreased, then your doctor will discuss another form of treatment such as radioactive iodine therapy or surgery. Again, radioactive iodine therapy or surgery will leave you with a nonfunctioning thyroid gland that will cause you to be hypothyroid. To balance this, you'll be placed on thyroid replacement hormone.

Finally, if you are being treated with antithyroid medication, you must not breast-feed. The drugs can pass to the child through the milk, and it is critical to avoid any risk of hypothyroidism in an infant, whose brain development depends on adequate thyroid hormone. In addition, should the mother's condition change and require radioactive iodine therapy, it would be difficult to abruptly wean the child, since the breast milk would be contaminated for at least sixty days.

Medications to Stay Away from While You Are Hyperthyroid

Following are some medications you should avoid while you are hypothyroid.

- Avoid cough and cold medicines with decongestants. These drugs can cause restlessness, while stimulating your heart. Because your heart is already being overstimulated by your hyperthyroid condition, you don't want to tempt fate and risk any added stimulation. (However, mild exercise and sexual activity are fine!)
- Avoid other stimulants such as caffeine (coffee, chocolate, soft drinks), alcohol, or tobacco. Again, these stimulants will increase your heart rate.
- Avoid anything with excess iodine. Some prescription and over-the-counter drugs contain iodine, such as certain asthma medications, vitamin pills, cough medicines, suntan lotions, and salt substitutes. Be sure to read labels before taking any other medications while you're hyperthyroid. You should also stay away from kelp (seaweed) and cut

down on seafood while you're hyperthyroid. The iodine in these substances can make your hyperthyroidism worse by triggering the thyroid gland to make more thyroxine with the extra iodine.

• Do not take Haldol if you're hyperthyroid. Haldol is a drug prescribed for certain psychiatric disorders (it is an antipsychotic) and is also widely used to control alcohol withdrawal in recovering alcoholics. Hyperthyroid patients taking Haldol may develop extreme stiffness or rigidity, which could lead to an inability to walk.

• If you are asthmatic, be sure to consult with your doctor or pharmacist about your asthma before going on beta-blockers to control your heart rate. Some beta-blockers can trigger asthma attacks.

Self-Healing and Complementary Therapies

While you're managing your thyroid condition using conventional treatments, there are a myriad of self-healing strategies and complementary therapies you can incorporate into your treatment, which may improve your sense of well-being and health. This section outlines other forms of healing that have been shown to be beneficial. Herbal supplements are not discussed in this section, as more and more problems are surfacing about their safety and efficacy, and they provide "mixed bags" of compounds. (However, aromatherapy is included here.) Although there are numerous herbs that have been shown to have benefits, it's important to discuss with your doctor any herbs you're taking in the event that they conflict in some way with other medications. For example, Saint-John's-wort, which was very popular in recent years, was shown, on further study, to interfere with certain medications, such as drugs for HIV. Although herbal medicine experts are very knowledgeable about combining various herbs, they are frequently not knowledgeable about thyroid health (although some claim expertise), and are not likely to understand herbal interactions with conventional pharmaceutical products you're taking.

You may find that your own physicians are not supportive of complementary therapies. Doctors make the mistake of assuming that "complementary" is synonymous with "alternative" and worry that their patients may abandon clearly curative therapies in the hopes that drinking a Chinese tea will cure their thyroid condition. On the other hand, keep in mind that "natural" is not necessarily "not harmful," and many conscientious physicians require a higher standard of scientific evidence before recommending complementary therapies that have not been evaluated in this fashion. What I mean by "complementary" is that you can have RAI and a massage, too!

Hands-On Healing

One of the most popular forms of hands-on healing involves *energy healing*, which can involve therapeutic touch or healing touch. An energy healer will use his or her hands to help guide your life force energy (called *chi*, *qi*, or *prana*). The hands may rest on the body, or just close to the body, not actually touching it. Energy healing is used to reduce pain and inflammation, improve sleep patterns and appetite, and reduce stress. It is supported by the American Holistic Nurses Association, and has been incorporated into conventional nursing techniques. Therapies that help to move or stimulate the life force energy include the following:

- Healing touch
- Tuana
- Mari-el
- Qi gong
- Reiki
- SHEN therapy
- Therapeutic touch

Massage

For many, dramatic emotional wellness is at their fingertips! Massage therapy can be beneficial whether you're receiving the massage from your spouse or a massage therapist trained in any one of dozens of techniques from shiatsu to Swedish massage. In the East, massage was extensively written about in *The Yellow Emperor's Classic of Internal Medicine*, published in 2700 B.C. (the text that frames the entire Chinese medicine tradition). In Chinese medicine, massage is recommended as a treatment for a variety of illnesses; tuana massage, a form of deep tissue massage, combined with acupuncture is very effective. A Swedish doctor and poet, Per Henrik, who borrowed techniques from ancient Egypt, China, and Rome, developed Swedish massage, the method Westerners are used to experiencing, in the nineteenth century. It's out of shiatsu in the East and Swedish massage in the West that all the many forms of massage were developed. While the philosophies and styles differ in each tradition, the common element is the same: to mobilize the natural healing properties of the body, which will help it maintain or restore optimal health. Shiatsu-inspired massage focuses on balancing the life force energy; Swedish-inspired massage works on more physiological principles. It relaxes muscles to improve blood flow throughout connective tissues, which ultimately strengthens the cardiovascular system. Massage is more technically referred to as *soft tissue manipulation*. But no matter what kind of massage you have, there exist numerous helpful gliding and kneading techniques used along with deep circular movements and vibrations that will relax muscles, improve circulation, and increase mobility. All are known to help relieve stress and, often, ease muscle and joint pain. In fact, a number of employers cover massage therapy in their health plans. Massage is becoming so popular that the number of licensed massage therapists enrolled in the American Massage Therapy Association has grown from twelve hundred in 1983 to more than thirty-eight thousand today.

Some benefits of massage include:

- Improved circulation
- Improved lymphatic system
- Faster recovery from musculoskeletal injuries
- Soothed aches and pains
- Reduced edema (water retention)
- Reduced anxiety

Types of massage include:

- Deep tissue massage
- Manual lymph drainage
- Neuromuscular massage
- Sports massage

- Swedish massage
- Shiatsu massage

Yoga

Yoga is not just about various stretches or postures, but is actually a way of life for many. It is part of a whole science of living known as the ayurveda. The ayurveda is an ancient Indian approach to health and wellness that's stood up quite well to the test of time (it's roughly three thousand years old). Essentially, it divides up the universe into three basic constitutions or "energies" that are known as *doshas*. The three doshas are based on wind (*vata*), fire (*pitta*), and earth (*kapha*). These doshas also govern our bodies, personalities, and activities. When our doshas are balanced, all functions well, but when they're not balanced, a state of disease (dis-ease as in "not at ease") can set in. Finding the balance involves changing your diet to suit your predominant dosha (foods are classified as kapha, vata, or pitta and we eat more or less of whatever we need for balance) and practicing yoga, which is a preventative health science that involves physical postures, exercises, and meditation. Essentially, yoga is the exercise component of ayurveda, and is designed to tone and soothe your mental and physical state. Most people benefit from introductory yoga classes, or even introductory yoga videos.

Qi Gong

Every morning, all over China, people of all ages gather at parks to do their daily qi gong exercises. Pronounced "ch'i kung," these are exercises that help get your life force energy flowing and unblocked. Qi gong exercises are modeled after movements in wildlife (such as birds or animals), movement of trees, and other things in nature. The exercises have a continuous flow, rather than the stillness of a posture seen in yoga.

The word *qi* means "vitality, energy and life force"; the word *gong* means "practice, cultivate, refine." Using the hands in various positions to gather in the qi, move the qi, or release the qi is one of the most important aspects of qi gong movements.

One of the first group of qi gong exercises you might learn are the "seasons"—fall, winter, spring, summer, and late summer (there are five seasons here). These exercises look more like a dance with precise, slow movements. The Chinese believe that practicing qi gong balances the body and improves physical and mental well-being. These exercises push the life force energy into the various meridian pathways that correspond to organs, incorporating the same map used in pressure point therapies, discussed next. Qi gong improves oxygen flow and enhances the lymphatic system. Qi gong is similar to tai chi, except it allows for greater flexibility in routine. The best place to learn qi gong is through a qualified instructor. You can generally find qi gong classes through the alternative healing community. Check health food stores and other centers that offer classes such as yoga or tai chi. Qi gong is difficult to learn from a book or video, so an instructor is best.

Pressure Point Therapies

Pressure point therapies involve using the fingertips to apply pressure to pressure points on the body. They're believed to help reduce stress, anxiety, pain, and other physical symptoms of stress or other ailments. There are different kinds of pressure point therapies; one of the best known is *acupuncture* and *reflexology*.

Acupuncture is an ancient Chinese healing art, which aims to restore the smooth flow of life energy (*qi*) to the body. Acupuncturists believe that your qi can be accessed from various points on your body, such as your ear. And each point is associated with a specific organ. So depending on your physical health, an acupuncturist will use a fine needle on a very specific point to restore qi to various organs. Each of the roughly two thousand points on your body has a specific therapeutic effect when stimulated. Acupuncture can relieve many of the physical symptoms and ailments caused by stress; it's now believed that acupuncture stimulates the release of endorphins, which is why it's effective in reducing stress, anxiety, pain, and so forth.

Western reflexology was developed by Dr. William Fitzgerald, an American ear, nose, and throat specialist, who described reflexology as "zone therapy." But in fact, reflexology is practiced in several cultures, including Egypt, India, Africa, China, and Japan. In the same way as the ears are a map to the organs in Chinese medicine, with valuable pressure points that stimulate the life force, here the feet play the same role. By applying pressure to certain parts of the feet, hands, and even ears, reflexologists can ease pain and tension and restore the body's life force energy. Like most Eastern healing arts, reflexology aims to release the flow of energy through the body along its various pathways. When this energy is trapped for some reason, illness can result. When the energy is released, the body can begin to heal itself. A reflexologist views the foot as a microcosm of the entire body. Individual reference points or reflex areas on the foot correspond to all major organs, glands, and parts of the body. Applying pressure to a specific area of the foot stimulates the movement of energy to the corresponding body part.

Shiatsu massage also involves using pressure points. A healer using shiatsu will travel the length of each energy pathway (also called *meridian*), applying thumb pressure to successive points along the way. The aim is to stimulate acupressure points while giving you some of his or her own life energy. Barefoot shiatsu involves the healer using his or her foot instead of hand to apply pressure. Jin Shin Jyutsu and Jin Shin Do are other pressure point therapies similar to acupuncture.

You can learn to work your own pressure points, too. Here are some simple pressure point exercises you can try:

1. With the thumb of one hand, slowly work your way across the palm of the other hand, from the base of the baby finger to the base of the index finger. Then rub the center of your palm with your thumb. Push on this point. This will calm your nervous system. Repeat this using the other hand.

2. To relieve a headache, grasp the flesh at the base of one thumb with the opposite index finger and thumb. Squeeze gently and massage the tissue in a circular motion. Then, pinch each fingertip. Switch to the other hand.

3. For general stress relief, find sore pressure points on your feet and ankles. Gently press your thumb into them, and work each sore point. The tender areas are signs of stress in particular parts of your body. By working them, you're relieving the stress and tension in various organs, glands, and tissues. You can also apply pressure with bunched and

extended fingers, the knuckles, the heel of the hand, or by using the entire hand in a gripping motion.

4. For self-massage of the hands, use the same techniques, paying special attention to tender points on the palms and wrists.

5. Use the same technique to self-massage the ears. Feel for tender spots on the flesh of the ears and work them with vigorous massage.

Aromatherapy

Essential oils, comprised from plants (mostly herbs and flowers), can do wonders to relieve stress naturally; many essential oils are known for their calming and antidepressant effects. The easiest way to use essential oils is in a warm bath; you simply drop a few drops of the oil into the bath, and sit and relax in it for about ten minutes. The aroma of the oils can also be inhaled (put a few drops in a bowl of hot water, lean over with a towel over your head, and breathe); diffused (using a lamp ring or a ceramic diffuser—that thing that looks like a fondue pot); or sprayed into the air as a mist. The following essential oils are known to have calming, sedative, and/or antidepressant effects: ylang ylang, neroli, jasmine, orange blossom, cedarwood, lavender (a few drops on your pillow will also help you sleep), chamomile, marjoram, geranium, patchouli, rose, sage, clary sage, and sandalwood. The following scents are considered stimulating and energizing: lemon, grapefruit, peppermint, rosemary, and pine.

Feng Shui

Pronounced "fung shway," this is the ancient practice of creating energy and harmony through your environmental surroundings (landscaping, interior design, and architecture). People tend to think of feng shui as something that can bring wealth to you (by having money corners) or romance (by hanging certain items over the bed), but this is in fact not what authentic feng shui consultants look for. Harmony has many elements to it, and where you live, how you live, and a host of other aspects of your surroundings can all affect how to arrange your environment. Feng shui consultants will assess the following:

1. *Entrance.* How is it lit? What do you have at your entrance (flowers, chimes, or a stack of old newspapers)?
2. *Grounds.* What kinds or colors of flowers are around your home? Are there rocks or sculpture around the grounds of your home?
3. *Specific areas inside your home.* These include your work space or home office, "chef station" or kitchen, bedroom, bathroom, and so on. Placement of mirrors, pictures, plants, lamps, candles, rugs, furniture, bed, or even aquariums are all considered significant. For example, round or octagonal mirrors are powerful.

In general, feng shui tries to optimize your outdoor spaces through the use of curvilinear and rectangular visual contours or edges, wildlife; landscaping/vegetation, aquatic habitat, and minimizing things that interfere with harmony such as signage, power lines, and so on. Inside the home, live plants, colors, lighting, and the positioning of furniture to maximize views of natural scenery are important. Feng shui is said to reduce stress, blood pressure, and adrenaline levels. Beginning with a book on feng shui is a good primer—there are dozens of these!

Meditation

Meditation simply requires you to stop thinking (about your life, problems, and so on) and just be. To do this, people usually find a relaxing spot, or sit quietly and breathe deeply for a few minutes. There is also what I call "active meditation" that can include the following:

- Taking a walk or hike
- Swimming
- Running or jogging
- Gardening
- Playing golf

- Listening to music
- Dancing
- Reading for pleasure
- Walking your dog
- Practicing breathing exercises (or simply listening to the sounds of your own breathing)
- Practicing stretching exercises
- Practicing yoga or qi gong

Appendix A

Thyroid Links
on the Web

Thyroid Websites of Interest

American Thyroid Association
www.thyroid.org

American Association of Clinical Endocrinologists
www.aace.com

EndocrineWeb.com
www.endocrineweb.com
  Site focuses on endocrine disorders and endocrine surgery.

Santa Monica Thyroid Diagnostic Center
www.thyroid.com
  This site was founded by Dr. Richard B. Gutler.

MyThyroid.com
www.mythyroid.com
  This is a patient-centered website, maintained by Dr. Daniel
J. Drucker, devoted to diseases of the thyroid.

General Thyroid Organizations

American Foundation of Thyroid Patients
www.thyroidfoundation.org

Thyroid Foundation of America, Inc.
www.allthyroid.org

Thyroid Foundation of Canada
www.thyroid.ca

Outside North America

European Thyroid Association
www.eurothyroid.com

Latin American Thyroid Society
www.lats.org

The following list provides patient organizations who are members of
Thyroid Federation International (TFI).

Australia

Australian Thyroid Foundation
www.thyroidfoundation.com.au

Thyroid Australia
www.thyroid.org.au

Brazil

Thyroid Foundation of Brazil
E-mail: medneto@uol.com.br

Denmark

Thyreoidea Landsforeningen
www.thyreoidea.dk

Finland

Thyroid Foundation of Finland
www.kolumbus.fi/kilpirauhasliitto

France

l'Association Française des Malades de la Thyroïde
www.thyro-asso.org

Germany

Schilddrüsen Liga Deutschland E.V. (SLD)
www.schilddruesenliga.de

Italy

Associazione Italiana Basedowiani e Tiroidei
emma99@libero.it

Japan

Thyroid Foundation of Japan
www.hata.ne.jp/tfj

Netherlands

Schildklierstichting Nederland
www.schildklier.nl

Norway

Norsk Thyreoideaforbund
www.stoffskifte.org

Republic of Georgia

Georgian Union of Diabetes and Endocrine Associations
E-mail: diabet@access.sanet.ge

Russia

Thyroid Foundation of St. Petersburg
E-mail: gasparyan@peterlink.ru

Sweden

Sköldkörtelförening i Stockholm
www.skoldkortelforeningen.se

Västsvenska Patientföreningen för Sköldkörtelsjuka
www.vpfs.info

United Kingdom

British Thyroid Foundation
www.btf-thyroid.org

Thyroid Cancer Sites

ThyCa, Inc. (The Thyroid Cancer Survivors' Association)
P.O. Box 1545
New York, NY 10159-1545
Phone: 877-588-7904
Fax: 503-905-9725
www.thyca.org
E-mail: thyca@thyca.org

Here you'll find local chapters, and links to the following support groups:

Advanced Thyroid Cancer Support Group
Anaplastic Support Group
Caregivers Support Group
Long-Term Survivors Support Group
Medullary Support Group
Pediatric Support Group
America Online Thyroid Cancer Support Group
The Thyroid Cancer Online E-mail Support Group

Canadian Thyroid Cancer Support Group (Thry'vors) Inc.
P.O. Box 23007
550 Eglinton Avenue West
Toronto, ON M5N 3A8
Canada
Phone: 416-487-8267
www.thryvors.org
thryvors@sympatico.ca
   To join Thry'vors support Listserv, go to:
   http://groups.yahoo.com/group/thryvors.

The Light of Life Foundation
www.checkyourneck.org
   Committed to support, education, and awareness for thyroid cancer patients, their families, and the lay public.

The Head and Neck Cancer Foundation
2345 Yonge Street, Suite 700
Toronto, ON M4P 2E5
Canada
Phone: 416-324-8178
Fax: 416-324-9021
www.headandneckcanada.com

Johns Hopkins Thyroid Tumor Center
www.thyroid-cancer.net

Thyrogen Website
www.thyrogen.com

The Thyroid Cancer Book
www.thyroidcancerbook.com
   This website is run by Your Health Press, which publishes *The Thyroid Cancer Book*, by M. Sara Rosenthal. The book includes the entire low iodine cookbook of The Light of Life Foundation. Website also has FAQs and many links.

Low Iodine Cookbooks and Recipes

www.lidcookbook.com
   This website is run by Your Health Press, which publishes *The Low Iodine Cookbook* by well-known cookbook author Norene Gilletz. Contains FAQs and links.

http://www.thyca.org
   This site offers a downloadable cookbook in PDF.

http://www.checkyourneck.org/cookbook.html
   This site offeres posted recipes. For this organization's complete cookbook, e-mail: cookbook@checkyourneck.org. (This cookbook is also included in its entirety in *The Thyroid Cancer Book*, available at www.thyroidcancerbook.com.)

www.hypoparathyroidism.org
   This source is good if you have calcium problems postsurgery.

www.cancernet.nci.nih.gov (National Cancer Institute)

Graves' Disease

National Graves' Disease Foundation
2 Tsitsi Court
Brevard, NC 28712

Phone: 704-877-5251

www.ngdf.org

You may call, visit the website, or send a self-addressed, stamped envelope (SASE) with your information request.

The TED Association

Solstice, Sea Road

Winchelsea Beach, East Sussex TN36 4LH

United Kingdom

Phone/fax: 01 797-222-338

tedassn@eclipse.co.uk

Thyroid Eye Disease

www.thyroid-eye-disease.com

This website is run by Your Health Press, which publishes the only patient book on TED: Thyroid Eye Disease: Understanding Graves' Ophthalmopathy by Elaine Moore. Includes FAQs and many links.

Appendix B

Links for Other Conditions Related to Thyroid Disease

Emotional Health

American Counseling Association
Phone: 703-823-9800
www.counseling.org

American Psychological Association
Phone: 202-336-5700
www.apa.org

National Depressive and Manic-Depressive Association
Phone: 800-82-NDMDA or 312-642-0049
www.ndmda.org

The National Association of Social Workers (NASW)
750 First Street NE, Suite 700
Washington, DC 20002-4241
Phone: 202-408-8600
Fax: 202-336-8311
TTD: 202-408-8396
www.naswdc.org

American Institute of Stress
Phone: 914-963-1200
www.stress.org

International Stress Management Association
Phone: 817-272-3869
www.stress-management-isma.org

The Anxiety Disorders Association of America
Phone: 240-485-1001
www.adaa.org

Women's Hormonal Conditions

The Hormone Foundation
Phone: 800-HORMONE (800-467-6663)
www.hormone.org
    The Hormone Foundation promotes the prevention, treatment,
and cure of hormone-related conditions.

North American Menopause Society
Phone: 440-442-7550
www.menopause.org

National Osteoporosis Foundation
www.nof.org

Heart Health

American Heart Association
Phone: 800-242-8721
www.americanheart.org

Obesity

American Obesity Association
Phone: 202-776-7711
www.obesity.org

Chronic Fatigue

The CFIDS Association of America
Phone: 704-365-2343
www.cfids.org

Infertility

RESOLVE: The National Infertility Association
www.resolve.org
    RESOLVE provides education, advocacy, and support for men and women facing the crisis of infertility.

Bibliography

Allardice, Pamela. *Essential Oils: The Fragrant Art of Aromatherapy.* Vancouver: Raincoast Books, 1999.

Allen, Paula Gunn. *Grandmothers of the Light: A Medicine Woman's Sourcebook.* Boston: Beacon Press, 1991.

Angier, Natalie. *Woman: An Intimate Geography.* New York: Houghton Mifflin Co., 1999.

Banda Purvis, Sarah. "Lessons Learned: The Myth of Workplace Equity." *Feminista!* 3, no. 2 (June 1999), http://www.feminista.com/v3n2/purvis.html.

Barnard, N. D., et al. "Diet and Sex-Hormone Binding Globulin, Dysmenorrhea, and Premenstrual Symptoms." *Obstetrics and Gynecology* 95 (2000): 245–50.

Beaudet, Marie P., and Claudio Perez. "The Health of Lone Mothers." *Health Reports* 11, no. 2 (Fall 1999): 21–32.

Becker, David. "Radiation and the Thyroid." *Thyrobulletin* 16, no. 3 (Autumn 1995).

Ben-Ari, Elia T. "Walking the Tightrope Between Work and Family." *BioScience* 50, no. 5 (May 2000): 472.

Benvenga, Salvatore, et al. "Delayed Intestinal Absorption of Levothyroxine." *Thyroid* 5, no. 4 (August 1995).

Bequaert Holmes, Helen. "A Call to Heal Medicine." *In Feminist Perspectives in Medical Ethics.* Indianapolis: Indiana University Press, 1992.

Bogner, U., et al. "Association Between Thyroid Cytotoxic Antibodies and Atrophic Thyroiditis." *Clinical Thyroidology* 8, no. 1 (January–April 1995).

Bower, Peter J., et al. "Manual Therapy: Hands-On Healing." *Patient Care* 31, no. 20 (December 15, 1997): 69.

Braverman, L., ed. *Diseases of the Thyroid.* Totawa, NJ: Humana Press, 1997.

Braverman, L., and R. Utiger, eds. *The Thyroid: A Fundamental Clinical Text*, 6th ed. Philadelphia: J. B. Lippincott, 1991.

Breggin, Peter R. *Toxic Psychiatry.* New York: St. Martin's Press, 1991.

Breggin, Peter R., and Ginger Ross Breggin. *Talking Back to Prozac.* New York: St. Martin's Press, 1994.

British Thyroid Foundation and the National Osteoporosis Society. "Thyroid Disease and Osteoporosis." Patient education brochure, 1992.

Brody, Jane E. "Tears: There May Not Be Enough." *New York Times,* December 23, 1997.

Brook, Paula. "Superwoman Goes Home: I Had It All. I'd Also Had Enough." *Saturday Night* 111, no. 5 (June 1996): 30–38.

Bunevicius, Robertas, et al. "Effects of Thyroxine as Compared with Thyroxine plus Triiodothyronine in Patients with Hypothyroidism." *New England Journal of Medicine* 340, no. 6 (February 11, 1999).

Caplan, Paula J. *They Say You're Crazy: How the World's Most Powerful Psychiatrists Decide Who's Normal.* New York: Addison Wesley, 1995.

Carlson, Betty Clark. "Managing Time for Personal Effectiveness: Achieving Goals with Less Stress." *ISMA-USA Newsletter* 1, no. 1 (Spring 1999).

Carrier, Patricia J., and Lorraine Davies. "The Importance of Power Relations for the Division of Household Labour." *Canadian Journal of Sociology* 24, no. 1 (Winter 1999): 35–51.

Center for Science in the Public Interest. "Better than Butter?" *Nutrition Action Healthletter* (December 2001), http://www.cspinet .org/nah/12_01/index.html (accessed May 30, 2002).

———. "Cutting Cholesterol in Kalamazoo." *Nutrition Action Healthletter* (January/February 2002).

———. "FDA Fiddles While Americans Die." *Nutrition Action Healthletter* (April 2002).

———. "Label Watch: Ingredient Secrets." Nutrition Action Healthletter (July/August 2001), http://www.cspinet.org/nah/07_01/ingre dients.html (accessed May 30, 2002).

———. "Rating the Diet Books." *Nutrition Action Healthletter* (May 2000), http://www.cspinet.org/nah/5_00/diet.htm (accessed May 30, 2002).

———. "Read My Lipids: How to Lower Your Risk of a Heart Attack." *Nutrition Action Healthletter* (October 2001), http:// www.cspinet.org/nah/10_01/index.html (accessed May 30, 2002).

———. "Tax Junk Foods." *Nutrition Action Healthletter* (December 2000).

———. "10 Super Foods You Should Eat!" *Nutrition Action Healthletter*, http://www.cspinet.org/nah/10foods_good.html (accessed May 30, 2002).

———. "Ten Tips for Staying Lean." *Nutrition Action Healthletter* (July 1999), http://www.cspinet.org/nah/7_99/ten_tips.htm (accessed May 30, 2002).

———. "Virtual Ingredients." *Nutrition Action Healthletter* (July/ August 2001).

———. "What a Pizza Delivers." *Nutrition Action Healthletter* (June 2002), http://www.cspinet.org/nah/06_02/pizza_051702 .pdf (accessed May 30, 2002).

———. "When in Rome: CSPI's Guide to Italian Food." *Nutrition Action Healthletter* (January/February 1994), http://www.cspinet .org/nah/ital.html (accessed May 30, 2002).

Chalfen, Betsy. "Fats: The Good, the Bad, and the Fake." *Sojourner* 21, no. 7 (March 1996): 20.

Chisholm, Patricia. "The Mother Load: Superwoman Is Burned Out. Should Mom Stay Home?" *Maclean's* (Toronto Edition) 112, no. 9 (March 1, 1999): 46.

Choi, P. Y. L., and P. Salmon. "Symptom Changes Across the Menstrual Cycle in Competitive Sportswomen, Exercisers, and Sedentary Women," *British Journal of Clinical Psychology* 34 (1995): 447–60.

Cicala, Roger S. *The Heart Disease Sourcebook*. Chicago: McGraw-Hill, 1998.

Clark, Orlo H., and Johann Elmhed. "Thyroid Surgery—Past, Present, and Future." *Thyroid Today* 8, no. 1 (March 1995).

Coney, Sandra. *The Menopause Industry: How the Medical Establishment Exploits Women*. Alameda, CA: Hunter House, 1994.

Cooper, David S. "Thyroid Nodules and Thyroid Cancer: Evaluation and Treatment." *Thyrobulletin* 16, no. 3 (Autumn 1995).

Cornell, Camilla. "The Toughest Job of All: You're Leaving the Nest and Returning to Work. Here's How to Ease the Emotional Adjustment." *Today's Parent* 15, no. 2 (March 1998): 48–54.

Cumming, David C., Ceinwen E. Cumming, and Dianne K. Dieren. "Menstrual Mythology and Sources of Information." *American Journal of Obstetrics and Gynecology* 164 (February 1991).

Cummings, Melanie. "Women Who Do Too Much (or Feel Guilty if They Don't)" *Herizons* 11, no. 4 (Fall 1997): 25–26.

Dalton, Katharina. *Once a Month: Understanding and Treating PMS*, 6th ed. Alameda, CA: Hunter House, 1999.

Daniels, Gilbert H. "Graves' Eye Disease." *Thyrobulletin* 15, no. 4 (January 1995).

Davies, Lorraine, and Donna D. McAlpine. "The Significance of Family, Work, and Power Relations for Mothers' Mental Health." *Canadian Journal of Sociology* 23, no. 4 (Fall 1998): 369–87.

Davies, Terry F. "New Thinking on the Immunology of Graves' Disease." *Thyroid Today* 15, no. 4 (1992).

Degroot, L. P., et al., eds. *The Thyroid and Its Diseases*, 5th ed. New York: Wiley and Sons, 1984.

Delanet, Kathy, and Marie R. Squillace. *Living with Heart Disease*. Chicago: McGraw-Hill, 1998.

Delange, F. "Iodine Deficiency Disorders and Their Prevention: A Worldwide Problem." Abstract from the 6th International Thyroid Symposium, Thyroid and Trace Elements, 1996.

"Depression and Thyroid Disease." *Thyroid Signpost* 1, no. 3 (June 1993).

"Differential Response to Antidepressants in Women with Premenstrual Syndrome/Premenstrual Dysphoric Disorder: A Randomized Controlled Trial." *Archives of General Psychiatry* 56 (October 1999): 932–39.

Dirusso, G., et al. "Complications of I-131 Radioablation for Well-Differentiated Thyroid Cancer." *Clinical Thyroidology* 8 (January–April 1995).

Dong, B. J., et al. "Bioequivalence of Generic and Brand-Name Levothyroxine Products in the Treatment of Hypothyroidism." *Journal of the American Medical Association* 277, no. 15 (April 16, 1997): 1199–1200.

Dottorini, M. E., et al. "Effect of Radioiodine for Thyroid Cancer on Carcinogenesis and Female Fertility." *Clinical Thyroidology* 8, no. 1 (January–April 1997).

Douglas, Susan, and Meredith Michaels. "Mommy Wars." *Ms. Magazine* (February/March 2000).

Edwards, C. M. B., J. P. D. Cox, and S. Robinson. "Psychological Well-Being of Patients on L-Thyroxine." *Clinical Endocrinology* 59 (2003): 2, 264–65.

Emanuel, Ezekiel J., and Linda L. Emanuel. "Four Models of the Physician-Patient Relationship." *Journal of the American Medical Association* 267, no. 16 (1992): 2221–26.

Enserink, Martin. "The Vanishing Promises of Hormone Replacement." *Science* 297, no. 5580 (July 19, 2002): 325–26.

Eskin, B. A. "Effects of Iodine Therapy on Breast Cancer and the Thyroid." Abstract from the 6th International Thyroid Symposium, Thyroid and Trace Elements, 1996.

Etchells, E., et al. "Disclosure." *Canadian Medical Association Journal* 155 (1996): 387–91.

Etchells, E., et al. "Voluntariness." *Canadian Medical Association Journal* 55 (1996): 1083–6.

Etchells, E., Gilbert Sharpe, et al. "Consent." *Canadian Medical Association Journal* 155 (1996): 177–80.

Feminist Therapy Institute. "Feminist Therapy Code of Ethics." In E. J. Rave and C. C. Larsen, eds., *Ethical Decision Making in Therapy: Feminist Perspectives.* New York: Guilford Press, 1995, 38–41.

Findlay, Deborah, and Leslia Miller. "Medical Power and Women's Bodies." In B. S. Bolaria and R. Bolaria, eds., *Women, Medicine and Health*. Halifax, NS: Fernwood Books, 1994.

Food and Drug Administration. "FDA Approves Sibutramine to Treat Obesity." FDA Talk Paper, Food and Drug Administration, U.S. Department of Health and Human Services, 1997.

Fransen, Jenny, and I. Jon Russell. *The Fibromyalgia Help Book*. St. Paul, MN: Smith House Press, 1996.

Friedman, Jeffrey M. "A War on Obesity, Not the Obese." *Science* 299, no. 5608 (2003): 856–58.

Fugh-Berman, Adrienne. *Alternative Medicine: What Works*. Tucson, AZ: Odonian Press, 1996.

Fukuda, et al. *Annals of Internal Medicine* 121 (December 15, 1994): 953–59.

Gaitan, Eduardo. "Goiter." *The Bridge* 10, no. 3 (Fall 1995).

Garton, M., et al. "Effect of L-Thyroxine Replacement on Bone Mineral Density and Metabolism in Premenopausal Women." *Clinical Thyroidology* 8, no. 1 (January–April 1995).

Gaz, Randall D. "Instructions for Patients Undergoing Thyroid Needle Biopsy." *Thyrobulletin* 14, no. 4 (Autumn 1993).

Genzyme Corporation. www.genzyme.com. Thyrogen prescribing information accessed February 17, 2000.

Gilligan, Carol. *In a Different Voice*, 2nd ed. Boston: Harvard University Press, 1993.

Ginsberg, Jody. "Wilson's Syndrome and T3." *Thyrobulletin* 15, no. 4 (January 1995).

Glinoer, D. "The Thyroid Gland and Pregnancy: Iodine Restriction and Goitrogenesis Revealed." *Thyroid International* 5 (1994).

Gomez, Joan. *Coping with Thyroid Problems*. London: Sheldon Press, 1998.

Greenspan, Miriam. *A New Approach to Women and Therapy*, 2nd ed. BlueRidge Summit, PA: Tab Books, 1993.

Greenwood, Sadja. *Menopause Naturally: Preparing for the Second Half of Life*. San Francisco, CA: Volcano Press, 1992.

Gunawant, Deepika, and Gopi Warrier. *Ayurveda: The Ancient Indian Healing Tradition*. London: Thorsons/Element, 1997.

Gura, Trisha. "Having It All." *Science* 299, no. 5608 (2003): 850.

"Hair Loss and Thyroid Disease." *Thyroid Signpost* 1, no. 1 (April 1993).

Havas, S., and J. M. Hershman. "Action of Lithium on the Thyroid." Abstract from the 6th International Thyroid Symposium, Thyroid and Trace Elements, 1996.

Hetzel, Basil S. "Iodine Deficiency and Excess: A World Problem." *Thyrobulletin* 16, no. 3 (Autumn 1995).

Hill, James O., et al. "Obesity and the Environment: Where Do We Go from Here?" *Science* 299, no. 5608 (2003): 853–55.

Houppert, Karen. *The Curse, Confronting the Last Unmentionable Taboo: Menstruation.* New York: Farrar, Straus and Giroux, 1999.

Hu, F. B., and W. C. Willett. "Optimal Diets for Prevention of Coronary Heart Disease." *Journal of the American Medical Association* 288, no. 20 (November 27, 2002): 2569–78.

Hurley, Jane, and Stephen Schmidt. "Going with the Grain." *Nutrition Action* 10, no. 11 (October 1994).

International Food Information Council. "IFIC Review: Uses and Nutritional Impact of Fat Reduction Ingredients." International Food Information Council, 1995.

———. "Sorting Out the Facts About Fat." International Food Information Council, 1997.

Ito, Masahiro, et al. "Childhood Thyroid Diseases Around Chernobyl Evaluated by Ultrasound Examination and Fine Needle Aspiration Cytology." *Thyroid* 5, no. 5 (1995).

Jamison, Kay Redfield. *An Unquiet Mind: A Memoir of Moods and Madness.* New York: Vintage Books, 1995.

Joffe, Russell, and Anthony Levitt. *Conquering Depression.* Hamilton, ON: Empowering Press, 1998.

Kalbfleisch, Robin. "Eldercare Major Source of Stress for Working Women." *Canadian Healthcare Manager* 6, no. 6 (October/November 1999): 11.

Kaplan, Michael, et al. "Editorial: In Search of the Impossible Dream? Thyroid Hormone Replacement Therapy That Treats All Symptoms in Hypothyroid Patients." *Journal of Clinical Endocrinology and Metabolism* 88, no. 10 (2003): 4540–42.

Kelner, Katrina, and Laura Helmuth. "Obesity—What Is to Be Done?" *Science* 299, no. 5608 (2003): 845.

Khatamee, M. D. "Infertility: A Preventable Epidemic?" *International Journal of Fertility* 33, no. 4 (1988): 246–51.

Kra, Siegfried J. *What Every Woman Must Know About Heart Disease.* New York: Warner Books, 1996.

Lark, Susan M. *Chronic Fatigue and Tiredness.* Los Altos, CA: Westchester Publishing Co., 1993.

Lee, John R. *What Your Doctor May Not Tell You About Menopause.* New York, Warner Books, 1996.

Leibenluft, Ellen. "Why Are So Many Women Depressed?" *Women's Health* 9, no. 2 (Summer 1998).

Leshin, Len. "The Thyroid and Down Syndrome." http://www.ds-health.com/thyroid.htm (accessed April 12, 1999).

Levine, R. J. *Ethics and Regulation of Clinical Research.* New Haven: Yale University Press, 1988.

Linden, Wolfgang, et al. "Recommendations on Stress Management." *Canadian Medical Association Journal* 160, no. 9 (May 4, 1999): S46–S49.

Loebig, Poerd, et al. "Regulation of Maternal Thyroid During Pregnancy by Human Chorionic Gonadotropin (hCG)." Abstract from the 6th International Thyroid Symposium, Thyroid and Trace Elements, 1996.

Martin, Raquel. *The Estrogen Alternative: Natural Hormone Therapy with Botanical Progesterone.* Rochester, VT: Healing Arts Press, 1997.

Martino, E., et al. "Increased Susceptibility to Hypothyroidism in Patients with Autoimmune Thyroid Disease Treated with Amiodarone." *Clinical Thyroidology* 8, no. 1 (January–April 1995).

Marx, Jean. "Cellular Warriors at the Battle of the Bulge." *Science* 299, no. 5608 (2003): 846–49.

Mastroianni, Anna C., Ruth Faden, and Daniel Federman, eds. *Women and Health Research: Ethical and Legal Issues of Including Women in Clinical Studies*, vol. 1. Washington, DC: National Academy Press, 1994.

Mazer, N. A. "Interaction of Estrogen Therapy and Thyroid Hormone Replacement in Postmenopausal Women." *Thyroid* 14, suppl. 1 (2004): 27–34.

McDermott, M. T. "Thyroid Disease and Reproductive Health." *Thyroid* 14, suppl. 1 (2004): 1–3.

Mitchell, Marvin L. "Congenital Hypothyroidism." *The Bridge* 10, no. 4 (Winter 1995).

Morrison, Judith H. *The Book of Ayurveda.* New York: Simon and Schuster, 1995.

Murray, Michael T. *Premenstrual Syndrome.* New York: Prima Publishing, 1997.

Nash, Madeleine J. "Cracking the Fat Riddle." *Time* (September 2, 2002): 46–55.

National Institute of Mental Health. "Anxiety Disorders." www.nimh .nih.gov/healthinformation/anxietymenu.cfm, accessed September 25, 2001.

Nestle, Marion. *Food Politics: How the Food Industry Influences Nutrition and Health.* Berkeley: University of California Press, 2002.

Nygaard, B., et al. "Acute Effects of Radioiodine Therapy on Thyroid Gland Size and Function in Patients with Multinodular Goiter." *Clinical Thyroidology* 8, no. 1 (January–April 1995).

"Olestra: Yes or No?" *Diabetes Dialogue* 43, no. 3 (Fall 1996).

Olveira, G., et al. "Altered Bioavailability Due to Changes in the Formulation of a Commercial Preparation of Levothyroxine in Patients with Differentiated Thyroid Carcinoma." *Clinical Endocrinology* 46 (June 1997): 707–11.

Osteoporosis Society of Canada. "Biophosphates." Fact Sheet Series no. 9, 1999.

———. "Calcitonin: Its Role in the Treatment of Osteoporosis." Press release, November 1999.

———. "Calcium." Fact Sheet Series no. 3, 1999.

———. "Hormone Therapy." Fact Sheet Series no. 8, 1999.

———. "Living with Osteoporosis." Fact Sheet Series no. 1, 1999.

———. "SERMs: Their Role in the Prevention of Osteoporosis." Press release, December 1998.

Palmer, Gabrielle. *The Politics of Breastfeeding.* London: Pandora Press, 1993.

Pellegrino, Edmund D., and D. C. Thomasma. "The Good Physician." In *For the Patient's Good.* New York: Oxford University Press, 1998.

Perros, P., et al. "Natural History of Thyroid Associated Ophthalmopathy." *Clinical Thyroidology* 8, no. 1 (January–April 1995).

Purdy, Laura M. *Reproducing Persons: Issues in Feminist Bioethics*. Ithaca, NY: Cornell University Press, 1996.

Quinn, Brian P. *The Depression Sourcebook*. Los Angeles: Lowell House, 1997.

Redmond, G. "Thyroid Dysfunction and Women's Reproductive Health." *Thyroid* 14, suppl. 134 (2004): 5–16.

Roberts, Francine M. *The Therapy Sourcebook*. Lincolnwood, IL: NTC/Contemporary Publishing, 1998.

Rosen, Irving B., and Paul Walfish. "You and Thyroid Cancer." *Thyrobulletin* 16, no. 4 (January 1996).

Rosen, Larry, and Michelle M. Weil. *Technostress: Coping with Technology @Work @Home @Play*. New York: John Wiley & Sons, 1997.

Rosenthal, M. Sara. *The Fertility Sourcebook*, 3rd ed. New York: McGraw-Hill, 2002.

———. *The Gynecological Sourcebook*, 4th ed. New York: McGraw-Hill, 2003.

———. *The Hypothyroid Sourcebook*. New York: McGraw-Hill, 2002.

———. *Managing PMS Naturally*. Toronto: Penguin Books, 2001.

———. *The Pregnancy Sourcebook*, 3rd ed. Los Angeles: Lowell House, 1999.

———. *The Skinny on Fat*. Toronto: McClelland and Stewart, 2004.

———. *The Thyroid Cancer Book*, 2nd ed. Toronto: Your Health Press, 2004.

———. *The Thyroid Sourcebook*, 4th ed. Los Angeles: Lowell House, 2000.

———. *Women and Depression*. Los Angeles: Lowell House, 2000.

———. *Women Managing Stress*. Toronto: Penguin Books, 2002.

Ross, Douglas S. "Fine Needle Aspiration Biopsy of Thyroid Nodules." *Thyrobulletin* 14, no. 4 (Autumn 1993).

Rushton, Anna, and Shirley A. Bond. *Natural Progesterone*. London: Thorsons, 1999.

St. Jeor, Sachiko T., et al., for the AHA Nutrition Committee. "Dietary Protein and Weight Reduction: A Statement for Healthcare Professionals from the Nutrition Committee of the Council on Nutrition, Physical Activity, and Metabolism of the American Heart Association." *Circulation* 104 (2001): 1869–74.

Saravanan, P., et al. "Psychological Well-Being in Patients on 'Adequate' Doses of L-Thyroxine: Results of a Large, Controlled, Community-Based Questionnaire Study." *Clinical Endocrinology* 57, no. 5 (November 2002): 577–78.

Sawka, A. M., et al. "Does a Combination Regimen of T4 and T3 Improve Depressive Symptoms Better than T4 Alone in Patients with Hypothyroidism? Results of a Double-Blind, Randomized, Controlled Trial." *Journal of Clinical Endocrinology and Metabolism* 88, no. 10 (2003): 4551–55.

Schlosser, Eric. *Fast Food Nation: The Dark Side of the American Meal.* New York: Houghton Mifflin, 2001.

Sherwin, Susan. *Patient No Longer: Feminist Ethics and Health Care.* Philadelphia: Temple University Press, 1984.

Shuttle, Penelope, and Peter Redgrove. *The Wise Wound: Menstruation and Everywoman.* New York: Marion Boyars, 1999.

Siegmund, W., et al. "Replacement Therapy with Levothyroxine plus Triiodothyronine (Bioavailable Molar Ratio 14:1) Is Not Superior to Thyroxine Alone to Improve Well-Being and Cognitive Performance in Hypothyroidism." *Clinical Endocrinology* 60 (2004): 6, 750–57.

Singer, Peter A. "Hashimoto's Thyroiditis." *Thyrobulletin* 16, no. 1 (Spring 1995).

Singh, A., et al. "Thyroid Antibodies as a Predictor of Early Reproductive Failure." *Clinical Thyroidology* 8, no. 1 (January–April 1995).

Sloca, Paul. "After 14 Years, Nuclear Fallout Study Leads to Questions, Few Answers." Associated Press, August 15, 1997, www.stardem.com.

Solomon, Diane. "Fine Needle Aspiration of the Thyroid: An Update." *Thyroid Today* 16, no. 3 (September 1993).

Surks, Martin I. *The Thyroid Book.* Yonkers, NY: Consumer Reports Books, 1994.

ThyCa: Thyroid Cancer Survivors' Association, Inc. "Thyroid Cancer Types, Stages and Treatment Overview." www.thyca.org (accessed April 2002).

Thyroid Carcinoma Task Force. "AACE/AAES Medical/Surgical Guidelines for Clinical Practice: Management of Thyroid Carcinoma." *Endocrine Practice* 7, no. 3 (May/June 2001).

Thyroid Foundation of America, Inc. "Commentary on Effects of Thyroxine as Compared with Thyroxine plus Triiodothyronine in Patients with Hypothyroidism." Position paper. www.tsh.org (accessed February 17, 2000).

Toft, Anthony D. "Other Forms of Hyperthyroidism." *Thyrobulletin* 16, no. 3 (Autumn 1995).

———. "Thyroid Hormone Replacement—One Hormone or Two?" (editorial). *The New England Journal of Medicine* 340, no. 6 (February 11, 1999).

Tuttle, R. Michael, Troy Patience, and Steven Budd. "Treatment with Propylthiouracil Before Radioactive Iodine Therapy Is Associated with a Higher Treatment Failure Rate than Therapy with Radioactive Iodine Alone in Graves' Disease." *Thyroid* 5, no. 4 (August 1995).

Utiger, Robert D. "Follow-Up of Patients with Thyroid Carcinoma." *The New England Journal of Medicine* 337, no. 13 (September 25, 1997).

Van Middlesworth, L. "Usual and Unusual Isotopes in the Thyroid." Abstract from the 6th International Thyroid Symposium, Thyroid and Trace Elements, 1996.

Varl, B., J. Drinovec, and M. Bagar-Posve. "Iodine Supply with Mineral Water." Abstract from the 6th International Thyroid Symposium, Thyroid and Trace Elements, 1996.

Walfish, Paul. "Thyroid Disease During and After Pregnancy." *Thyrobulletin* 16, no. 3 (Autumn 1995).

Walsh, John, et al. (2003). "Combined Thyroxine/Liothyronine Treatment Does Not Improve Well-Being, Quality of Life, or Cognitive Function Compared to Thyroxine Alone: A Randomized Controlled Trial in Patients with Primary Hypothyroidism." *Journal of Clinical Endocrinology and Metabolism* 88, no. 10: 4543–50.

Weed, Susun S., *Wise Woman Ways: Menopausal Years*. Woodstock, NY: Ash Tree Publishing, 1992.

Wesche, M. F., et al. "Long-Term Effect of Radioiodine Therapy on Goiter Size in Patients with Nontoxic Multinodular Goiter." *Clinical Thyroidology* 8, no. 1 (January–April 1995).

Westcott, Patsy. *Thyroid Problems: A Practical Guide to Symptoms and Treatment*. London: Thorsons/HarperCollins, 1995.

Willett, W. C., et al. "Intake of Trans Fatty Acids and Risk of Coronary Heart Disease Among Women." *Lancet* 341 (1993): 581–85.

Wolf, Naomi. *Misconceptions.* New York: Doubleday, 2001.

Vigilante, K., and Mary Flynn. "Low Fat Lies, High Fat Frauds." Washington, DC: Lifeline Press, 1999.

Zimmerman, Mary K. "The Women's Health Movement: A Critique of Medical Enterprise and the Position of Women." In M. Farle and B. Hess, eds., *Analyzing Gender.* Thousand Oaks, CA: Sage, 1987.

Your Health Press Series

The following books are published by M. Sara Rosenthal. They are available through online bookstores or by calling toll-free 866-752-6820.

Stopping Cancer at the Source (2001)
Women and Unwanted Hair (2001)
Living Well with Celiac Disease (2002) by Claudine Crangle
The Thyroid Cancer Book (2nd Edition, 2003)
Living Well with Ostomy (2003) by Elizabeth Rayson
Thyroid Eye Disease (2003) by Elaine Moore
Healing Injuries the Natural Way (2004) by Michelle Schoffro Cook
Menopause Before 40: Coping with Premature Ovarian Failure
    (2004) by Karin Banerd

Index